phase 1
low-carb recipes

Meredith® Books

Phase 1 Low-Carb Recipes

Editor: Stephanie Karpinske
Contributing Editor: Janet Figg
Assistant Art Director: Erin Burns
Copy Chief: Terri Fredrickson
Publishing Operations Manager: Karen Schirm
Edit and Design Production Coordinator: Mary Lee Gavin
Editorial Assistants: Cheryl Eckert, Kairee Windsor
Marketing Product Managers: Aparna Pande, Isaac Petersen, Gina Rickert, Stephen Rogers,
    Brent Wiersma, Tyler Woods
Book Production Managers: Pam Kvitne, Marjorie J. Schenkelberg, Rick von Holdt, Mark Weaver
Contributing Copy Editor: Amanda Knief
Contributing Proofreaders: Judy Friedman, Susan J. Kling, Donna Segal
Photographers: Andy Lyons, Blaine Moats
Food Stylists: Paige Boyle, Charles Worthington
Indexer: Elizabeth Parson
Test Kitchen Director: Lynn Blanchard
Test Kitchen Product Supervisor: Jennifer Kalinowski
Test Kitchen Home Economists: Marilyn Cornelius, Juliana Hale, Laura Harms, Maryellyn Krantz,
    Jill Moberly, Dianna Nolin, Colleen Weeden, Lori Wilson, Charles Worthington

Meredith® Books
Executive Director, Editorial: Greg Kayko
Executive Director, Design: Matt Strelecki
Senior Editor/Group Manager: Jan Miller
Senior Associate Design Director: Mick Schnepf

Publisher and Editor in Chief: James D. Blume
Editorial Director: Linda Raglan Cunningham
Executive Director, Marketing: Jeffrey Myers
Executive Director, New Business Development: Todd M. Davis
Executive Director, Sales: Ken Zagor
Director, Operations: George A. Susral
Director, Production: Douglas M. Johnston
Business Director: Jim Leonard

Vice President and General Manager: Douglas J. Guendel

Better Homes and Gardens® Magazine
Editor in Chief: Karol DeWulf Nickell
Deputy Editor, Food and Entertaining: Nancy Hopkins

Meredith Publishing Group
President: Jack Griffin
Senior Vice President: Bob Mate

Meredith Corporation
Chairman and Chief Executive Officer: William T. Kerr
President and Chief Operating Officer: Stephen M. Lacy

In Memoriam: E.T. Meredith III (1933-2003)

Our Better Homes and Gardens® Test Kitchen seal on the back cover of this book assures you that every recipe in *Phase 1 Low-Carb Recipes* has been tested in the Better Homes and Gardens® Test Kitchen. This means that each recipe is practical and reliable, and meets our high standards of taste appeal. We guarantee your satisfaction with this book for as long as you own it.

All of us at Meredith® Books are dedicated to providing you with the information and ideas you need to create delicious foods. We welcome your comments and suggestions. Write to us at: Meredith Books, Cookbook Editorial Department, 1716 Locust St., Des Moines, IA 50309-3023.

If you would like to purchase any of our cooking, crafts, gardening, home improvement, or home decorating and design books, check wherever quality books are sold. Or visit us at: bhgbooks.com

Pictured on front cover: Chicken Breasts with Caper Vinaigrette (recipe, page 225)

table of contents

phase 1 basics

Do juicy grilled steaks topped with herbed butter and savory eggs scrambled with ham and cheddar cheese sound too good to be diet foods? Not if you're on a low-carb diet. You can eat foods on a low-carb diet that many other dieters only dream about.

Although variations exist, most low-carb diet plans have similar traits. You won't be counting calories; instead, you'll be counting grams of carbohydrate and/or limiting the types of carbohydrates you eat. Low-carb diets start with a week or two of strictly limiting your carbohydrates, often called phase 1. This early plan is meant to jump-start your new low-carb lifestyle and take away your cravings for carbs. The next step is often called phase 2, during which you gradually add more carbs into your diet while maintaining ongoing weight loss.

What's phase 1 all about?

Many foods contain carbohydrates, but not all carbohydrates are alike. Some are sugars; others are fiber or starches. They may be classified further as refined or unrefined. Unrefined carbs undergo minimal processing and commonly have high amounts of vitamins and minerals. Refined carbohydrates are highly processed, which often means they have less fiber, vitamins, and minerals.

No matter what the source, all carbs, except for fiber, get converted to glucose and are absorbed into your blood. Your body burns the glucose for energy and stores any excess as fat or glycogen, a stored form of glucose. When your body takes glucose from your blood, there's a big drop in your blood sugar levels. That causes hunger and cravings for more high-carbohydrate foods. Severely limiting carbohydrate intake, such as in phase 1 of a low-carb diet, helps reduce big drops in blood sugar levels and control carbohydrate cravings.

Ketosis and carb cravings

We can burn both fat and carbs for energy, but the body prefers carbs. When you strictly limit your carbohydrate consumption, you do not have enough carbs to meet your body's energy needs. Instead, your body burns its own fat for energy—a state called ketosis. Ketones, a by-product of ketosis, also suppress your appetite, helping you stick to your low-carb diet.

Changing your metabolism from carbohydrate burning to fat burning doesn't happen all at once. Most people require a few days to make the switch. During that time, it's important to stay focused. You may yearn for carbohydrates for the first day or two. However, the protein and fat you consume should keep you from experiencing hunger pangs. After a few days of eating only phase 1 foods, your carbohydrate cravings likely will disappear.

Phase 1 foods

Acceptable phase 1 foods depend on which diet plan you choose. The strictest diets allow you only about 20 grams of carbohydrate per day. That's equivalent to about 3 cups of salad greens or cooked low-carbohydrate vegetables. (See the list on page 15 for acceptable low-carb vegetables.) Most other carbohydrate-containing foods are forbidden. You may eat poultry, fish, shellfish, meat, eggs, olive oil, butter, salad dressings with less than 2 grams of carbohydrate per serving, low-carb condiments (mustard, mayonnaise), and caffeine-free, sugar-free beverages.

Some low-carb diet plans don't encourage counting grams of carbohydrate, but instead restrict carbohydrate intake to those foods with a low glycemic index. Foods with a low glycemic index don't cause blood sugar levels to rise and fall as quickly as carbs with a high glycemic index. Phase 1 on these diets prohibits all breads, pasta, rice, high-carb vegetables (potatoes, beans, peas, corn, and winter squash), baked goods, and fruit. You can consume meats, fish, poultry, eggs, cheese, greens, and non-starchy vegetables. On these diets, you also may have caffeinated coffee or tea.

Since the phases of low-carb diets vary in the type of foods allowed, it's best to check your plan to make sure you're following it correctly.

Discuss your diet with your physician.

As with any dietary change, talk to your doctor about a low-carb eating plan before you begin. He or she may want to review your diet plan and evaluate your current health status before giving approval. People who have kidney disease or a history of kidney disease, as well as pregnant or nursing women should not go on a low-carb diet plan unless they are under a physician's care. Drastic reductions in carbohydrate consumption require your kidneys to work more. On a very low-carb diet, your body will first use up its glycogen (the storage form of glucose) from your liver and muscles. Glycogen contains a lot of water. Converting it to glucose for use by your body causes it to release the water and results in frequent urination. After your body goes into the fat-burning stage, ketones, from the breakdown of fat, are released into your blood. Your body requires plenty of water to flush the ketones out, causing additional work for your kidneys. Finally, consuming additional fat and protein to make up for the missing carbs releases more metabolic by-products than normal, further increasing the workload of your kidneys.

5

Stay on track! Tips for Phase 1 success

Phase 1 of any low-carb diet is the most stringent. It's the first couple of weeks of a new lifestyle and involves changing your daily habits. The following tips will help keep you on track:

• **Clear your schedule.**

If possible, pick a relatively calm week to start phase 1 of your new diet. Avoid travel times, vacations, and weeks with especially stressful schedules. It's easier to stay focused on a new eating plan when your routine is normal.

• **Stick to the diet rules.**

Diet plans work best when you follow the rules. When you're switching your body from carb-burning to fat-burning as in phase 1, it takes just one incident of diet cheating to put your body back into its carb-burning mode.

• **Start with breakfast.**

Many dieters skip breakfast. Some don't take the time and others just don't feel hungry. None of these excuses are valid. Breakfast is the first food you consume after a nightlong fast. A good breakfast revs up your metabolism, helping you burn more calories for the rest of the day.

If you're short on time in the mornings, plan ahead and keep your refrigerator stocked with grab-and-go, diet-friendly foods. Hard-cooked eggs can be prepared in advance and kept refrigerated until needed. Precooked bacon slices and precooked sausage patties cut morning prep time.

If you don't feel hungry in the mornings, try nontraditional breakfast choices. Cold, sliced chicken or turkey; grilled hamburger patties; or sliced cheese may get you out of your breakfast slump.

• **Enlist the support of family and friends.**

Some of your friends and family members won't understand a low-carb diet. They may encourage you to eat high-carb foods, especially at the holidays or other special occasions.

To avoid these pitfalls, enlist the help and support of your family and friends. Explain your low-carb diet and what foods are allowed. Discuss the health benefits you expect to gain from following your diet plan.

Encourage family members, even if they're not overweight, to adopt some aspects of your low-carb eating plan. It's good for anyone to cut back on refined carbohydrates (snack foods, baked goods, sugar). Instead, they can choose more unrefined carbohydrates, such as vegetables, whole grains, and fresh fruits.

• **Keep snacks handy.**

During phase 1, some diet plans suggest you eat snacks midmorning and midafternoon, while other plans suggest eating every six hours. That means you're going to need some readily available snacks that are acceptable for phase 1. Consider keeping hard-cooked eggs, cooked shrimp, grilled chicken breast strips, sliced cheese, roast beef or pork slices, canned tuna, roasted turkey slices, or ham slices in your refrigerator. When you're at work, take snacks with you in an insulated container with an ice pack. It's also a good idea to keep bottled water and a variety of sugar-free drink mixes available.

• Pack your lunch.

Lunchtime away from home can ruin the best dietary intentions. Avoid those enticements by packing your lunch. To avoid the morning rush, make your lunch while cooking the previous night's dinner.

Any of the foods listed previously as possible snacks also work well for brown-bag lunches. Eat them alone or use them to top mixed greens. Pack low-carb salad dressing in a small separate container. Other phase 1 lunch ideas include sugar- and fruit-free chicken, tuna, egg, or shrimp salads or thinly sliced roast turkey, grilled steak, or broiled chicken breast wrapped in lettuce leaves.

• Add exercise to your routine.

Although you might not want to start exercising during the first week of phase 1, try adding a daily walk or other exercise during the second week. It increases your fat burning and weight loss, while toning and strengthening your muscles. After you finish working out, your metabolism remains at an elevated level for a period of time, increasing your calorie expenditure.

If you haven't exercised recently, talk to your physician before starting. Be sure your doctor knows that you're following a low-carb diet plan. Once you have physician approval, start out slowly and gradually increase your exercise intensity and duration. Your goal should be at least one-half to one hour of exercise five days a week.

Exercising first thing in the morning keeps subsequent distractions from pre-empting your activity plans. However, if morning exercise doesn't work for you, schedule your drill later in the day. Check out your calendar every week and plan time.

Participating in a variety of activities keeps boredom at bay and allows you to work different muscle groups. Plan to exercise with friends or coworkers, if possible. They'll increase your motivation and encourage you to do it even on the days you really don't feel like exercising.

• Stock your kitchen for low-carb eating.

A refrigerator or pantry that's filled with chips, doughnuts, candy, pretzels, and cookies only provides unneeded temptations for a low-carb dieter. Throw out any edibles that encourage you to stray. Purchase plenty of your favorite foods that fit into phase 1. Keep several kinds of cheese in your refrigerator. Make sure you have plenty of eggs, meat, fish, shellfish, and poultry. Buy fresh salad greens and low-carb vegetables. For convenience, wash and store the greens and veggies as soon as you get home. Canned tuna, crabmeat, and salmon are handy to have on hand. They're nonperishable and ready to eat. Keep a variety of sugar-free spices, herbs, and condiments available. They'll add interest to ordinary meats, poultry, and fish.

Q & A

Many people have questions about low-carb dieting. Here are answers to some frequently asked questions about phase 1 of a low-carb diet. Refer to your specific low-carb plan for more detailed help about the diet you're following.

When should I stop phase 1 and start phase 2 of my low-carb diet?

Most low-carb diets suggest you follow phase 1 for at least two weeks. However, after two weeks, you may not feel comfortable adding carbs back into your diet. Or you may enjoy the success of phase 1 so much that you're not willing to make changes. You can continue with phase 1 until you feel ready to start adding some carbs back into your diet. On the other hand, if you find it easier to stick with a low-carb diet while eating a wider variety of foods, you may choose to proceed to phase 2 after two weeks. Everyone responds differently to changes in their diet so wait and see what works best for you.

When I diet, I usually count calories. How many calories are in a phase 1 diet?

Low-carb dieting doesn't emphasize calorie counting. Instead, phase 1 of most low-carb diets either limits you to 20 grams of carbohydrate per day or limits the kinds of carbohydrate you consume. However, it is possible to consume too many calories during phase 1 of a low-carb diet. If you are unable to lose weight, it's possible that you are eating more calories than you expend in a day. In that case, examine your portion sizes. Although there are no restrictions on how much of an acceptable food you may eat, you still should watch your portions and not overindulge. Instead, eat just until you feel pleasantly full but not overly stuffed.

What do food labels tell me about carbohydrates in foods?

Hundreds of new low-carb foods are filling grocery store shelves, leading to confusion about food labeling. The Food and Drug Administration (FDA) defines "total carbohydrate," "sugars," "dietary fiber," "sugar alcohol," and "other carbohydrates." Those terms are all found on the Nutrition Facts label. As a low-carb dieter, you want to pay attention to total carbohydrate and dietary fiber. That's because most low-carb diets refer to net carbs when they set carbohydrate limits. You may calculate the grams of net carbs by subtracting the grams of dietary fiber from the grams of total carbohydrate. Fiber is deducted from the total carbohydrate because your body does not digest fiber.

Some food manufacturers print grams of net carbs, effective carbs, or impact carbs on their package labels. The FDA does not currently regulate these terms. Generally they all mean the same thing: grams of total carbohydrate minus grams of dietary fiber. Sometimes sugar alcohols are also deducted because they have minimal effect on your blood-sugar levels, although they still may have calories, depending on the sugar alcohol that was used.

If I stay under my diet's carb limitations during phase 1, can I have a piece of bread?

No. Phase 1 relies on both limiting total carbohydrate intake and eating the "right" kinds of carbs. Bread, even whole wheat bread, contains many refined carbohydrates or the kind of carbs that may cause rapid spikes in your blood-sugar levels and lead to hunger. Another goal of phase 1 is to teach you to eat only nutrient-dense carbs, such as vegetables, which provide antioxidant vitamins and health-promoting phytonutrients.

Can I drink soda during phase 1?

Water, whether it's bottled or tap, is your best beverage choice during phase 1. However, if you want to add diet soda or other beverages, be sure they fit into your chosen diet plan. Some diets require that beverages be both sugar- and caffeine-free. Other diets require only that beverages be sugar-free. And some phase 1 diets say to avoid artificial sweeteners.

Will I get adequate fiber in my diet during phase 1?

During phase 1 of a low-carb diet, you limit your consumption of fruits, vegetables, whole grains, nuts, and seeds. All of these restricted foods are fiber-rich, making it difficult to get enough dietary fiber. If you have constipation during phase 1, you may want to sprinkle a tablespoon of wheat bran, psyllium husks, or ground flaxseed over your allowed greens or vegetables. They are all high fiber and won't have to be counted in your daily total of carbohydrates because they do not impact your blood-sugar levels.

My diet plan suggests that I go into ketosis. What does that mean?

After your body uses up available glucose and glycogen, it burns its own fat to supply energy. That's called ketosis. In ketosis, you get energy from ketones, little carbon fragments that are the fuel created by the breakdown of fat stores. Ketones naturally reduce hunger, making it likely you'll eat less. When you strictly limit your carbohydrate intake, it takes about two days for your body to burn its stored glycogen and start to burn fat (ketosis). Read more about ketosis on page 4.

My low-carb diet says to avoid trans fats. What are they?

Trans fats are formed when vegetable oils are made into solid or semisolid fats during a process called hydrogenation. Manufacturers use hydrogenation to increase the stability of fats and the shelf life of many packaged foods. Although some trans fats are found naturally in foods, most dietary trans fats come from snack foods and baked goods made with "partially hydrogenated vegetable oil" or "vegetable shortening." In the body, trans fats raise LDL (bad) cholesterol and lower HDL (good) cholesterol, increasing the risks for heart disease. Therefore, it's a good idea to limit your consumption of trans fats, whether you're on a low-carb diet or not.

Phase 1 Menus

Most low-carb diets suggest you follow phase 1 for at least two weeks. That's why a sample two-week menu plan is provided below. But everyone is different and some people may choose to extend this phase for another week or so. If you're feeling good and losing weight, you may not want to add carbs back into your diet after two weeks. If you have questions about how long you should stay on phase 1, check your specific plan or talk to your physician about it.

Week 1

Day 1

Breakfast

Poached Eggs Florentine (p. 25)	2g
3 slices crisp-cooked bacon	0g
Hot herbed caffeine-free tea	0g

Lunch

Spicy Sausage Soup (p. 203)	5g
1 cup cucumber sticks	2g
½ cup (4% fat) cottage cheese	3g
Sparkling water	0g

Dinner

Cheesy Tuscan Chicken Pockets (p. 233)	2g
Green Beans Amandine (p. 359)	3g
Italian Coleslaw (p. 389)	3g
Iced caffeine-free sugar-free tea	0g

Snack

1 ounce mozzarella cheese	1g
Total net carbs	**21g**

Day 2

Breakfast

Pepper & Cheese Omelet (p. 53)	5g
2 links sausage	1g
Hot herbed caffeine-free tea	0g

Lunch

4 ounces roasted turkey breast, cut into strips	0g
Herbed Goat Cheese Salad (p. 60)	1g
Iced caffeine-free, sugar-free coffee	0g

Dinner

Broiled Halibut with Dijon Cream (p. 302)	4g
Bacon & Spinach Salad (p. 376)	2g
Chilled sparkling water	0g

Snack

1 cup raw cauliflower	2g
½ cup raw green sweet pepper strips	3g
Total net carbs	**18g**

Day 3

Breakfast

Meat Lover's Scrambled Eggs (p. 19)	2g
Hot herbed caffeine-free tea	0g

Lunch

Ham Salad (p. 196)	3g
wrapped in butterhead lettuce leaves	0g
1 cup raw broccoli florets	2g
Chilled caffeine-free diet soda made with sucralose	0g

Dinner

Moroccan Rib Roast (p. 78)	1g
2 cups steamed fresh spinach	6g
2 slices fresh tomato	3g
Chilled mineral water	0g

Snack

1 ounce Swiss cheese	1g
Total net carbs	**18g**

Day 4

Breakfast

Spicy Scrambled Eggs (p. 48)	2g
3 slices crisp-cooked bacon	0g
Hot herbed caffeine-free coffee	0g

Lunch

Chicken Salad with Olives & Peppers (p. 248)	3g
1 cup leaf lettuce	1g
Iced caffeine-free, sugar-free tea	0g

Dinner

Pork Au Poivre with Mustard & Sage (p. 153)	3g
Tossed Crisp Vegetable Salad (p. 387)	4g
1 cup steamed broccoli	4g
Hot herbed caffeine-free tea	0g

Snack

Herb-Salt Sprinkle (with radishes) (p. 370)	0g
1 ounce cheddar cheese	0g
Total net carbs	**17g**

Day 5

Breakfast

Easy Baked Eggs (p. 18)	1g
2 ounces Canadian-style bacon	1g
Hot caffeine-free coffee	0g

Lunch

Chili-Lime Pork Salad (p. 187)	4g
Chilled mineral water	0g

Dinner

Lemon-Herb Swordfish Steaks (p. 300)	2g
Peppers Stuffed with Goat Cheese (p. 358)	3g
Iced caffeine-free, sugar-free coffee	0g

Snack

2 ounces Gouda cheese	2g
1 cup red sweet pepper strips	7g
Total net carbs	**20g**

Day 6

Breakfast

Spinach Omelet with Red Pepper Relish (p. 30)	3g
2 links sausage	1g
Hot herbed caffeine-free tea	0g

Lunch

Shrimp & Greens Soup (p. 338)	5g
1 cup cucumber sticks	2g
Chilled sparkling water	0g

Dinner

Lemon-Soy Marinated Flank Steak (p. 67)	1g
Grilled Summer Squash with Cheese (p. 368)	1g
Iced caffeine-free, sugar-free tea	0g

Snack

Cheese & Turkey Wrap (p. 58)	3g
Total net carbs	**16g**

Day 7

Breakfast

Scrambled Eggs with Smoked Salmon & Chives (p. 22)	1g
Hot herbed caffeine-free tea	0g

Lunch

Blue Cheese-Stuffed Chicken Breasts (p. 243)	2g
Lemony Mixed Vegetables (p. 355)	2g
Tossed Salad (1 cup torn leaf lettuce, ½ cup cauliflower florets, ½ cup chopped red sweet pepper, and 2 tablespoons low-carb salad dressing)	6g
Chilled mineral water	0g

Dinner

Brats with Onion-Pepper Relish (p. 204)	4g
1 cup cucumber slices	2g
Iced caffeine-free, sugar-free tea	0g

Snack

Decadent Deviled Eggs (p. 56)	1g
Total net carbs	**18g**

Week 2
Day 1
Breakfast

Ham & Swiss Skillet (p. 42)	2g
Hot caffeine-free coffee	0g

Lunch

Italian Pork Burger (p. 192)	1g
Creamy Lemon-Pepper Coleslaw (p. 390)	3g
½ cup green sweet pepper slices	3g
Chilled caffeine-free diet soda made with sucralose	0g

Dinner

Steak with Roasted Garlic & Herbs (p. 99)	2g
Brussels Sprouts with Prosciutto (p. 361)	3g
Iced caffeine-free, sugar-free tea	0g

Snack

Tossed salad (1 cup torn romaine lettuce, 2 sliced radishes, ¼ cup cauliflower florets, 1 tablespoon real bacon bits, 1 ounce shredded mozzarella cheese, and 2 tablespoons low-carb salad dressing)	4g
Total net carbs	**18g**

It doesn't fit into my diet!

This book contains hundreds of recipes, menu plans, information, and charts to get you started on your newly adopted, low-carb lifestyle. Because low-carb diet plans vary in "allowed" foods, especially in phase 1, you may find a few recipes that are "off-limits" on your specific diet plan. However, with more than 300 recipes in this book, you're sure to find plenty of other taste-tempting inspirations that fit the requirements of your diet plan.

Day 2
Breakfast

Broccoli-Pepper Frittata (p. 45)	3g
2 turkey breakfast sausage patties	1g
Hot herbed caffeine-free tea	0g

Lunch

Pork with Cabbage Slaw (p. 189)	2g
Iced caffeine-free, sugar-free tea	0g

Dinner

Pan-Seared Scallops with Lemon Vinaigrette (p. 342)	5g
Roasted Asparagus in Mustard Dill Sauce (p. 353)	3g
2 slices fresh tomato	3g
Chilled sparkling water	0g

Snack

2 ounces provolone cheese	1g
Total net carbs	**18g**

Day 3
Breakfast

Crustless Mexican Quiche (p. 28)	4g
Hot herbed caffeine-free tea	0g

Lunch

Ham-&-Salad Spirals (p. 197)	4g
1 cup raw broccoli florets	2g
Chilled mineral water	0g

Dinner

Garlic & Mint Chicken Breasts (p. 239)	2g
Tossed salad (1 cup torn leaf lettuce, ½ cup sliced celery, ½ cup sliced cucumber, ½ cup sliced mushrooms, 1 tablespoon sliced green onion, and 2 tablespoons low-carb salad dressing)	5g
Iced caffeine-free, sugar-free tea	0g

Snack

Bacon-Chive Deviled Eggs (p. 57)	1g
Total net carbs	**18g**

Day 4

Breakfast

French Omelet (p. 26)	1g
2 ounces Canadian-style bacon	1g
Hot caffeine-free coffee	0g

Lunch

Cajun-Style Pork Chops (p. 141)	2g
Lemon Broccoli (p. 362)	2g
Iced caffeine-free, sugar-free tea	0g

Dinner

Spicy Beef Tenderloin (p. 77)	5g
Garlicky Mushrooms (p. 357)	4g
1 cup cucumber sticks	2g
Chilled mineral water	0g

Snack

Bacon-&-Cheese-Stuffed Mushrooms (p. 369)	3g
Total net carbs	**20g**

Day 5

Breakfast

Scrambled Eggs with Sausage & Feta Cheese (p. 50)	3g
Hot caffeine-free coffee	0g

Lunch

Smoked Pork Salad (p. 190)	4g
Chilled sparkling water	0g

Dinner

Minty Halibut with Squash (p. 311)	3g
Broiled Roma Tomatoes with Goat Cheese (p. 372)	2g
Hot herbed caffeine-free tea	0g

Snack

Marinated Vegetables, Cheese, & Sausage (p. 59)	5g
Total net carbs	**17g**

Day 6

Breakfast

Sweet Pepper-Gruyère Omelet (p. 21)	4g
Hot herbed caffeine-free tea	0g

Lunch

Callaloo Soup (p. 339)	2g
½ cup raw cauliflower florets	1g
½ cup cucumber sticks	1g
Chilled mineral water	0g

Dinner

Mustard-Marinated Chicken (p. 262)	3g
Swiss Chard with Peppered Bacon (p. 352)	3g
Hot caffeine-free coffee	0g

Snack

Marinated Feta Salad (p. 61)	4g
Total net carbs	**18g**

Day 7

Breakfast

Seafood Omelet with Avocado Salsa (p. 41)	3g
Hot herbed caffeine-free tea	0g

Lunch

Ham, Sweet Pepper & Zucchini Soup (p. 198)	5g
1 ounce cheddar cheese	0g
Iced caffeine-free, sugar-free tea	0g

Dinner

Bistro Beef & Mushrooms (p. 88)	4g
Herb-Lover's Salad (p. 375)	1g
Hot caffeine-free coffee	0g

Snack

½ cup (4% fat) cottage cheese	3g
Cheese-and-Pepper Ham Salad (p. 196)	3g
Total net carbs	**19g**

Low-Carb Restaurant Guide

Schedules crammed with work, volunteer jobs, and family activities make it nearly impossible for most of us to cook three meals a day. Even if you dine out frequently, you still can follow your diet. Here are a few strategies to help you while on a low-carb diet:

• Don't arrive at the restaurant famished.

Even though it might be tempting to skip a meal before dining out, it only increases your hunger so you end up eating more. Instead, eat a high-protein snack an hour or two before arriving at the restaurant.

• Drink plenty of water.

Drinking water before you get to the restaurant or shortly after you arrive contributes to a feeling of fullness, making it likely you'll eat less.

• Study menus.

When dining at local restaurants, ask for a copy of the menu to take home or check to see if the restaurant posts its menu online. Soon you'll have menus from all of the restaurants you frequent. Read the menus, noting restaurants that offer the best choices for your diet plan.

Classic steakhouses and seafood restaurants offer an abundance of phase-1-friendly foods. Generally, Greek or Middle Eastern restaurants serve great grilled kabobs containing meats or poultry and low-carb vegetables—perfect low-carb fare. Ask the waiter to omit any couscous, hummus, or pita bread that might come with the meal. Chinese, Japanese, or Thai restaurants serve many entrées appropriate for phase 1, as long as you skip the rice or noodles. Although Mexican and Italian restaurants may be a challenge, most will provide salads and broiled meats or fish upon request. Even pizza places usually serve salads that fit into phase 1 dieting. No matter which cuisine you select, be sure to avoid any sauces containing sugar, honey, or cornstarch.

• Ask how food is prepared.

Ask your waiter if foods contain sugar, cornstarch, bread crumbs, or other items that don't fit within your diet.

• Request alternative foods.

Many restaurant meals start with a basket of bread or chips—both foods you should avoid. Ask your waiter to hold these foods or for a possible substitution, such as a dish of olives in place of a bread basket or a side salad instead of a baked potato.

• Make fast food fit.

If you're going to eat fast food, you've got to make the food fit into your diet. Choose burgers or grilled chicken sandwiches without the bun. Top them with mayonnaise or mustard, but skip the high-sugar catsup or barbecue sauce. For salads, choose low-carb vegetables topped with hard-cooked egg, turkey, and an oil-and-vinegar salad dressing. Pass up croutons, cole slaw, fruits, gelatin, and pasta salads—they often are loaded with carbs.

Allowable Vegetables

Most phase 1 diet plans include vegetables but some limit the type and amount allowed. The list below includes vegetables low in carbohydrates and most likely to be included in a phase 1 diet. See your particular plan for more information.

The following vegetables are very low in carbs so many phase 1 plans allow up to three cups a day.

Alfalfa sprouts

Arugula

Bok choy

Celery

Chicory

Chives

Cucumber

Daikon

Endive

Escarole

Fennel

Jicama

Lettuce

Mushrooms

Peppers

Radicchio

Radishes

Romaine lettuce

The vegetables listed below are higher in carbohydrates and may be limited to one cup per day for some phase 1 plans.

Artichokes

Artichoke hearts

Asparagus

Bamboo shoots

Bean sprouts

Broccoli

Broccoli rabe

Brussels sprouts

Cabbage

Cauliflower

Celery

Collard greens

Eggplant

Kale

Leeks

Okra

Onion

Pumpkin

Rhubarb

Sauerkraut

Scallions

Snow peas

Spaghetti squash

Spinach

String or wax beans

Summer squash

Tomato

Turnips

Water chestnuts

Zucchini

Check out the charts

At the end of each chapter, we've included handy cooking charts for eggs, meat, poultry, fish, and seafood. These charts provide basic cooking instructions and timings for many high-protein foods prepared on phase 1 of your low-carb diet. On busy weeknights, just choose your protein, then look at the chart to decide how to cook it or to see which is the fastest method.

At the end of the book, you'll find a carb counter's journal. This section is intended to help you track your carbs each day while on phase 1. You can mark in the book or make copies to take with you. It's an easy and convenient way to keep track of your phase 1 diet.

Free Foods

Many high-protein foods contain no carbs so they are often called "free foods," meaning you can eat them without counting them toward your carb limit. Although most meats are allowed, avoid lunch meats made with added nitrites or sugars. Artificial meats, such as imitation crabmeat, are also a no-no since many of them have added carbs. Consult your specific plan for more information.

Meat

All meat, including:

Bacon

Beef

Ham

Lamb

Pork

Veal

Venison

Fish

All fish, including:

Flounder

Salmon

Sardines

Sole

Trout

Tuna

Fowl

All fowl, including:

Chicken

Cornish Hen

Duck

Goose

Pheasant

Quail

Turkey

Shellfish

All shellfish, including:

Clams

Crabmeat

Lobster

Mussels

Oysters

Shrimp

Squid

Eggs

Eggs cooked any style, including:

Deviled

Fried

Hard-boiled

Omelets

Poached

Scrambled

Soft-boiled

Cheese

Most full-fat firm, soft, and semi-soft cheeses, including:

Blue cheese

Cheddar

Cream cheese

Feta

Fontina

Goat cheese

Monterey Jack

Mozzarella

Parmesan

Provolone

Swiss

Eggs & Cheese

Versatile and high in protein, eggs and cheese are great alternatives to meat. Check out the variety of recipes in this chapter and you'll see just how easy it is to mix up a meal with these basic ingredients. You'll find everything from Egg-Filled Ham Cups for lazy Sunday mornings to a Spinach & Asiago Cheese Frittata for entertaining guests.

Easy Baked Eggs

Prep: 10 minutes Bake: 25 minutes Oven: 325°F Makes: 3 servings

Butter

6 eggs

Snipped fresh chives

Salt and black pepper

6 tablespoons shredded

cheddar, Swiss, or Monterey

Jack cheese (1½ ounces)

1. Generously grease three 10-ounce casseroles with butter. Carefully break 2 eggs into each casserole; sprinkle with chives, salt, and pepper. Set casseroles in a 13×9×2-inch baking pan; place on an oven rack. Pour hot water around casseroles in pan to a depth of 1 inch.

2. Bake in a 325° oven for 20 minutes. Sprinkle shredded cheese on top of eggs; bake for 5 to 10 minutes more or until eggs are firm, whites are opaque, and cheese melts.

1_g carbs 0_g fiber 1_g net carbs

Nutrition Facts per serving: 161 cal., 11 g total fat (3 g sat. fat), 426 mg chol., 186 mg sodium, 1 g carbo., 0 g fiber, 13 g pro.

Meat Lover's Scrambled Eggs

Start to Finish: 20 minutes   Makes: 4 servings

1. In a medium bowl beat together eggs, water, salt, and pepper with a rotary beater; set aside.

2. In a large skillet cook and stir bacon and sausage over medium heat until bacon is crisp and sausage is no longer pink. Drain, reserving 1 tablespoon drippings in skillet. Set bacon and sausage aside.

3. Add egg mixture to drippings in skillet. Cook over medium heat without stirring until mixture begins to set on the bottom and around edge. Sprinkle bacon, sausage, and ham over egg mixture.

4. With a spatula or a large spoon, lift and fold the partially cooked egg mixture so the uncooked portion flows underneath. Continue cooking over medium heat for 2 to 3 minutes or until egg mixture is cooked through but is still glossy and moist. Sprinkle with shredded cheese and if desired, green onion. Remove from heat. Let stand 1 to 2 minutes or until cheese melts.

8 **eggs**

½ **cup water, heavy**
   cream, or light cream

¼ **teaspoon salt**

⅛ **teaspoon black pepper**

4 **slices bacon, chopped**

4 **ounces bulk pork sausage**

½ **cup chopped cooked**
   ham and/or Polish sausage

½ **cup shredded cheddar cheese**

   Thinly sliced green onion

   (optional)

2 g carbs   **0** g fiber   **2** g net carbs

Nutrition Facts per serving: 380 cal., 29 g total fat (11 g sat. fat), 473 mg chol., 707 mg sodium, 2 g carbo., 0 g fiber, 25 g pro.

Egg-Filled Ham Cups

Start to Finish: 30 minutes Oven: 350°F Makes: 4 servings

4   thin slices cooked ham

(about 4 ounces)

4   eggs

Salt and black pepper

4   teaspoons heavy cream

or light cream

Shredded cheese or snipped

fresh herbs (optional)

1. Lightly butter four 6-ounce custard cups. Place cups on a baking sheet. Line each cup with a slice of ham, pleating ham as needed to fit.

2. Carefully break 1 egg into the center of each custard cup. Sprinkle with salt and pepper. Pour 1 teaspoon of cream over each egg; cover with foil.

3. Bake in a 350° oven for 20 to 25 minutes or until eggs are firm and whites are opaque. If desired, garnish with shredded cheese.

See photo, page 34.

2g
carbs

0g
fiber

2g
net carbs

Nutrition Facts per serving: 137 cal., 9 g total fat (4 g sat. fat), 235 mg chol., 476 mg sodium, 2 g carbo., 0 g fiber, 11 g pro.

Sweet Pepper-Gruyère Omelet

Start to Finish: 10 minutes Makes: 1 serving

1. In an 8-inch nonstick skillet with flared sides cook sweet pepper in hot butter over medium heat until tender. Remove sweet pepper with a slotted spoon; set aside.

2. Meanwhile, in a small bowl beat together eggs, water, salt, and black pepper with a fork until combined but not frothy.

3. Add egg mixture to the hot skillet. Stir egg mixture gently but continuously with a spatula until mixture resembles small pieces of cooked egg surrounded by liquid egg. Stop stirring. Cook 30 to 60 seconds more or until egg mixture is set but shiny. Sprinkle cheese across center of omelet. Spoon cooked sweet peppers over cheese. With a spatula lift and fold an edge of the omelet about a third of the way toward the center. Remove from heat. Fold the opposite edge toward the center. Transfer to a warm plate.

⅓ cup chopped red and/or green sweet pepper

1 tablespoon butter

2 eggs

2 tablespoons water

Dash salt

Dash black pepper

¼ cup shredded Gruyère or Swiss cheese (1 ounce)

5 g carbs

1 g fiber

4 g net carbs

Nutrition Facts per serving: 387 cal., 31 g total fat (16 g sat. fat), 489 mg chol., 487 mg sodium, 5 g carbo., 1 g fiber, 22 g pro.

Scrambled Eggs with Smoked Salmon & Chives

Start to Finish: 15 minutes Makes: 4 servings

6 eggs

⅓ cup water

3 tablespoons snipped

   fresh chives

1 tablespoon butter

1 3- to 4-ounce package thinly

   sliced, smoked salmon

   (lox-style), cut into

   bite-size strips

   Snipped fresh chives

   (optional)

1. In a medium bowl beat together eggs, water, and chives with a rotary beater. In a large skillet melt butter over medium heat; pour in egg mixture. Cook over medium heat without stirring until mixture begins to set on the bottom and around edge.

2. With a spatula or large spoon, lift and fold partially cooked egg mixture so the uncooked portion flows underneath. Fold in salmon; continue cooking over medium heat for 2 to 3 minutes or until egg mixture is cooked through but is still glossy and moist. If desired, garnish with fresh chives.

See photo, page 35.

1 g carbs   0 g fiber   1 g net carbs

Nutrition Facts per serving: 164 cal., 11 g total fat (4 g sat. fat),
332 mg chol., 551 mg sodium, 1 g carbo., 0 g fiber, 13 g pro.

Cheese Frittata with Mushrooms & Dill

Start to Finish: 25 minutes Makes: 4 servings

1. In a medium bowl combine eggs, cheese, water, salt, and pepper; set aside.

2. In a 10-inch nonstick skillet melt butter over medium-high heat. Add mushrooms; cook for 4 to 5 minutes or until liquid evaporates. Stir in green onions, parsley, and dill.

3. Pour egg mixture over vegetables in skillet. Cook over medium heat. As mixture sets, run a spatula around edge of skillet, lifting egg mixture so uncooked portion flows underneath. Continue cooking and lifting edges until egg mixture is almost set. Remove from heat.

4. Cover and let stand for 3 to 4 minutes or until top is set. Cut into wedges.

6 beaten eggs

⅓ cup shredded Gruyère
   or Swiss cheese

¼ cup water, heavy cream,
   or light cream

¼ teaspoon salt

⅛ teaspoon black pepper

2 tablespoons butter

1½ cups thinly sliced fresh
   mushrooms (4 ounces)

¼ cup sliced green onions (2)

1 tablespoon snipped fresh
   flat-leaf parsley

1 tablespoon snipped
   fresh dill

3g carbs   **0**g fiber   **3**g net carbs

Nutrition Facts per serving: 216 cal., 17 g total fat (5 g sat. fat), 331 mg chol., 332 mg sodium, 3 g carbo., 0 g fiber, 13 g pro.

Brie & Mushroom Scrambled Eggs

Start to Finish: 30 minutes Makes: 6 servings

½ of a 4- to 5-ounce round Brie
   or Camembert cheese

8 eggs

2 tablespoons water, heavy
   cream, or light cream

1 tablespoon snipped fresh
   chives or thinly sliced
   green onion tops

¼ teaspoon salt

⅛ teaspoon black pepper

2 ounces sliced pancetta or
   3 slices bacon
   Olive oil

1½ cups fresh mushrooms, sliced

6 ounces fresh arugula, lightly
   steamed (4½ cups)

1. Remove rind from cheese, if desired. Cut cheese into bite-size pieces; set aside.

2. In a medium bowl beat together eggs, water, chives, salt, and pepper with a rotary beater; set aside. In a large skillet cook pancetta over medium heat until crisp. Drain on paper towels, reserving drippings in skillet. Crumble pancetta and set aside. Measure drippings in skillet; add oil, if necessary, to equal 2 tablespoons.

3. Add mushrooms to skillet; cook over medium heat until tender. Return pancetta to skillet.

4. Pour egg mixture over mushroom mixture in skillet. Cook without stirring until mixture begins to set on the bottom and around edge. Using a large spatula, lift and fold the partially cooked eggs so that the uncooked portions are underneath.

5. Continue cooking over medium heat for 2 to 3 minutes or until egg mixture is cooked through but is still glossy and moist. Top with Brie. Remove from heat. Cover and let stand for 1 to 2 minutes to soften cheese.

6. Place arugula in a steamer basket in a skillet over a small amount of gently boiling water. Cover and steam about 1 minute or until arugula is just wilted. Drain well. Divide arugula among 4 plates. Spoon egg mixture alongside.

2 g carbs   1 g fiber   1 g net carbs

Nutrition Facts per serving: 217 cal., 17 g total fat (5 g sat. fat), 298 mg chol., 432 mg sodium, 2 g carbo., 1 g fiber, 13 g pro.

Poached Eggs Florentine

Start to Finish: 25 minutes Makes: 4 servings

1. Half fill a large skillet with water. Bring water to boiling; reduce heat to simmering (bubbles should begin to break the surface of the water).

2. Break 1 egg into a measuring cup. Carefully slide egg into simmering water, holding the lip of the cup as close to the water as possible. Repeat with remaining eggs.

3. Simmer eggs, uncovered, for 3 to 5 minutes or until the whites are completely set and yolks begin to thicken but are not hard. Remove eggs with a slotted spoon. Season to taste with salt and pepper.

4. Meanwhile, in a large skillet bring 2 tablespoons water to boiling. Add spinach. Cover and cook for 1 minute or until wilted, stirring with tongs once or twice. Stir in the $\frac{1}{4}$ teaspoon salt, the $\frac{1}{8}$ teaspoon pepper, and nutmeg.

5. Using a slotted spoon, divide spinach mixture among 4 plates. Top with poached eggs and sprinkle with cheese.

4 **eggs**

   Salt and black pepper

8 **cups fresh spinach**

$\frac{1}{4}$ **teaspoon salt**

$\frac{1}{8}$ **teaspoon black pepper**

   Dash ground nutmeg

2 **tablespoons finely shredded**

   Parmesan cheese

3g carbs **1**g fiber **2**g net carbs

Nutrition Facts per serving: 157 cal., 10 g total fat (4 g sat. fat), 223 mg chol., 618 mg sodium, 3 g carbo., 1 g fiber, 14 g pro.

French Omelet

Start to Finish: 10 minutes Makes: 1 serving

2 eggs

2 tablespoons water

⅛ teaspoon salt

Dash black pepper

1 tablespoon butter

1. In a small bowl combine eggs, water, salt, and pepper. Beat with a fork until combined but not frothy. Heat an 8-inch nonstick skillet with flared sides over medium-high heat until skillet is hot.

2. Add butter to skillet. When butter melts, add egg mixture to skillet; lower heat to medium. Stir eggs gently but continuously with a wooden or plastic spatula until mixture resembles small pieces of cooked egg surrounded by liquid egg. Stop stirring. Cook for 30 to 60 seconds more or until egg is set but shiny.

3. If desired, spoon filling (see option below) across the center. With a spatula lift and fold an edge of the omelet about a third of the way toward the center. Remove from the heat. Fold the opposite edge of omelet toward the center and transfer to a warm plate.

Cheese Omelet: Prepare as above, except omit salt. In step 3, sprinkle ¼ cup shredded cheddar, Swiss, or Monterey Jack cheese across center of omelet for filling.

Nutrition Facts per serving: 370 cal., 32 g total fat (17 g sat. fat), 487 mg chol., 426 mg sodium, 2 g carbo., 0 g dietary fiber, 20 g pro.

1 g carbs   0 g fiber   1 g net carbs

Nutrition Facts per serving: 257 cal., 22 g total fat (11 g sat. fat), 458 mg chol., 541 mg sodium, 1 g carbo., 0 g fiber, 13 g pro.

Zucchini Frittata

Start to Finish: 25 minutes Oven: 400°F Makes: 4 to 6 servings

1. In a medium bowl combine eggs, parsley, water, rosemary, salt, and pepper; set aside. In a large ovenproof skillet cook and stir zucchini and leek in hot butter just until tender.

2. Pour egg mixture over vegetables in skillet. Cook over medium heat. As mixture sets, run a spatula around edge of skillet, lifting egg mixture so uncooked portion flows underneath. Continue cooking and lifting until egg mixture is almost set (surface will be moist).

3. Place pan in a 400° oven. Bake, uncovered, about 4 minutes or until top is just set. Cut the half circle of Camembert horizontally (if using); cut each half into 2 or 3 wedges and place on the frittata. Allow cheese to melt slightly before serving.

6 eggs

2 tablespoons snipped fresh parsley

2 tablespoons water, heavy cream, or light cream

½ teaspoon snipped fresh rosemary or ⅛ teaspoon dried rosemary, crushed

½ teaspoon salt

⅛ teaspoon black pepper

1 cup thinly sliced zucchini (1 small)

½ cup thinly sliced leek (1 medium)

1 tablespoon butter

½ of a 4½-ounce package Camembert cheese or 2 tablespoons freshly shredded Parmesan cheese

5g carbs   **1**g fiber   **4**g net carbs

Nutrition Facts per serving: 201 cal., 14 g total fat (5 g sat. fat), 331 mg chol., 534 mg sodium, 5 g carbo., 1 g fiber, 13 g pro.

Crustless Mexican Quiche

Prep: 15 minutes Bake: 30 minutes Stand: 10 minutes
Oven: 325°F Makes: 6 servings

Nonstick cooking spray

½ pound bulk chorizo or

   hot pork sausage

4 beaten eggs

1½ cups light cream

1½ cups shredded Monterey

   Jack cheese with

   jalapeño peppers

⅓ cup bottled salsa

1. Lightly coat a 9-inch pie plate with cooking spray; set aside.

2. In a small skillet cook chorizo until brown; drain off fat. Meanwhile, in a medium bowl stir together eggs and cream; stir in cooked chorizo. Add cheese; mix well. Pour egg mixture into the prepared pie plate.

3. Bake in a 325° oven about 30 minutes or until a knife inserted near the center comes out clean. Let stand about 10 minutes before serving. Top each serving with salsa.

See photo, page 36.

4 g carbs   **0** g fiber   **4** g net carbs

Nutrition Facts per serving: 406 cal., 33 g total fat (16 g sat. fat), 222 mg chol., 714 mg sodium, 4 g carbo., 0 g fiber, 22 g pro.

Oven Omelet

Start to Finish: 25 minutes Oven: 400°F Makes: 6 servings

1. Lightly coat a 15×10×1-inch baking pan with nonstick coating; set aside. In a medium bowl beat together eggs, water, salt, and pepper with a rotary beater until combined but not frothy.

2. Place the prepared pan on an oven rack. Carefully pour the egg mixture into the pan. Bake in a 400° oven about 7 minutes or until egg mixture is set but still glossy.

3. Cut the omelet into six 5-inch squares. Using a large spatula, remove square and invert onto warm serving plates. Spoon some cheese on half of each square; fold other half over filling, forming a triangle or a rectangle.

Nonstick cooking spray

12 eggs

¼ cup water

½ teaspoon salt

⅛ teaspoon black pepper

1 cup shredded cheddar, Monterey Jack, or Colby cheese (4 ounces)

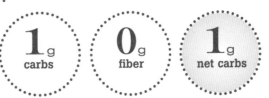

1 g carbs   **0** g fiber   **1** g net carbs

Nutrition Facts per serving: 226 cal., 16 g total fat (7 g sat. fat), 446 mg chol., 421 mg sodium, 1 g carbo., 0 g fiber, 17 g pro.

Spinach Omelet with Red Pepper Relish

Start to Finish: 20 minutes Makes: 2 servings

⅓ cup chopped red sweet pepper

1 tablespoon finely chopped onion

1½ teaspoons cider vinegar

⅛ teaspoon black pepper

4 eggs

Dash salt

Dash cayenne pepper

2 tablespoons butter

¼ cup shredded sharp cheddar cheese (1 ounce)

1 tablespoon snipped fresh chives or flat-leaf parsley

1 cup spinach leaves

1. For red pepper relish, in a small bowl combine sweet pepper, onion, vinegar, and black pepper. Set aside.

2. In a large bowl combine eggs, salt, and cayenne pepper. Beat with a fork until combined. Heat a 10-inch nonstick skillet with flared sides over medium-high heat until skillet is hot.

3. Add butter to skillet. When butter melts, add egg mixture to skillet; lower heat to medium. Stir egg mxiture gently but continuously with a spatula until mixture resembles small pieces of cooked egg surrounded by liquid egg. Stop stirring. Cook 30 to 60 seconds more or until egg mixture is set but shiny.

4. Sprinkle with cheese and chives. Top with ¾ cup of the spinach and 2 tablespoons of the relish. Lift and fold an edge of omelet about a third of the way toward the center. Remove from heat. Fold the opposite edge toward the center. Top with the remaining spinach and remaining relish. Cut the omelet in half. Transfer to warm plates.

4g carbs   **1**g fiber   **3**g net carbs

Nutrition Facts per serving: 325 cal., 27 g total fat (12 g sat. fat), 470 mg chol., 397 mg sodium, 4 g carbo., 1 g fiber, 17 g pro.

Brunch Scrambled Eggs

Start to Finish: 20 minutes Makes: 6 servings

1. Drain thawed spinach well, pressing out excess liquid; set aside.

2. In a large bowl beat together eggs, water, dried oregano, salt, and pepper with a rotary beater. In a large skillet melt butter over medium heat; pour in egg mixture. Cook without stirring until mixture begins to set on the bottom and around edge. Using a large spatula, lift and fold partially cooked egg mixture so uncooked portion flows underneath. Stir in spinach, Colby cheese, and half of the feta cheese. Continue cooking over medium heat for 2 to 3 minutes or until egg mixture is cooked through but is still glossy and moist. Transfer to a serving bowl; sprinkle with remaining feta cheese.

See photo, page 37.

1 10-ounce package frozen
      chopped spinach, thawed

12 eggs

½ cup water, heavy cream,
      or light cream

½ teaspoon dried oregano or
      thyme, crushed

¼ teaspoon salt

⅛ teaspoon black pepper

2 tablespoons butter

1 cup shredded Colby or cheddar
      cheese (4 ounces)

1 cup crumbled feta cheese
      (4 ounces)

3g carbs   **1**g fiber   **2**g net carbs

Nutrition Facts per serving: 318 cal., 24 g total fat (12 g sat. fat), 468 mg chol., 653 mg sodium, 3 g carbo., 1 g fiber, 21 g pro.

Oven Omelets with Pesto

Start to Finish: 30 minutes Oven: 400°F Makes: 6 servings

1 recipe Spinach Pesto

Nonstick cooking spray

12 eggs

¼ cup water

¾ teaspoon salt

⅛ teaspoon black pepper

1 medium zucchini, halved

lengthwise and thinly sliced

1 tablespoon olive oil

1 medium Roma tomato,

seeded and chopped

Grated Parmesan cheese

(optional)

1. Prepare Spinach Pesto; set aside. Lightly coat a 15×10×1-inch baking pan with nonstick coating; set aside.

2. In a medium bowl beat together eggs, water, salt, and pepper with a rotary beater until combined but not frothy. Place the prepared pan on an oven rack. Carefully pour the egg mixture into the pan. Bake in a 400° oven about 7 minutes or until egg mixture is set but still glossy.

3. Meanwhile, in a large skillet cook zucchini in hot oil just until tender. Remove from heat. Stir in about half of the Spinach Pesto.

4. Cut the omelet into six 5-inch squares. Using a large spatula, remove squares and invert onto warm serving plates. Spoon zucchini mixture on half of each square; fold other half over filling, forming a triangle or a rectangle. Top with remaining pesto; sprinkle with chopped tomato and if desired, Parmesan cheese.

Spinach Pesto: In a food processor bowl combine ½ cup packed torn fresh spinach; ¼ cup packed fresh basil leaves; 2 tablespoons grated Parmesan cheese; 1 small clove garlic, quartered; and dash salt. Cover and process with several on-off turns until a paste forms, stopping the machine several times and scraping sides. With machine running, gradually add 1 tablespoon olive oil. Process until mixture is the consistency of soft butter.

3 g carbs

1 g fiber

2 g net carbs

Nutrition Facts per serving: 202 cal., 15 g total fat (4 g sat. fat), 424 mg chol., 485 mg sodium, 3 g carbo., 1 g fiber, 14 g pro.

See photo, page 33.

Oven
Omelets with
Pesto
p. 32

Egg-Filled
Ham Cups
p. 20

Scrambled Eggs with Smoked Salmon & Chives p. 22

Crustless
Mexican
Quiche
p. 28

Brunch
Scrambled
Eggs
p. 31

Ham &
Swiss Skillet
p. 42

Pepperoni
Pizza Frittata
p. 49

Seafood Omelet with Avocado Salsa p. 41

Seafood Omelet with Avocado Salsa

Start to Finish: 20 minutes Makes: 4 servings

1. For avocado salsa, in a medium bowl combine avocado, red onion, cilantro, lime juice, and salt and black pepper to taste.

2. In a large bowl combine eggs, water, green onions, the ¼ teaspoon salt, ¼ teaspoon black pepper, and cayenne pepper. Beat with a fork until combined but not frothy. Heat an 8-inch nonstick skillet with flared sides over medium-high heat until skillet is hot.

3. Add 1 tablespoon of the butter to skillet. When butter melts, add ½ cup of the egg mixture; lower heat to medium. Stir egg mixture gently but continuously with a spatula until mixture resembles small pieces of cooked egg surrounded by liquid egg. Stop stirring. Cook 30 to 60 seconds more or until egg mixture is set but shiny.

4. Spoon one-fourth of the crab meat across center of eggs. With a spatula lift and fold edge of the omelet about a third of the way toward the center. Remove from heat. Fold the opposite edge toward the center; transfer to a warm plate. Repeat with remaining butter, egg mixture, and filling. Serve with avocado salsa.

See photo, page 40.

1 medium avocado, halved, seeded, peeled, and chopped

1 tablespoon finely chopped red onion

1 tablespoon snipped fresh cilantro

1 tablespoon lime juice

   Salt and black pepper

8 eggs

½ cup water

¼ cup chopped green onion

¼ teaspoon salt

¼ teaspoon black pepper

¼ teaspoon cayenne pepper

4 tablespoons butter

1 6-ounce can crabmeat, drained, flaked, and cartilage removed, or 7-ounce package frozen peeled, cooked tiny shrimp, thawed and patted dry

6 g carbs   **3** g fiber   **3** g net carbs

Nutrition Facts per serving: 373 cal., 29 g total fat (10 g sat. fat), 493 mg chol., 665 mg sodium, 6 g carbo., 3 g fiber, 22 g pro.

Ham & Swiss Skillet

Start to Finish: 25 minutes Makes: 6 servings

12 eggs

½ teaspoon dried thyme,

    crushed

    Dash salt

    Dash black pepper

1 cup coarsely chopped

    zucchini or yellow summer

    squash

1 tablespoon butter

1½ cups coarsely chopped

    cooked ham

½ cup shredded Swiss cheese

    (2 ounces)

    Snipped fresh chives

    (optional)

1. In a medium bowl combine eggs, thyme, salt, and pepper; set aside. In a 10-inch broilerproof skillet cook zucchini in hot butter until tender, stirring occasionally. Stir in ham.

2. Pour egg mixture over zucchini mixture in skillet. Cook over medium-low heat without stirring until mixture begins to set on the bottom and around the edge. As egg mixture sets, run a spatula around the edge of skillet, lifting eggs so the uncooked portion flows underneath. Continue cooking and lifting edges until egg mixture is almost set (surface will be moist). Sprinkle with cheese.

3. Place the skillet under the boiler 4 to 5 inches from the heat. Broil for 1 to 2 minutes or just until top is set and cheese melts. If desired, sprinkle with chives. Cut into wedges.

See photo, page 38.

3g carbs   **1**g fiber   **2**g net carbs

Nutrition Facts per serving: 260 cal., 17 g total fat (7 g sat. fat), 456 mg chol., 638 mg sodium, 3 g carbo., 1 g fiber, 21 g pro.

Spinach & Asiago Cheese Frittata

Start to Finish: 30 minutes Oven: 350°F Makes: 6 servings

1. In a 10-inch ovenproof skillet, cook leek and garlic in hot oil over medium heat about 2 minutes or until tender, stirring frequently. Add spinach; cook and stir about 1 minute more or until spinach is limp. Remove from heat. Stir in sweet pepper strips, $\frac{1}{2}$ cup of the Asiago cheese, thyme, salt, and black pepper. Add eggs, stirring to mix well.

2. Bake in a 350° oven for 13 to 15 minutes or until a knife inserted near the center comes out clean. Sprinkle remaining Asiago cheese over the top of the frittata. Cut into wedges.

1 leek, thinly sliced

2 cloves garlic, minced

1 tablespoon olive oil or

   cooking oil

4 cups torn fresh spinach

$\frac{2}{3}$ cup bottled roasted red sweet

   pepper, cut into thin strips

$\frac{3}{4}$ cup shredded Asiago cheese

   (3 ounces)

$1\frac{1}{2}$ teaspoons snipped fresh thyme or

   $\frac{1}{4}$ teaspoon dried thyme, crushed

$\frac{1}{8}$ teaspoon salt

$\frac{1}{8}$ teaspoon black pepper

6 slightly beaten eggs

2g carbs   **1**g fiber   **1**g net carbs

Nutrition Facts per serving: 101 cal., 8 g total fat (3 g sat. fat), 114 mg chol., 170 mg sodium, 2 g carbo., 1 g fiber, 6 g pro.

Tomato & Basil Frittata

Start to Finish: 25 minutes Oven: 350°F Makes: 2 servings

5 egg whites

1 egg

1 tablespoon snipped fresh
   basil or ½ teaspoon dried
   basil, crushed

⅛ teaspoon salt

   Dash black pepper

   Nonstick spray coating

½ cup chopped fresh spinach

2 green onions, sliced

1 clove garlic, minced

1 small tomato, chopped

¼ cup shredded reduced-fat
   cheddar cheese (1 ounce)

1. In a medium bowl lightly beat together egg whites and whole egg. Stir in basil, salt, and pepper; set aside.

2. Spray an unheated 8-inch ovenproof skillet with nonstick coating. Preheat the skillet over medium heat. Add spinach, green onions, and garlic. Cook for 1 to 2 minutes or until spinach begins to wilt. Remove skillet from heat; drain, if necessary.

3. Pour egg mixture over spinach mixture in the skillet. Bake, uncovered, in a 350° oven for 6 to 8 minutes or until egg mixture is set. Sprinkle with chopped tomato and cheese. Bake for 1 to 2 minutes more or until the cheese melts. Cut the frittata into wedges.

5 g carbs   **1** g fiber   **4** g net carbs

Nutrition Facts per serving: 143 cal., 5 g total fat (2 g sat. fat),
116 mg chol., 430 mg sodium, 5 g carbo., 1 g fiber, 17 g pro.

Broccoli-Pepper Frittata

Start to Finish: 30 minutes Makes: 6 servings

1. In a medium bowl combine eggs and water; set aside. In a 10-inch skillet heat oil. Add broccoli, sweet pepper, onion, Italian seasoning, salt, and black pepper. Cook and stir over medium heat for 4 to 5 minutes or until vegetables are crisp-tender.

2. Pour egg mixture over vegetable mixture in skillet. As mixture sets, run a spatula around edge of skillet, lifting egg mixture so uncooked portion flows underneath. Continue cooking and lifting edges until eggs are nearly set (surface will be moist).

3. Remove skillet from heat; sprinkle with cheese. Cover and let stand for 3 minutes or until set. Cut into wedges.

10 beaten eggs

2 tablespoons water, heavy cream, or light cream

1 tablespoon cooking oil

1 cup fresh or frozen broccoli florets, thawed

½ of a large red sweet pepper, seeded and thinly sliced (¾ cup)

¼ cup chopped onion

½ teaspoon dried Italian seasoning, crushed

¼ teaspoon salt

⅛ teaspoon black pepper

2 tablespoons finely shredded Parmesan cheese

4g carbs   **1**g fiber   **3**g net carbs

Nutrition Facts per serving: 202 cal., 14 g total fat (5 g sat. fat), 360 mg chol., 407 mg sodium, 4 g carbo., 1 g fiber, 15 g pro.

Salmon, Herb & Cheese Oven Frittata

Prep: 20 minutes Bake: 15 minutes Oven: 400°F Makes: 6 servings

8   beaten eggs

½   cup heavy cream or light

     cream

½   cup snipped fresh basil

¼   cup snipped fresh chives

¼   cup snipped fresh tarragon

¼   teaspoon salt

¼   teaspoon freshly ground

     black pepper

3   ounces thinly sliced smoked

     salmon, chopped

1   3-ounce package cream

     cheese, cut into ½-inch

     pieces

2   teaspoons olive oil

1. In a large bowl combine eggs, cream, basil, chives, tarragon, salt, and pepper. Stir in smoked salmon and cream cheese.

2. Brush the bottom and sides of a 12-inch ovenproof skillet with oil. Pour in egg mixture. Bake in a 400° oven for 15 to 18 minutes or just until center is set. Cut into wedges.

2 g carbs   **0** g fiber   **2** g net carbs

Nutrition Facts per serving: 249 cal., 21 g total fat (10 g sat. fat), 328 mg chol., 524 mg sodium, 2 g carbo., 0 g fiber, 13 g pro.

Benedict-Style Eggs & Mushrooms

Start to Finish: 25 minutes Makes: 4 servings

1. Remove stems from shiitake mushrooms and discard; halve mushrooms. In a large skillet cook mushrooms in hot oil until tender. Sprinkle with salt and pepper.

2. Meanwhile, grease another large skillet. Half fill skillet with water. Bring to boiling; reduce heat to simmering (bubbles should begin to break surface). Break 1 egg into a measuring cup. Carefully slide egg into simmering water, holding the lip of the cup as close to the water as possible. Repeat with remaining eggs. Simmer, uncovered, for 3 to 5 minutes or until whites are completely set and yolks begin to thicken but are not hard.

3. To serve, divide mushrooms among 4 plates. Using a slotted spoon, remove eggs from water and place on top of mushrooms. Spoon Easy Hollandaise Sauce over eggs.

Easy Hollandaise Sauce: In a small saucepan stir together $^1/_4$ cup dairy sour cream, $^1/_4$ cup mayonnaise, 1 teaspoon lemon juice, and $^1/_2$ teaspoon Dijon-style mustard. Cook and stir over low heat until warm; do not boil.

4 cups fresh shiitake or
  button mushrooms

2 tablespoons olive oil or butter

$^1/_4$ teaspoon salt

$^1/_8$ teaspoon black pepper

4 eggs

1 recipe Easy Hollandaise Sauce

6 g carbs   **1** g fiber   **5** g net carbs

Nutrition Facts per serving: 259 cal., 23 g total fat (4 g sat. fat), 222 mg chol., 302 mg sodium, 6 g carbo., 1 g fiber, 8 g pro.

Spicy Scrambled Eggs

Start to Finish: 10 minutes Makes: 4 servings

8 eggs

½ cup heavy cream or light

   cream

½ teaspoon salt

¼ teaspoon freshly ground

   black pepper

1 tablespoon butter

½ cup shredded cheddar cheese

   (2 ounces)

¼ cup bottled hot salsa

2 teaspoons snipped

   fresh cilantro

   Chopped green onion or

   avocado (optional)

1. In a medium bowl beat together eggs, cream, salt, and pepper with a rotary beater.

2. In a large skillet melt butter over medium heat; pour in egg mixture. Cook over medium heat without stirring until egg mixture begins to set on the bottom and around edge.

3. Sprinkle cheddar cheese on egg mixture. With a spatula or a large spoon, lift and fold the partially cooked egg mixture so the uncooked portion flows underneath. Continue cooking over medium heat for 2 to 3 minutes or until egg mixture is cooked through but is still glossy and moist. Remove from heat.

4. In a small bowl stir together salsa and cilantro. Serve eggs with salsa mixture and if desired, green onion.

2g carbs **0**g fiber **2**g net carbs

Nutrition Facts per serving: 337 cal., 29 g total fat (15 g sat. fat), 487 mg chol., 587 mg sodium, 2 g carbo., 0 g fiber, 17 g pro.

Pepperoni Pizza Frittata

Start to Finish: 30 minutes Makes: 4 servings

1. In a medium bowl combine eggs, oregano, salt, and pepper; set aside. Lightly coat a large broilerproof skillet with cooking spray. Heat skillet over medium heat.

2. Pour egg mixture into skillet. As mixture sets, run a spatula around edge of skillet, lifting egg mixture so uncooked portion flows underneath. Continue cooking and lifting edges until almost set (surface will be moist).

3. Remove skillet from heat. Sprinkle egg mixture with chopped tomatoes. Place skillet under the broiler 4 to 5 inches from heat. Broil for 1 to 2 minutes or just until top is set. Remove from broiler; top with pepperoni and ¼ cup of the cheese. Return to broiler. Broil 1 to 2 minutes more or until cheese melts. Sprinkle with remaining ¼ cup cheese. Cut into wedges.

See photo, page 39.

- 6 slightly beaten eggs
- ¾ teaspoon dried oregano, crushed
- ¼ teaspoon salt
- ¼ teaspoon black pepper
- Nonstick cooking spray
- ¾ cup chopped Roma tomatoes
- ⅓ cup chopped pepperoni
- ½ cup shredded mozzarella cheese (2 ounces)

3g carbs   **1**g fiber   **2**g net carbs

Nutrition Facts per serving: 212 cal., 15 g total fat (6 g sat. fat), 338 mg chol., 512 mg sodium, 3 g carbo., 1 g fiber, 15 g pro.

Scrambled Eggs with Sausage & Feta Cheese

Start to Finish: 20 minutes Makes: 4 servings

8 eggs

½ cup water, heavy cream,

    or light cream

6 ounces smoked turkey

    sausage, sliced or chopped

2 tablespoons butter

1 4-ounce package crumbled

    feta cheese with garlic

    and herbs

1. In a medium bowl beat together eggs and water with rotary beater; set aside.

2. In a large skillet cook sausage in hot butter over medium heat for 2 to 3 minutes or until sausage just begins to brown. Pour in egg mixture. Cook over medium heat without stirring until egg mixture begins to set on the bottom and around edge.

3. With a spatula or a large spoon, lift and fold the partially cooked egg mixture so the uncooked portion flows underneath. When eggs are almost set, sprinkle with feta cheese. Continue cooking over medium heat for 1 minute or until egg mixture is cooked through but is still glossy and moist.

3g carbs   **0**g fiber   **3**g net carbs

Nutrition Facts per serving: 339 cal., 26 g total fat (11 g sat. fat),
493 mg chol., 870 mg sodium, 3 g carbo., 0 g fiber, 23 g pro.

Mexican Beef Hash with Eggs

Start to Finish: 30 minutes Makes: 4 servings

1. In a large nonstick skillet cook onions, jalapeños, and garlic in 1 tablespoon hot oil over medium heat until tender. Stir in beef, cumin, lime peel, and lime juice. Cook and stir until heated through. Divide beef mixture among 4 plates, keep warm.

2. In the same skillet, heat the remaining 1 tablespoon oil over medium heat. Carefully break 4 eggs into skillet. When whites are set, add water. Cover skillet and cook until desired doneness (3 to 4 minutes for soft-set yolks or 4 to 5 minutes for firm-set yolks). Remove from skillet; keep warm. Repeat with remaining eggs.

3. Top each serving of beef mixture with 2 fried eggs. Season to taste with salt and black pepper. Top with sour cream and shredded cheese.

*****Note:** Because hot chile peppers, such as jalapeños, contain volatile oils that can burn your skin and eyes, wear plastic or rubber golves when working with chile peppers. If your bare hands do touch the peppers, wash your hands well with soap and water.

¼ **cup thinly sliced green onions (2)**

2 **fresh jalapeño or serrano peppers,**

  seeded and finely chopped*

2 **cloves garlic, minced**

2 **tablespoons cooking oil**

8 **ounces cooked beef, chopped**

1 **teaspoon ground cumin**

¼ **teaspoon finely shredded lime peel**

1 **tablespoon lime juice**

8 **eggs**

1 **tablespoon water**

  Salt and black pepper

¼ **cup dairy sour cream**

¼ **cup shredded cheddar**

  cheese (1 ounce)

3g carbs   **1**g fiber   **2**g net carbs

Nutrition Facts per serving: 366 cal., 24 g total fat (8 g sat. fat), 475 mg chol., 374 mg sodium, 3 g carbo., 1 g fiber, 32 g pro.

Swiss Cheese & Ham Frittata

Start to Finish: 25 minutes Makes: 4 servings

6 slightly beaten eggs

⅛ teaspoon salt

⅛ teaspoon black pepper

1 cup diced cooked ham
(about 5 ounces)

¾ cup chopped red sweet
pepper

¼ cup chopped onion

1 tablespoon cooking oil

2 Roma tomatoes, thinly
sliced (optional)

½ cup shredded Swiss or white
cheddar cheese

Snipped fresh basil (optional)

1. In a medium bowl combine eggs, salt, and black pepper; set aside. In a medium broilerproof skillet cook ham, sweet pepper, and onion in hot oil over medium heat until vegetables are tender and ham is lightly browned, stirring occasionally.

2. Pour egg mixture over ham mixture in skillet. Cook over medium heat. As egg mixture sets, run a spatula around the edge of the skillet, lifting egg mixture so uncooked portion flows underneath. Continue cooking and lifting edges until egg mixture is almost set (surface will be moist).

3. Place skillet under broiler 4 to 5 inches from heat. Broil for 1 to 2 minutes or until top is just set. If desired, arrange tomato slices on top of frittata. Sprinkle with cheese. Broil 1 minute more. If desired, sprinkle with fresh basil. Cut into wedges.

5 g carbs   1 g fiber   4 g net carbs

Nutrition Facts per serving: 263 cal., 18 g total fat (6 g sat. fat),
350 mg chol., 668 mg sodium, 5 g carbo., 1 g fiber, 19 g pro.

Pepper & Cheese Omelet

Start to Finish: 30 minutes Makes: 4 servings

1. In a medium bowl, beat eggs and cream with a fork until combined; set aside.

2. In a 10-inch nonstick skillet with flared sides cook sweet peppers and jalapeño pepper in 1 tablespoon oil over medium heat for 2 to 3 minutes or until tender. Stir in tomato. Remove vegetable mixture from skillet; set aside.

3. In same skillet heat 1 teaspoon oil over medium heat. Add half of the egg mixture. Stir egg mixture gently but continuously with a spatula until mixture resembles small pieces of cooked egg surrounded by liquid egg. Stop stirring. Cook 30 to 60 seconds more or until egg mixture is set but shiny.

4. Spoon half of the vegetable mixture across the center of the omelet. Top with half of the cheddar cheese and half of the Swiss cheese. Fold sides of omelet over filling. Heat for 1 to 2 minutes more to melt the cheese. Transfer omelet to a serving plate; keep warm.

5. Repeat with another 1 teaspoon oil and remaining egg mixture, vegetable mixture, and cheeses.

6 eggs

¼ cup heavy cream

⅓ cup chopped green sweet pepper

⅓ cup chopped red sweet pepper

1 fresh jalapeño pepper, seeded
   and finely chopped (see note,
   page 51)

   Olive oil or cooking oil

1 medium tomato, seeded
   and chopped

¼ cup shredded cheddar cheese
   (1 ounce)

¼ cup shredded Swiss cheese
   (1 ounce)

5g carbs   **0**g fiber   **5**g net carbs

Nutrition Facts per serving: 280 cal., 23 g total fat (11 g sat. fat), 359 mg chol., 166 mg sodium, 5 g carbo., 0 g fiber, 14 g pro.

Smoked Salmon Frittata

Start to Finish: 25 minutes Makes: 4 servings

6   eggs

¼   teaspoon black pepper

    Nonstick cooking spray

¼   cup sliced green onions (2)

1   4-ounce piece smoked

    salmon, flaked, with skin and

    bones removed

2   tablespoons snipped fresh dill

    or 1 teaspoon dried dill

1   ounce semi-soft goat cheese

    (chèvre), crumbled

1. In a medium bowl combine eggs and pepper; set aside.

2. Lightly coat a large broilerproof skillet with cooking spray. Cook onion in skillet over medium heat until tender. Stir in salmon and dill. Pour egg mixture over salmon mixture in skillet. As egg mixture sets, run a spatula around edge of skillet, lifting egg mixture so uncooked portion flows underneath. Continue cooking and lifting edges until egg mixture is almost set (surface will be moist).

3. Place skillet under the broiler 4 to 5 inches from the heat. Broil for 1 to 2 minutes or just until top is set. Sprinkle with cheese. Cut into wedges.

1_g carbs 0_g fiber 1_g net carbs

Nutrition Facts per serving: 166 cal., 10 g total fat (4 g sat. fat),
329 mg chol., 344 mg sodium, 1 g carbo., 0 g fiber, 16 g pro.

Smoked Oyster-Stuffed Eggs

Start to Finish: 35 minutes Makes: 4 servings

1. Drain oysters well; pat with paper towels to remove oil. Coarsely chop oysters.

2. Halve hard-cooked eggs lengthwise and remove yolks. Set whites aside. Place yolks in a bowl; mash with a fork. Add mayonnaise, the 2 tablespoons chives, mustard, pepper, and chopped oysters; mix well.

3. Stuff egg white halves with oyster mixture. Garnish with snipped chives. If desired, serve with mixed greens and low-carb salad dressing.

*To hard-cook eggs: Place eggs in a single layer in a large saucepan. Add enough cold water to just cover eggs. Bring to a rapid boil over high heat (water will have large, rapidly breaking bubbles). Remove from heat, cover, and let stand for 15 minutes; drain. Run cold water over eggs or place in ice water to cool enough to handle; drain again. To peel, gently tap each egg on the countertop. Roll the eggs between the palms of your hands. Peel off eggshell, starting at the large end.

1 3- to 3¾-ounce can smoked oysters

8 hard-cooked eggs*

6 tablespoons mayonnaise

2 tablespoons snipped fresh chives

1 tablespoon Dijon-style mustard

¼ teaspoon freshly ground black pepper

1 tablespoon snipped fresh chives

Tossed mixed salad greens (optional)

Bottled low-carb salad dressing (optional)

4 g carbs   0 g fiber   4 g net carbs

Nutrition Facts per serving: 353 cal., 29 g total fat (6 g sat. fat), 444 mg chol., 414 mg sodium, 4 g carbo., 0 g fiber, 17 g pro.

Decadent Deviled Eggs

Start to Finish: 20 minutes Makes: 3 servings

6 hard-cooked eggs

   (see note, page 55)

⅓ cup mayonnaise

2 teaspoons Dijon-style mustard

1 teaspoon snipped fresh chives

1 6- to 6½-ounce can crabmeat,

   drained, flaked, and

   cartilage removed

   Salt and black pepper

   Fresh chives (optional)

   Tossed mixed salad greens

   (optional)

   Bottled low-carb salad

   dressing (optional)

1. Halve hard-cooked eggs lengthwise and remove yolks. Set whites aside. Place yolks in a bowl; mash with a fork. Add mayonnaise, mustard, and the 1 teaspoon chives; mix well. Gently stir in crabmeat. If desired, season to taste with salt and pepper.

2. Stuff egg white halves with crab mixture. If desired, garnish with additional chives. If desired, serve with tossed greens and low-carb salad dressing.

1 g carbs   0 g fiber   1 g net carbs

Nutrition Facts per serving: 391 cal., 31 g total fat (6 g sat. fat), 492 mg chol., 586 mg sodium, 1 g carbo., 0 g fiber, 24 g pro.

Bacon-Chive Deviled Eggs

Start to Finish: 20 minutes Makes: 6 servings

1. Halve hard-cooked eggs lengthwise and remove yolks. Set whites aside. Place yolks in a bowl; mash with a fork. Add mayonnaise, chives, and mustard; mix well. Season to taste with salt and pepper.

2. Stuff egg white halves with yolk mixture. Serve immediately or cover and chill for up to 24 hours. Just before serving, top with crumbled bacon. If desired, serve with tossed greens and low-carb salad dressing.

12 hard-cooked eggs

   (see note, page 55)

½ cup mayonnaise

2 tablespoons snipped

   fresh chives

2 teaspoons Dijon-style mustard

   Salt and black pepper

3 tablespoons crumbled crisp-

   cooked bacon (about

   3 slices)

   Tossed mixed salad greens

   (optional)

   Bottled low-carb salad

   dressing (optional)

1 g.	0 g	1 g
carbs	fiber	net carbs

Nutrition Facts per serving: 313 cal., 27 g total fat (6 g sat. fat), 441 mg chol., 363 mg sodium, 1 g carbo., 0 g fiber, 14 g pro.

57

Cheese & Turkey Wrap

Start to Finish: 25 minutes Makes: 6 servings

1 4-ounce package semi-soft
   goat cheese (chèvre)

½ of an 8-ounce package
   cream cheese, cubed

¼ cup heavy cream

½ cup shredded cheddar
   cheese (2 ounces)

2 tablespoons dairy sour cream

1 green onion, chopped

1 teaspoon Worcestershire
   sauce

6 ounces thinly sliced turkey,
   turkey ham, or beef

6 small lettuce leaves

1 small zucchini, cut lengthwise
   into narrow strips

1. In a food processor bowl combine goat cheese, cream cheese, and heavy cream; cover and process until smooth.

2. Add cheddar cheese, sour cream, onion, and Worcestershire sauce to goat cheese mixture. Cover and process until nearly smooth.

3. Place a slice of turkey on each lettuce leaf; spread with cheese mixture. Top each with one or two zucchini strips. Roll up.

3g carbs   **0**g fiber   **3**g net carbs

Nutrition Facts per serving: 231 cal., 19 g total fat (12 g sat. fat), 66 mg chol., 520 mg sodium, 3 g carbo., 0 g fiber, 13 g pro.

Marinated Vegetables, Cheese & Sausage

Prep: 30 minutes Marinate: 4 hours Makes: 6 servings

1. Cook artichoke hearts according to package directions. Drain and cool. Place in a large nonmetal bowl. Cut cheese and sausage into $\frac{1}{2}$-inch cubes; add to bowl. Add mushroom halves, olives, and zucchini sticks.

2. In a screw-top jar combine vinegar, oil, Italian seasoning, crushed red pepper, dry mustard, and garlic. Cover and shake well; pour over ingredients in bowl. Cover and chill for 4 to 24 hours, stirring occasionally. Just before serving, gently stir in cherry tomato halves. If desired, serve over tossed greens.

10-ounce package frozen artichoke hearts

6 ounces Muenster or provolone cheese

6 ounces unsliced, cooked Polish sausage

2 cups mushrooms, halved

1 cup pimiento-stuffed green olives

1 small zucchini, cut into $1\frac{1}{2}$-inch sticks

$\frac{1}{2}$ cup vinegar

$\frac{1}{3}$ cup salad oil

$1\frac{1}{2}$ teaspoons dried Italian seasoning, crushed

1 teaspoon crushed red pepper

$\frac{1}{2}$ teaspoon dry mustard

1 clove garlic, minced

$\frac{1}{2}$ cup cherry tomatoes, halved

Tossed mixed salad greens (optional)

9g carbs   **4**g fiber   **5**g net carbs

Nutrition Facts per serving: 369 cal., 32 g total fat (11 g sat. fat), 47 mg chol., 965 mg sodium, 9 g carbo., 4 g fiber, 14 g pro.

Herbed Goat Cheese Salad

Start to Finish: 25 minutes Makes: 6 servings

1 tablespoon snipped
fresh rosemary

2 teaspoons snipped
fresh thyme

1 teaspoon coarsely ground
black pepper

1 8-ounce roll goat cheese
(chèvre)

$1/8$ teaspoon salt

$1/3$ cup white wine vinegar

$1/4$ cup extra virgin olive oil

9 cups torn mixed salad greens

3 radishes, thinly sliced

1. Set aside $1/2$ teaspoon of the rosemary, $1/4$ teaspoon of the thyme, and $1/8$ teaspoon of the pepper. Combine the remaining herbs and pepper on a 12-inch square of waxed paper or plastic wrap. Roll goat cheese in the herbs to coat. Slice cheese into thin rounds.

2. In a screw-top jar combine reserved herbs and pepper and the salt; add vinegar and oil. Shake well to mix.

3. Divide greens and radish slices among 6 plates. Top each with goat cheese rounds. Shake dressing; drizzle over salads.

2g carbs **1**g fiber **1**g net carbs

Nutrition Facts per serving: 196 cal., 17 g total fat (7 g sat. fat),
17 mg chol., 197 mg sodium, 2 g carbo., 1 g fiber, 8 g pro.

Marinated Feta Salad

Prep: 20 minutes Stand: 30 minutes Chill: 3 days Makes: 4 servings

1. In a small bowl combine olive oil, herbs, garlic, lemon juice, cracked peppercorns, and poppy seeds. Stir until well mixed. Add cheese cubes; toss gently to coat. Divide mixture between two clean half-pint jars with lids.

2. Cover and store in the refrigerator for 3 to 5 days. To use, let stand at room temperature for 30 minutes before serving. Serve on mixed greens with turkey strips and low-carb salad dressing.

2 tablespoons olive oil

2 tablespoons assorted
   snipped fresh herbs, such as
   dill, thyme, basil, oregano,
   and/or parsley

2 cloves garlic, minced

1 tablespoon lemon juice

1 teaspoon dried whole mixed
   peppercorns, cracked

½ teaspoon poppy seeds

8 ounces feta cheese, cubed

   Tossed mixed salad greens (optional)

   Cooked turkey or ham, cut into strips
   (optional)

   Bottled low-carb salad
   dressing (optional)

4 g carbs 0 g fiber 4 g net carbs

Nutrition Facts per serving: 214 cal., 19 g total fat (9 g sat. fat),
50 mg chol., 626 mg sodium, 4 g carbo., 0 g fiber, 8 g pro.

Cooking Eggs

Eggs make a quick, inexpensive meal that's also high in protein and other nutrients. Plus, there are so many different ways to make them. Follow the methods below for the best-ever soft-cooked, poached, and fried eggs.

Soft-Cooked Eggs

Start to Finish: 10 minutes

Makes: 4 soft-cooked eggs

  4 eggs

     Cold water

Place eggs in a single layer in a medium saucepan. Add enough cold water to just cover the eggs. Bring to a rapid boil over high heat (water will have large rapidly breaking bubbles). Remove from heat, cover, and let stand for 3 to 4 minutes; drain.

  Run cold water over the eggs or place them in ice water just until cool enough to handle; drain. Cut off tops and serve in egg cups. Or cut the eggs in half and use a spoon to scoop the eggs into serving dishes.

Nutrition Facts per egg: 78 cal., 5 g total fat (2 g sat. fat), 212 mg chol., 62 mg sodium, 1 g carbo., 0 g fiber, 6 g pro.

Poached Eggs

Start to Finish: 10 minutes

Makes: 4 poached eggs

  1 to 2 teaspoons instant chicken Bouillon granules (optional)

  4 eggs

If desired, lightly grease a medium skillet (for 4 eggs) or a 1-quart saucepan (for 1 or 2 eggs) with cooking oil or shortening. Half fill the skillet with water. If desired, stir in chicken bouillon granules. Bring the water to boiling; reduce heat to simmering (bubbles should begin to break surface).

  Break 1 egg into a measuring cup. Carefully slide egg into simmering water, holding the lip of the cup as close to the water as possible. Repeat with remaining eggs, allowing each egg an equal amount of space.

  Simmer eggs, uncovered, for 3 to 5 minutes or until whites are completely set and yolks begin to thicken but are not hard. Remove eggs with a slotted spoon. Season with salt and black pepper.

Nutrition Facts per egg: 78 cal., 5 g total fat (2 g sat. fat), 212 mg chol., 62 mg sodium, 1 g carbo., 0 g fiber, 6 g pro

Fried Eggs

Start to Finish: 10 minutes

Makes: 4 fried eggs

  2 teaspoons butter, margarine, or nonstick cooking spray

  4 eggs

  1 to 2 teaspoons water

In a large skillet melt butter over medium heat. (Or coat an unheated skillet with nonstick cooking spray before heating.) Break eggs into skillet. When whites are set, add water. Cover skillet and cook eggs for 3 to 4 minutes or until yolks begin to thicken but are not hard.

Nutrition Facts per egg: 92 cal., 7 g total fat (3 g sat. fat), 218 mg chol., 84 mg sodium, 1 g carbo., 0 g fiber, 6 g pro.

Beef, Lamb & Veal

Other diets may tell you to eat little to no meat, but not on a phase 1 diet plan. These hearty meat recipes will cure your cravings for a satisfying meal. How about a steak topped with rich blue cheese butter or veal chops studded with pungent garlic cloves? These are definitely not your typical diet foods!

London Broil

Prep: 20 minutes Marinate: 4 hours Broil: 15 minutes
Makes: 4 to 6 servings

1 1- to 1½-pound beef
   flank steak

¼ cup cooking oil

2 tablespoons vinegar or
   lemon juice

¼ teaspoon salt

¼ teaspoon black pepper

1 clove garlic, minced

1. Score meat on both sides by making shallow diagonal cuts at 1-inch intervals in a diamond pattern. Place meat in a self-sealing plastic bag set in a shallow dish.

2. For marinade, in a small bowl combine oil, vinegar, salt, pepper, and garlic. Pour over meat; close bag. Marinate in the refrigerator for 4 to 24 hours, turning bag occasionally. Drain meat, discarding marinade.

3. Preheat boiler. Place meat on the unheated rack of a broiler pan. Broil 3 to 4 inches from the heat for 15 to 18 minutes for medium doneness (160°F), turning once halfway through grilling. Thinly slice meat diagonally across the grain.

1 g carbs   0 g fiber   1 g net carbs

Nutrition Facts per serving: 227 cal., 15 g total fat (4 g sat. fat),
63 mg chol., 133 mg sodium, 1 g carbo., 0 g fiber, 22 g pro.

64

Jerk London Broil

Prep: 15 minutes Marinate: 30 minutes Grill: 17 minutes
Makes: 6 servings

1. Score meat on both sides by making shallow diagonal cuts at 1-inch intervals in a diamond pattern. Place in a shallow dish. For marinade, in a blender container combine green onions, lime juice, oil, Scotch bonnet pepper (if desired), jerk seasoning, ginger, and garlic. Cover and blend until smooth. Spread over meat. Cover and marinate at room temperature for 30 minutes or in the refrigerator for 6 to 24 hours.

2. For a charcoal grill, grill meat on the rack of an uncovered grill directly over medium coals for 17 to 21 minutes for medium doneness (160°F), turning once halfway through grilling. (For a gas grill, preheat grill. Reduce heat to medium. Place meat on grill rack over heat. Cover and grill as above.)

3. Thinly slice meat diagonally across the grain.

1 1¼- to 1½-pound beef flank steak

4 green onions

¼ cup lime juice

2 tablespoons cooking oil

1 Scotch bonnet pepper, stem and seeds removed (optional) (see note, page 51)

2 teaspoons Jamaican jerk seasoning

1 1-inch piece fresh ginger, sliced

3 cloves garlic

2g carbs **0**g fiber **2**g net carbs

Nutrition Facts per serving: 187 cal., 11 g total fat (3 g sat. fat), 44 mg chol., 117 mg sodium, 2 g carbo., 0 g fiber, 18 g pro.

Spiced Loin Steaks

Prep: 20 minutes Chill: 8 hours Grill: 10 minutes Makes: 8 servings

1 tablespoon coriander seeds

1 teaspoon fennel seeds

1 teaspoon cumin seeds

2 cloves garlic, minced

½ teaspoon kosher salt or

   ¼ teaspoon salt

¼ teaspoon black pepper

4 boneless beef top loin steaks,

   cut 1 inch thick

2 tablespoons dry red wine

1 tablespoon olive oil

1. In a small skillet toast coriander, fennel, and cumin seeds over medium-low heat for 1 to 3 minutes or until seeds become fragrant and lightly colored. Cool completely. In a spice or coffee grinder pulse seeds until coarsely ground.* In a small bowl combine garlic, salt, and pepper; add ground spices. Sprinkle mixture over both sides of meat; rub in with your fingers. Transfer meat to a glass dish. Cover with plastic wrap and chill for 8 to 24 hours.

2. In a small bowl combine wine and oil; brush on both sides of meat.

3. For a charcoal grill, grill meat on rack of an uncovered grill directly over medium coals until desired doneness, turning once halfway through grilling. Allow 10 to 12 minutes for medium-rare (145°F) or 12 to 15 minutes for medium doneness (160°F). (For a gas grill, preheat grill. Reduce heat to medium. Place meat on grill rack over heat. Cover and grill as above.)

*Note: If you don't have a spice or coffee grinder, grind seeds, one type at a time, using a mortar and pestle.

1 g carbs   0 g fiber   1 g net carbs

Nutrition Facts per serving: 189 cal., 9 g total fat (3 g sat. fat), 66 mg chol., 179 mg sodium, 1 g carbo., 0 g fiber, 25 g pro.

Lemon-Soy Marinated Flank Steak

Prep: 15 minutes Marinate: 6 hours Grill: 17 minutes Makes: 4 servings

1. Score meat on both sides making shallow cuts at 1-inch intervals in a diamond pattern. Place meat in a self-sealing plastic bag set in a shallow dish. For marinade, in a small bowl combine green onions, water, wine, soy sauce, lemon juice, oil, garlic, celery seeds, and pepper. Pour over meat; seal bag. Marinate in the refrigerator for 6 to 24 hours, turning bag occasionally. Drain meat and discard marinade.

2. For a charcoal grill, grill meat on the rack of an uncovered grill directly over medium coals for 17 to 21 minutes for medium doneness (160°F), turning once halfway through grilling. (For a gas grill, preheat grill. Reduce heat to medium. Place meat on grill rack over heat. Cover and grill as above.)

3. Thinly slice the meat diagonally across the grain.

1 1¼- to 1½-pound beef flank steak

2 green onions, sliced (¼ cup)

¼ cup water

¼ cup dry red wine

¼ cup soy sauce

3 tablespoons lemon juice

2 tablespoons cooking oil

2 cloves garlic, minced

½ teaspoon celery seeds

½ teaspoon black pepper

1g carbs   **0**g fiber   **1**g net carbs

Nutrition Facts per serving: 251 cal., 12 g total fat (5 g sat. fat), 57 mg chol., 382 mg sodium, 1 g carbo., 0 g fiber, 32 g pro.

Spinach-Stuffed Flank Steak

Prep: 20 minutes Broil: 12 minutes Makes: 4 servings

1 1-pound beef flank steak

¼ teaspoon salt

⅛ teaspoon black pepper

½ of a 10-ounce package

    frozen chopped spinach,

    thawed and well drained

¼ cup grated Parmesan cheese

2 tablespoons snipped

    fresh basil

1. Score meat on both sides by making shallow diagonal cuts at 1-inch intervals in a diamond pattern. Place meat between 2 pieces of plastic wrap. Using the flat side of a meat mallet, pound meat into about a 12×8-inch rectangle. Remove plastic wrap. Sprinkle meat with salt and pepper.

2. Spread spinach over meat. Sprinkle with Parmesan cheese and basil. Roll up meat from short side. Secure with wooden toothpicks at 1-inch intervals, starting ½ inch from one end of the meat. Cut between the toothpicks into eight 1-inch slices.

3. Preheat broiler. Place slices, cut sides down, on the unheated rack of a broiler pan. Broil 3 to 4 inches from the heat for 12 to 16 minutes for medium doneness (160°F). To serve, remove toothpicks.

1 g carbs   1 g fiber   0 g net carbs

Nutrition Facts per serving: 207 cal., 9 g total fat (4 g sat. fat), 50 mg chol., 331 mg sodium, 1 g carbo., 1 g fiber, 28 g pro.

Flank Steak with Parsley & Lemon

Prep: 15 minutes Marinate: 6 hours Broil: 15 minutes Makes: 4 servings

1. Score meat on both sides by making shallow diagonal cuts at 1-inch intervals in a diamond pattern. Place meat in a self-sealing plastic bag set in a shallow dish. Cover lemon peel and chill until needed. For marinade, in a small bowl whisk together lemon juice, water, oil, 2 cloves garlic, salt, and pepper. Pour over meat; seal bag. Marinate in the refrigerator for 6 to 8 hours, turning bag occasionally.

2. Drain meat, discarding marinade. Preheat broiler. Place meat on the unheated rack of a broiler pan. Broil 3 to 4 inches from heat for 15 to 18 minutes for medium doneness (160°F), turning once halfway through broiling.

3. Meanwhile, in a small bowl combine parsley, lemon peel, and 1 clove garlic. Thinly slice meat diagonally across the grain. Sprinkle with parsley mixture.

1 1¼- to 1½-pound beef flank steak

2 teaspoons finely shredded
   lemon peel

½ cup lemon juice

¼ cup water

¼ cup olive oil

2 cloves garlic, minced

½ teaspoon salt

¼ teaspoon freshly ground
   black pepper

3 tablespoons snipped fresh parsley

1 clove garlic, minced

1g carbs   **0**g fiber   **1**g net carbs

Nutrition Facts per serving: 263 cal., 14 g total fat (5 g sat. fat), 57 mg chol., 170 mg sodium, 1 g carbo., 0 g fiber, 31 g pro.

Grilled Flank Steak with Horseradish Mayonnaise

Prep: 15 minutes   Marinate: 4 hours   Grill: 17 minutes   Makes: 4 servings

1   1¼- to 1¾-pound beef

    flank steak

¼   cup white or red wine vinegar

¼   cup olive oil

1   tablespoon snipped fresh

    basil or 1 teaspoon dried

    basil, crushed

2   cloves garlic, minced

½   teaspoon salt

¼   teaspoon freshly ground

    black pepper

1   recipe Horseradish

    Mayonnaise

1. Score meat on both sides by making shallow diagonal cuts at 1-inch intervals in a diamond pattern. Place meat in a self-sealing plastic bag set in a shallow dish. For marinade, in a small bowl whisk together vinegar, oil, basil, garlic, salt, and pepper. Pour over meat; seal bag. Marinate in the refrigerator for 4 hours or overnight, turning bag occasionally. Drain meat, discarding marinade.

2. For a charcoal grill, grill meat on the rack of an uncovered grill directly over medium coals for 17 to 21 minutes for medium doneness (160°F), turning once halfway through grilling. (For a gas grill, preheat grill. Reduce heat to medium. Place meat on grill rack over heat. Cover and grill as above.) Thinly slice meat diagonally across the grain. Serve with Horseradish Mayonnaise.

Horseradish Mayonnaise: In a small bowl stir together ½ cup mayonnaise, 1 to 2 tablespoons prepared horseradish, and 2 tablespoons snipped fresh chives or chopped green onion.

1 g carbs   **0** g fiber   **1** g net carbs

Nutrition Facts per serving: 488 cal., 39 g total fat (8 g sat. fat),
77 mg chol., 415 mg sodium, 1 g carbo., 0 g fiber, 31 g pro.

Beef Tenderloins with Wine Sauce

Start to Finish: 25 minutes Makes: 4 servings

1. Press pepper onto both sides of meat. In a large skillet cook meat in hot butter over medium to medium-high heat until desired doneness, turning once halfway through cooking. Allow 10 to 13 minutes for medium-rare (145°F) to medium doneness (160°F). Transfer meat to a serving platter, reserving drippings in skillet. Keep meat warm.

2. For sauce, stir onion into reserved drippings in skillet. Cook for 3 to 4 minutes or until onion is tender. Remove from heat. Carefully add broth, wine, and marjoram, stirring to loosen any brown bits in bottom of skillet. Return to heat. Bring to boiling; reduce heat. Boil gently, uncovered, about 2 minutes or until mixture is reduced to about ¼ cup. Serve sauce over meat.

½ teaspoon cracked black pepper

4 beef tenderloin steaks,

   cut 1 inch thick

1 tablespoon butter

¼ cup chopped onion

¼ cup beef broth

¼ cup dry red wine

1 teaspoon dried marjoram,

   crushed

2 g carbs **0** g fiber **2** g net carbs

Nutrition Facts per serving: 315 cal., 15 g total fat (6 g sat. fat), 120 mg chol., 176 mg sodium, 2 g carbo., 0 g fiber, 38 g pro.

Herbed Beef Tenderloin

Prep: 15 minutes Grill: 45 minutes Stand: 15 minutes Makes: 8 servings

¼ cup snipped fresh parsley

2 tablespoons Dijon-style
  mustard

1 tablespoon snipped
  fresh rosemary

2 teaspoons snipped
  fresh thyme

2 cloves garlic, minced

1 teaspoon olive oil or cooking oil

½ teaspoon coarsely ground
  black pepper

1 2-pound beef tenderloin roast

½ cup dairy sour cream

2 teaspoons Dijon-style mustard

1. In a small bowl stir together parsley, 2 tablespoons mustard, rosemary, thyme, garlic, oil, and pepper. Rub over top and sides of meat.

2. For a charcoal grill, arrange hot coals around a drip pan. Test for medium-high heat above pan. Place meat on grill rack over drip pan. Insert a meat thermometer in center of meat. Cover and grill 45 minutes or until thermometer registers 135°F for medium-rare. (For a gas grill, preheat grill. Reduce heat to medium-high. Adjust for indirect cooking. Grill as above.)

3. Remove meat from grill. Cover with foil; let stand for 15 minutes before carving. (The meat's temperature will rise 10°F during standing).

4. Meanwhile, stir together sour cream and 2 teaspoons mustard. Thinly slice meat. Serve with sour cream mixture.

2 g carbs   **0** g fiber   **2** g net carbs

Nutrition Facts per serving: 224 cal., 12 g total fat (5 g sat. fat),
75 mg chol., 180 mg sodium, 2 g carbo., 0 g fiber, 25 g pro.

Favorite Beef Tenderloin

Prep: 15 minutes Chill: 8 hours Roast: 50 minutes Stand: 15 minutes
Oven: 425°F Makes: 12 to 16 servings

1. In a small bowl combine thyme, white pepper, garlic salt, seasoned salt, and oregano. Sprinkle over all sides of meat; rub in with your fingers. Place meat in a self-sealing plastic bag; seal bag. Chill for 8 to 24 hours.

2. Remove meat from bag and place on rack in a foil-lined roasting pan. Drizzle with Worcestershire sauce. Insert a meat thermometer into center of meat. Roast in 425° oven until desired doneness. Allow 50 to 60 minutes for medium-rare (135°F) or 60 to 70 minutes for medium doneness (150°F).

3. Cover meat with foil and let stand for 15 minutes before carving. (The meat's temperature will rise 10°F during standing.)

1 tablespoon dried thyme, crushed

1 teaspoon ground white pepper

1 teaspoon garlic salt

1 teaspoon seasoned salt

¼ teaspoon dried oregano, crushed

1 4- to 6-pound beef tenderloin roast

2 tablespoons Worcestershire sauce

1g carbs   **0**g fiber   **1**g net carbs

Nutrition Facts per serving: 237 cal., 11 g total fat (4 g sat. fat),
92 mg chol., 304 mg sodium, 1 g carbo., 0 g fiber, 31 g pro.

Tenderloins with Rosemary & Port

Start to Finish: 20 minutes Makes: 4 servings

4 beef tenderloin steaks, cut

   ¾ inch thick

   Salt and coarsely ground

   black pepper

1 tablespoon olive oil or

   cooking oil

1½ teaspoons snipped

   fresh rosemary

⅓ cup port wine

⅓ cup water

¼ cup whipping cream

1. Sprinkle both sides of meat with salt and pepper. In a large skillet heat oil over medium-high heat. Add meat. Reduce heat to medium and cook until desired doneness, turning once halfway through cooking. Allow 7 to 9 minutes for medium-rare (145°F) to medium doneness (160°F). Transfer meat to a serving platter; keep warm.

2. For sauce, add rosemary to drippings in skillet. Cook and stir for 1 minute to loosen any brown bits in bottom of skillet. Remove skillet from heat. Carefully stir port and water into skillet. Return skillet to heat. Bring to boiling. Boil, uncovered, about 3 minutes or until mixture is reduced by half. Stir in whipping cream. Return to boiling; boil gently for 2 to 3 minutes or until slightly thickened. Spoon sauce over meat.

3g carbs   **0**g fiber   **3**g net carbs

Nutrition Facts per serving: 295 cal., 18 g total fat (7 g sat. fat), 90 mg chol., 132 mg sodium, 3 g carbo., 0 g fiber, 24 g pro.

Beef Tenderloin with Peppercorn Sauce

Prep: 20 minutes   Grill: 45 minutes   Stand: 15 minutes   Makes: 6 servings

1. In a small bowl stir together 1 tablespoon pepper, thyme, and salt. Sprinkle over meat; rub mixture in with your fingers.

2. For a charcoal grill, arrange hot coals around a drip pan. Test for medium-high heat above pan. Place meat on grill rack over pan. Cover and grill for 45 to 60 minutes for medium-rare (135°F). (For a gas grill, preheat grill. Reduce heat to medium-high. Adjust for indirect cooking. Grill as above, except place meat on a rack in a roasting pan.)

3. Meanwhile, for sauce, in a large skillet combine whipping cream, broth, ¹/₂ teaspoon pepper, and garlic. Bring to boiling. Reduce heat. Simmer, uncovered, for 10 to 12 minutes or until liquid is reduced to 1 cup, stirring occasionally. Stir in whiskey; cook 1 minute more. Remove from heat; cover to keep warm.

4. Remove meat from grill. Cover with foil; let stand for 15 minutes before slicing. (The meat's temperature will rise 10°F during standing.)

5. Slice meat and serve with sauce.

1   tablespoon coarsely ground
      black pepper

1¹/₂ teaspoons dried thyme, crushed

1   teaspoon salt

1   2-pound beef tenderloin roast

2   cups whipping cream

¹/₂ cup beef broth

¹/₂ teaspoon coarsely ground
      black pepper

2   cloves garlic, minced

2   tablespoons whiskey or brandy

4 g carbs   **0** g fiber   **4** g net carbs

Nutrition Facts per serving: 539 cal., 2 g total fat (23 g sat. fat), 202 mg chol., 562 mg sodium, 4 g carbo., 0 g fiber, 33 g pro.

Coriander-Studded Tenderloin Steak

Prep: 10 minutes Broil: 12 minutes Makes: 4 servings

4 beef tenderloin steaks, cut

    1 inch thick

Salt

1 tablespoon reduced-sodium

    soy sauce

1 tablespoon olive oil

1 tablespoon snipped

    fresh chives

2 cloves garlic, minced

½ teaspoon coriander seeds or

    cumin seeds, crushed

½ teaspoon celery seeds,

    crushed

½ teaspoon coarsely ground

    black pepper

1. Sprinkle meat lightly with salt. In a small bowl combine soy sauce, oil, chives, garlic, coriander seeds, celery seeds, and pepper. Brush mixture over both sides of each steak.

2. Preheat broiler. Place meat on the unheated rack of a broiler pan. Broil 3 to 4 inches from heat until desired doneness, turning once halfway through broiling. Allow 12 to 14 minutes for medium-rare (145°F) or 15 to 18 minutes for medium doneness (160°F).

1 g carbs   0 g fiber   1 g net carbs

Nutrition Facts per serving: 164 cal., 9 g total fat (3 g sat. fat), 42 mg chol., 256 mg sodium, 1 g carbo., 0 g fiber, 18 g pro.

Spicy Beef Tenderloin

Prep: 20 minutes Roast: 35 minutes Stand: 15 minutes Oven: 425°F Makes: 8 servings

1. For rub, in a small bowl combine chili powder, salt, pepper, cumin, and oregano. Sprinkle rub evenly over all sides of roast; rub in with your fingers. Place meat on a rack in a shallow roasting pan. Insert a meat thermometer into center of meat. Roast, uncovered, in a 425° oven until desired doneness. Allow 35 to 40 minutes for medium-rare (135°F) or 45 to 50 minutes for medium doneness (150°F).

2. Cover meat with foil and let stand 15 minutes before slicing. (The meat's temperature will rise 10°F during standing.)

¾ teaspoon chili powder

¾ teaspoon salt

½ teaspoon coarsely ground black pepper

¼ teaspoon ground cumin

¼ teaspoon dried oregano, crushed

1 3-pound beef tenderloin roast

5g carbs

0g fiber

5g net carbs

Nutrition Facts per serving: 335 cal., 15 g total fat (6 g sat. fat), 101 mg chol., 364 mg sodium, 5 g carbo., 0 g fiber, 41 g pro.

Moroccan Rib Roast

Prep: 15 minutes Grill: 2 hours Stand: 15 minutes Makes: 8 to 10 servings

2   tablespoons coriander seeds,
    crushed

2   tablespoons finely shredded
    lemon peel

1   tablespoon olive oil

1   teaspoon whole cumin seeds,
    crushed

½   to 1 teaspoon crushed
    red pepper

½   teaspoon coarse salt

1   4- to 5-pound beef rib roast

8   cloves garlic, peeled and cut
    into slivers

1. In a small bowl stir together coriander seeds, lemon peel, oil, cumin seeds, crushed red pepper, and salt. Rub mixture into surface of meat with your fingers.

2. Cut ½-inch-wide slits randomly into top and sides of meat. Insert garlic slivers deep into slits. If desired, cover and chill roast for up to 24 hours.

3. Insert a meat thermometer into center of roast, not touching bone. For a charcoal grill, arrange medium coals around a drip pan. Test for medium-low heat above pan. Place roast on grill rack over drip pan. Cover and grill until desired doneness. Allow 2 to 2¾ hours for medium-rare (145°F) or 2½ to 3¼ hours for medium doneness (150°F). (For a gas grill, preheat grill. Reduce heat to medium. Adjust for indirect cooking. Grill as above except place meat in a roasting pan.)

4. Remove meat from grill. Cover with foil; let stand for 15 minutes before carving. (The meat's temperature will rise 10°F during standing.)

2 g carbs   **1** g fiber   **1** g net carbs

Nutrition Facts per serving: 228 cal., 11 g total fat (4 g sat. fat), 68 mg chol., 196 mg sodium, 2 g carbo., 1 g fiber, 29 g pro.

Marinated Rump Roast

Prep: 20 minutes Marinate: 2 days Grill: 1½ hours Makes: 12 to 14 servings

1. Place meat in a large self-sealing plastic bag set in a large, deep bowl. For marinade, in a medium bowl combine water, vinegar, onions, lemon, bay leaves, cloves, peppercorns, and salt. Pour over meat; seal bag. Marinate in the refrigerator for 2 to 3 days, turning bag occasionally. Drain meat, reserving marinade.

2. For a charcoal grill, arrange medium coals around a drip pan. Test for medium-low heat above pan. Place meat on grill rack over drip pan. Cover and grill for 1½ to 2 hours for medium doneness (160°), brushing occasionally with reserved marinade during the first hour of grilling and adding additional coals as needed. (For a gas grill, preheat grill. Reduce heat to medium-low. Adjust for indirect cooking. Grill as above except place meat in a roasting pan.)

1 3-pound boneless beef rump
   roast (rolled and tied)

2½ cups water

2½ cups vinegar

2 medium onions, sliced

1 medium lemon, sliced

2 or 3 bay leaves

12 whole cloves

6 whole black peppercorns

1 teaspoon salt

Nutrition Facts per serving: 147 cal., 5 g total fat (2 g sat. fat),
72 mg chol., 83 mg sodium, 0 g carbo., 0 g fiber, 24 g pro.

Southwestern Tri-Tip Roast

Prep: 10 minutes Chill: 6 hours Bake: 30 minutes Stand: 15 minutes
Oven: 425°F Makes: 6 to 8 servings

1 tablespoon dried chipotle
   pepper, seeded and finely
   chopped (see note, page 51)

1 tablespoon fresh oregano or
   1 teaspoon dried oregano,
   crushed

1 tablespoon olive oil

1 teaspoon ground cumin

½ teaspoon salt

2 cloves garlic, crushed

1½- to 2-pound beef tri-tip
   (bottom sirloin) roast

1. For rub, in a bowl combine chipotle pepper, oregano, oil, cumin, salt, and garlic. Sprinkle over surface of meat; rub in with your fingers. Cover and chill for 6 to 24 hours.

2. Place meat on a rack in a shallow roasting pan. Insert a meat thermometer into center of meat. Roast in a 425° oven until desired doneness. Allow 30 to 35 minutes for medium-rare (140°F) or 40 to 45 minutes for medium doneness (155°F).

3. Cover meat with foil and let stand 15 minutes before carving. (The meat's temperature will rise 5°F during standing.)

1 g carbs   0 g fiber   1 g net carbs

Nutrition Facts per serving: 293 cal., 22 g total fat (8 g sat. fat),
76 mg chol., 231 mg sodium, 1 g carbo., 0 g fiber, 23 g pro.

Peppered Rib Roast

Prep: 10 minutes Grill: 2 hours Stand: 15 minutes Makes: 10 to 12 servings

1. Brush meat with oil. For rub, in a small bowl combine pepper, shallots, salt, basil, and thyme. Rub mixture over surface of meat. Insert a meat thermometer into center of roast not touching bone.

2. For a charcoal grill, arrange medium coals around drip pan. Test for medium-low heat above pan. Place meat, bone side down, on grill rack over drip pan. Cover; grill until desired doneness. Allow 2 to 2³⁄₄ hours for medium-rare (135°F) or 2¹⁄₂ to 3¹⁄₄ hours for medium doneness (150°F). (For a gas grill, preheat grill. Reduce heat to medium. Adjust for indirect cooking. Grill as above, except place meat in a roasting pan.)

3. Remove meat from grill. Cover with foil; let stand for 15 minutes before carving. (The meat's temperature will rise 10°F during standing.)

1 **6-pound beef rib roast**

1 **tablespoon olive oil**

4 **teaspoons coarsely ground pepper**

2 **tablespoons finely chopped shallots**

1 **teaspoon coarse salt**

1 **teaspoon dried basil, crushed**

1 **teaspoon dried thyme, crushed**

1g carbs   **0**g fiber   **1**g net carbs

Nutrition Facts per serving: 310 cal., 18 g total fat (7 g sat. fat), 100 mg chol., 305 mg sodium, 1 g carbo., 0 g fiber, 34 g pro.

Fennel-Stuffed Roast

Prep: 40 minutes Roast: 1½ hours Stand: 15 minutes
Oven: 325°F Makes: 8 to 10 servings

1 2- to 3-pound beef eye
   round roast

4 slices bacon

1½ cups very thinly sliced
   fennel bulb

1 medium shallot, chopped

2 cloves garlic, minced

3 tablespoons snipped fresh
   basil or 1½ teaspoons
   dried basil, crushed

   Salt and black pepper

1. Butterfly meat by making a lengthwise cut down center, cutting to within ½ inch of the other side. Spread open. Place knife in the "V" of the first cut. Cut away from the first cut and parallel to the cut surface to within ½ inch of the other side of the meat. Repeat on opposite side of "V." Cover with plastic wrap. Using the flat side of a meat mallet, pound to ¾-inch thickness. Remove plastic wrap. Set aside.

2. In a large skillet, cook bacon. Drain on paper towels, reserving 2 tablespoons drippings in skillet. Cook fennel in reserved drippings over medium heat for 5 minutes, stirring occasionally. Add shallot and garlic; cook and stir for 1 or 2 minutes or until fennel is tender. Remove from heat. Crumble bacon. Stir bacon and basil into fennel mixture.

3. Spread fennel mixture on meat. Roll up from a short side. Tie with 100-percent-cotton string at 1½-inch intervals. Sprinkle with salt and pepper. Place on a rack in a shallow roasting pan. Insert a meat thermometer into center of roast. Roast, uncovered, in a 325° oven. Allow 1½ to 1¾ hours for medium-rare (135°F). Cover meat with foil; let stand for 15 minutes. (The meat's temperature will rise 10°F during standing.) Slice to serve.

2 g carbs   1 g fiber   1 g net carbs

Nutrition Facts per serving: 171 cal., 6 g total fat (2 g sat. fat), 64 mg chol., 141 mg sodium, 2 g carbo., 1 g fiber, 26 g pro.

Rib Roast with Dijon-Sour Cream Sauce

Prep: 25 minutes Marinate: 6 hours Roast: 1¾ hours
Stand: 15 minutes Oven: 350°F Makes: 8 servings

1. Place meat, bone side up, in a large self-sealing plastic bag set in a shallow dish. For marinade, in a small bowl combine wine, lemon juice, rosemary, marjoram, and garlic salt. Pour over meat; seal bag. Marinate in the refrigerator for 6 to 24 hours, turning bag occasionally. Drain meat, discarding marinade. Insert a meat thermometer into the center of the roast, not touching bone.

2. Place meat, fat side up, in a shallow roasting pan. Roast, uncovered, in a 350° oven until desired doneness. Allow 1¾ to 2½ hours for medium-rare (135°F) or 2¼ to 2¾ hours for medium doneness (150°F).

3. Cover with foil; let stand for 15 minutes. (The meat's temperature will rise 10°F during standing.) Slice meat and serve with Dijon-Sour Cream Sauce.

Dijon-Sour Cream Sauce: In a small bowl, stir together one 8-ounce carton dairy sour cream, 2 tablespoons Dijon-style mustard, and ½ teaspoon lemon-pepper seasoning. Cover and chill until serving time.

1 **4-pound beef rib roast**

¾ **cup dry red wine**

¼ **cup lemon juice**

2 **teaspoons dried rosemary, crushed**

2 **teaspoons dried marjoram, crushed**

¼ **teaspoon garlic salt**

1 **recipe Dijon-Sour Cream Sauce**

2g carbs **0**g fiber **2**g net carbs

Nutrition Facts per serving: 274 cal., 15 g total fat (7 g sat. fat), 80 mg chol., 255 mg sodium, 2 g carbo., 0 g fiber, 30 g pro.

Fork-Tender Beef with Broth

Prep: 20 minutes Cook: 10 to 12 hours (low) or 5 to 6 hours (high) Makes: 3 servings

2 large onions, sliced (2 cups)

4 cloves garlic, halved

8 fresh parsley sprigs

4 large bay leaves

8 whole black peppercorns

1½ teaspoons salt

3 pounds meaty beef soup
   bones (beef shank
   crosscuts or short ribs)

5 cups water

1 egg white (optional)

¼ cup water (optional)

1. In a 4- to 6-quart slow cooker combine onions, garlic, parsley, bay leaves, peppercorns, and salt. Add soup bones and 5 cups water.

2. Cover; cook on low-heat setting for 10 to 12 hours or on high-heat setting for 5 to 6 hours.

3. Remove bones from cooker. Strain broth through a sieve or colander lined with two layers of 100-percent-cotton cheesecloth. Discard solids in cheesecloth. If desired, clarify broth by combining egg white and ¼ cup water in a large saucepan. Add hot broth. Bring to boiling; let stand 5 minutes. Strain broth through two layers of 100-percent-cotton cheesecloth.

4. If using broth at once, skim off fat. If storing broth for later use, chill broth in a bowl for 6 hours. Lift off fat. Pour broth into an airtight container; discard residue in the bottom of the bowl; seal. Chill in the refrigerator for up to 3 days or freeze for up to 3 months.

5. When bones are cool enough to handle, remove meat from bones. Discard bones. Place the meat in an airtight container; seal. Chill in the refrigerator for up to 3 days or freeze for up to 3 months.

2 g carbs   **0** g fiber   **2** g net carbs

Nutrition Facts per serving: 169 cal., 7 g total fat (2 g sat. fat),
58 mg chol., 749 mg sodium, 2 g carbo., 0 g fiber, 24 g pro.

Basil-Stuffed Steak

Prep: 25 minutes Grill: 32 minutes Makes: 6 servings

1. With a sharp knife, make 5 lengthwise slits three-quarters of the way through meat.

2. In a small bowl, combine salt, pepper, and parsley flakes. Sprinkle over meat; rub in with your fingers. In the same bowl, combine basil, onion, garlic, rosemary, and thyme. Press basil mixture into the slits. Using 100-percent-cotton string, tie meat loosely at 2-inch intervals to close the slits and hold in the filling. Drizzle with oil.

3. For a charcoal grill, arrange medium-hot coals around a drip pan. Test for medium heat above pan. Place meat on grill rack over drip pan. Cover and grill until desired doneness. Allow 32 to 36 minutes for medium-rare (145°F) and 36 to 40 minutes for medium doneness (160°F). (For a gas grill, preheat grill. Reduce heat to medium. Adjust grill for indirect cooking. Grill as above.)

4. Transfer meat to carving board; remove strings. Cut meat into ½-inch slices.

1 2- to 2½-pound boneless beef sirloin steak, cut about 1½ inches thick

½ teaspoon salt

¼ teaspoon black pepper

¼ teaspoon dried parsley flakes

1 cup lightly packed fresh basil leaves, coarsely chopped

¼ cup finely chopped onion

4 cloves garlic, minced

1½ teaspoons fresh rosemary, finely snipped, or ½ teaspoon dried rosemary, crushed

⅛ teaspoon fresh thyme, finely snipped, or dried thyme, crushed

1 teaspoon olive oil

2 g carbs   **0** g fiber   **2** g net carbs

Nutrition Facts per serving: 201 cal., 6 g total fat (2 g sat. fat), 71 mg chol., 275 mg sodium, 2 g carbo., 0 g fiber, 33 g pro.

Peppercorn Beef

Prep: 15 minutes Marinate: 2 hours Grill: 10 minutes Makes: 4 servings

4 beef tenderloin steaks or
   1 to 1½ pounds boneless
   beef top loin steak, cut 1
   inch thick

⅓ cup dry red wine

3 tablespoons olive oil

2 tablespoons red wine vinegar

¼ cup snipped fresh garlic
   chives or ¼ cup snipped
   fresh chives plus 1 teaspoon
   bottled minced garlic

½ teaspoon salt

1 tablespoon cracked multicolor
   or black peppercorns

1. Place meat in a large self-sealing plastic bag set in a shallow dish. For marinade, in a small bowl stir together wine, oil, vinegar, garlic chives, and salt. Pour marinade over meat; seal bag. Marinate in the refrigerator for 2 hours, turning bag occasionally. Drain meat, discarding marinade. Pat peppercorns into both sides of meat.

2. For a charcoal grill, grill meat on the rack of an uncovered grill directly over medium coals until desired doneness, turning once halfway through grilling. Allow 10 to 12 minutes for medium-rare (145°F) or 12 to 15 minutes for medium doneness (160°F). (For a gas grill, preheat grill. Reduce heat to medium. Place meat on grill rack over heat. Cover and grill as above.)

3. If using top loin steak, cut into 4 serving-size pieces.

1g carbs   **0**g fiber   **1**g net carbs

Nutrition Facts per serving: 267 cal., 14 g total fat (4 g sat. fat),
87 mg chol., 212 mg sodium, 1 g carbo., 0 g fiber, 30 g pro.

Filet Mignon with Mustard Sauce

Prep: 15 minutes Grill: 10 minutes Makes: 2 servings

1. Sprinkle cracked black pepper and salt over both sides of steaks, pressing into meat with your fingers. For a charcoal grill, grill meat on the rack of an uncovered grill directly over medium coals until desired doneness, turning once halfway through grilling. Allow 10 to 12 minutes for medium-rare (145°F) or 12 to 15 minutes for medium doneness (160°F). (For a gas grill, preheat grill. Reduce heat to medium. Place meat on grill rack over heat. Cover and grill as above.) Serve meat with Mustard Sauce.

Mustard Sauce: In a small saucepan bring $\frac{1}{2}$ cup whipping cream to boiling. Reduce heat; simmer, uncovered, for 3 minutes or until slightly thickened. Stir in 1 tablespoon Dijon-style mustard. Season to taste with salt and freshly ground black pepper.

1 teaspoon whole black peppercorns, cracked

$\frac{1}{4}$ teaspoon salt

2 beef tenderloin steaks, cut 1 inch thick

1 recipe Mustard Sauce

4g carbs

0g fiber

4g net carbs

Nutrition Facts per serving: 638 cal., 41 g total fat (21 g sat. fat), 256 mg chol., 694 mg sodium, 4 g carbo., 0 g fiber, 62 g pro.

Bistro Beef & Mushrooms

Start to Finish: 25 minutes Makes: 4 servings

1 tablespoon Dijon-style
   mustard or coarse-grain
   brown mustard

4 beef tenderloin steaks, cut
   ¾ inch thick

2 tablespoons olive oil or
   roasted garlic olive oil

8 ounces fresh crimini, shiitake,
   portobello, or button
   mushrooms, sliced
   (about 3 cups)

⅓ cup dry red wine or sherry

1 tablespoon Worcestershire
   sauce for chicken

2 teaspoons snipped fresh
   thyme

1. Spread mustard evenly over both sides of steaks. In a large skillet heat 1 tablespoon of the oil over medium heat. Add meat; cook until desired doneness, turning once halfway through cooking. Allow 7 to 9 minutes for medium-rare (145°F) to medium doneness (160°F). Transfer meat to a serving platter; keep warm.

2. Add remaining 1 tablespoon oil to drippings in skillet. Add mushrooms; cook and stir for 4 minutes. Stir in wine, Worcestershire sauce, and thyme. Simmer, uncovered, for 3 minutes. Spoon over meat.

5g
carbs

1g
fiber

4g
net carbs

Nutrition Facts per serving: 263 cal., 14 g total fat (4 g sat. fat),
64 mg chol., 176 mg sodium, 5 g carbo., 1 g fiber, 23 g pro.

Garlic-&-Wine-Marinated Beef

Prep: 25 minutes Marinate: 4 hours Grill: 1¼ hours
Stand: 15 minutes Makes: 8 servings

1. With the point of a paring knife, make small slits in meat. Insert garlic slices into slits. Place meat in a self-sealing plastic bag set in a shallow dish. For marinade, in a small bowl combine wine, onion, oil, and vinegar. Pour over meat; seal bag. Marinate in the refrigerator for 4 to 24 hours, turning bag occasionally.

2. Drain meat, discarding marinade. Sprinkle roast with salt and pepper. Insert a meat thermometer into the center of roast.

3. For a charcoal grill, arrange medium coals around a drip pan. Test for medium-low heat above the pan. Place meat on grill rack over drip pan. Cover and grill until desired doneness. Allow 1¼ to 1½ hours for medium-rare (140°F) or 1½ to 1¾ hours for medium doneness (155°F). (For a gas grill, preheat grill. Reduce heat to medium-low. Adjust for indirect cooking. Grill as above, except place meat on a rack in a roasting pan.)

4. Remove meat from grill. Cover with foil; let stand for 15 minutes before slicing. (The meat's temperature will rise 5°F during standing.) Thinly slice meat.

1 **2-pound beef round tip roast**

    or sirloin tip roast

8 **cloves garlic, sliced**

⅔ **cup dry red wine**

½ **cup finely chopped onion (1 medium)**

2 **tablespoons olive oil**

2 **tablespoons red wine vinegar**

¼ **teaspoon salt**

¼ **teaspoon black pepper**

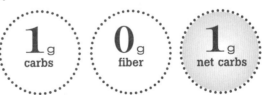

1g carbs   **0**g fiber   **1**g net carbs

Nutrition Facts per serving: 166 cal., 6 g total fat (2 g sat. fat), 68 mg chol., 133 mg sodium, 1 g carbo., 0 g fiber, 24 g pro.

Steak au Poivre

Start to Finish: 30 minutes Makes: 4 servings

1 tablespoon cracked
   black pepper

4 beef tenderloin steaks or
   ribeye steaks, cut
   1 inch thick

2 tablespoons butter

2 tablespoons brandy or
   beef broth

⅓ cup whipping cream

⅓ cup beef broth

2 teaspoons Dijon-style mustard
   (optional)

1. Use your fingers to press pepper onto both sides of the steaks. In a large skillet cook meat in hot butter over medium heat to desired doneness, turning once halfway through cooking. Allow 10 to 13 minutes for medium-rare (145°F) to medium doneness (160°F). Transfer meat to a serving platter, reserving the drippings in the skillet. Keep warm.

2. For sauce, add brandy to drippings, stirring to loosen any brown bits in bottom of skillet. Stir in whipping cream, beef broth, and if desired, mustard. Cook and stir for 4 to 5 minutes or until mixture is reduced to ⅓ cup. Pour sauce over meat.

See photo, page 106.

2g carbs   **0**g fiber   **2**g net carbs

Nutrition Facts per serving: 298 cal., 20 g total fat (8 g sat. fat), 91 mg chol., 246 mg sodium, 2 g carbo., 0 g fiber, 23 g pro.

Steaks with Blue Cheese Butter

Start to Finish: 28 minutes Makes: 4 servings

1. For blue cheese butter, in a small bowl stir together butter, blue cheese, parsley, basil, and garlic. Set aside.

2. For a charcoal grill, grill meat on the rack of an uncovered grill directly over medium coals to desired doneness, turning once. Allow 18 to 21 minutes for medium-rare (145°F) or 22 to 25 minutes for medium doneness (160°F). (For a gas grill, preheat grill. Reduce heat to medium. Place meat on grill rack over heat. Cover and grill as above.

3. Cut meat into serving-size pieces. Sprinkle with salt and pepper; top with blue cheese butter.

See photo, page 107.

½ cup butter, softened

½ cup crumbled blue cheese (2 ounces)

1 tablespoon snipped fresh parsley

1 teaspoon dried basil, crushed

1 clove garlic, minced

2 beef porterhouse or T-bone
   steaks, cut 1½ inches thick

Salt and black pepper

0_g carbs 0_g fiber 0_g net carbs

Nutrition Facts per serving: 452 cal., 29 g total fat (14 g sat. fat), 149 mg chol., 494 mg sodium, 0 g carbo., 0 g fiber, 45 g pro.

Sherried Fillet Steaks

Start to Finish: 15 minutes Makes: 4 servings

4 beef tenderloin steaks, cut

   ½ inch thick

1 tablespoon cooking oil

½ cup dry sherry

¼ teaspoon salt

¼ teaspoon cracked black

   pepper

2 tablespoons whipping cream

1 teaspoon snipped

   fresh tarragon

1. In a large skillet cook meat in hot oil over medium-high heat until desired doneness, turning once halfway through cooking. Allow 5 to 7 minutes for medium-rare (145°F) to medium doneness (160°F). Transfer meat to a serving platter; keep warm. Drain off fat.

2. For sauce, remove skillet from heat. Carefully add sherry to the skillet. Stir in salt and pepper. Return skillet to heat. Bring to boiling, reduce heat. Simmer, uncovered, for 1 to 2 minutes or until reduced by half. Stir in whipping cream. Return to boiling and boil gently, uncovered, for 2 minutes or until reduced to ¼ cup. Spoon sauce over meat; sprinkle with tarragon.

3g carbs **0**g fiber **3**g net carbs

Nutrition Facts per serving: 267 cal., 14 g total fat (5 g sat. fat), 80 mg chol., 201 mg sodium, 3 g carbo., 0 g fiber, 24 g pro.

Ribeyes with Grilled Garlic

Prep: 20 minutes Grill: 30 minutes Makes: 4 servings

1. Tear off a 24×12-inch piece of heavy foil. Fold in half to make a 12-inch square. Remove the papery outer layers from garlic head. Cut off and discard tip about ½ inch from top of garlic head to expose the garlic cloves. Place garlic head in center of foil. Bring the foil up around the garlic on all sides, forming a cup. Drizzle garlic with oil; sprinkle with rosemary. Twist foil, completely enclosing garlic in the foil.

2. For a charcoal grill, grill garlic packet on the rack of an uncovered grill directly over medium coals for 20 minutes. Sprinkle meat lightly with salt and pepper. Add meat to grill next to garlic packet; grill meat and garlic packet until meat reaches desired doneness and garlic cloves are very tender, turning meat once halfway through grilling. Allow 10 to 12 minutes for medium-rare (145°F) or 12 to 15 minutes for medium doneness (160°F). (For a gas grill, preheat grill. Reduce heat to medium. Place garlic packet on a grill rack. Cover and grill for 20 minutes. Add meat next to garlic packet, cover and grill as above.)

3. Place meat on serving platter. Open foil packet. Squeeze the softened cloves of garlic from head; spread over meat. Drizzle oil from packet over meat. Sprinkle with basil.

1 **whole head garlic**

2 **tablespoons olive oil**

1 **tablespoon snipped fresh**
    rosemary or ½ teaspoon
    dried rosemary, crushed

2 **boneless beef ribeye steaks,**
    cut 1 inch thick
    Salt and black pepper

2 **tablespoons snipped fresh**
    basil

3g carbs   **0**g fiber   **3**g net carbs

Nutrition Facts per serving: 329 cal., 17 g total fat (5 g sat. fat), 81 mg chol., 237 mg sodium, 3 g carbo., 0 g fiber, 38 g pro.

Red Wine-Marinated Steaks

Prep: 20 minutes Marinate: 2 hours Grill: 10 minutes Makes: 4 servings

2 beef T-bone steaks, cut
       1 inch thick

½ cup dry red wine

2 tablespoons olive oil or
       cooking oil

1 tablespoon snipped fresh
       thyme or marjoram or
       1½ teaspoons dried thyme
       or marjoram, crushed

½ teaspoon salt

¼ teaspoon coarsely ground
       black pepper

2 cloves garlic, minced

1. Place meat in a large self-sealing plastic bag set in a shallow dish. For marinade, stir together wine, oil, thyme, salt, pepper, and garlic. Pour over meat. Close bag. Marinate in the refrigerator for 2 to 6 hours, turning bag occasionally.

2. Drain meat, discarding marinade. For a charcoal grill, grill meat on the rack of an uncovered grill directly over medium coals to desired doneness, turning once halfway through grilling. Allow 10 to 12 minutes for medium-rare (145°F) or 12 to 15 minutes for medium doneness (160°F). (For a gas grill, preheat grill. Reduce heat to medium. Place meat on grill rack over heat. Cover and grill as above.) To serve, cut meat into serving-size pieces.

0g carbs   **0**g fiber   **0**g net carbs

Nutrition Facts per serving: 221 cal., 8 g total fat (3 g sat. fat), 60 mg chol., 150 mg sodium, 0 g carbo., 0 g fiber, 33 g pro.

Grilled Steaks with a Twist

Prep: 15 minutes Marinate: 30 minutes Grill: 10 minutes Makes: 4 servings

1. Place meat in a self-sealing plastic bag set in a shallow dish. For marinade, combine green onions, gin, oil, and lemon peel. Pour over steaks; seal bag. Marinate in the refrigerator for 30 minutes to 4 hours, turning bag occasionally.

2. Drain steaks, discarding marinade. Press peppercorns onto both sides of steaks.

3. For a charcoal grill, grill meat on the rack of an uncovered grill directly over medium-hot coals until desired doneness, turning once. Allow 10 to 12 minutes for medium-rare (145°F) and 12 to 15 minutes for medium doneness (160°F). Season to taste with salt. To serve, garnish with lemon twists.

4 boneless beef top loin steaks,
  cut 1 inch thick

4 green onions, chopped (¼ cup)

¼ cup gin

1 tablespoon olive oil

1 teaspoon finely shredded
  lemon peel

1 teaspoon tricolor peppercorns,
  crushed

Salt

Lemon twists

2 g carbs   1 g fiber   1 g net carbs

Nutrition Facts per serving: 398 cal., 17 g total fat (5 g sat. fat), 133 mg chol., 262 mg sodium, 2 g carbo., 1 g fiber, 49 g pro.

Chili-Rubbed Steaks

Prep: 10 minutes Chill: 1 hour Grill: 10 minutes Makes: 4 servings

2 beef ribeye steaks, cut

   1 inch thick

1 tablespoon chili powder

1 tablespoon olive oil

1½ teaspoons dried oregano,

   crushed

½ teaspoon salt

½ teaspoon ground cumin

1. Place meat in a single layer in a shallow dish. For rub, in a small bowl combine chili powder, oil, oregano, salt, and cumin. Spoon mixture over meat; rub in with your fingers. Cover and chill for 1 to 2 hours.

2. For a charcoal grill, grill meat on the rack of an uncovered grill directly over medium coals until desired doneness, turning once halfway through grilling. Allow 10 to 12 minutes for medium-rare (145°F) or 12 to 15 minutes for medium doneness (160°F). (For a gas grill, preheat grill. Reduce heat to medium. Place meat on grill rack over heat. Cover and grill as above.)

3. To serve, cut meat into serving-size pieces.

1 g carbs 1 g fiber 0 g net carbs

Nutrition Facts per serving: 323 cal., 16 g total fat (5 g sat. fat),
92 mg chol., 376 mg sodium, 1 g carbo., 1 g fiber, 42 g pro.

Argentinean-Style Steaks

Prep: 15 minutes Grill: 10 minutes Makes: 4 servings

1. For a charcoal grill, grill meat on the rack of an uncovered grill directly over medium coals until desired doneness, turning once halfway through grilling. Allow 10 to 12 minutes for medium-rare (145°F) or 12 to 15 minutes for medium doneness (160°F). (For a gas grill, preheat grill. Reduce heat to medium. Place meat on grill rack over heat. Cover and grill as above.)

2. Meanwhile, for sauce, stir together oil, parsley, oregano, garlic, salt, and cayenne pepper. Spoon sauce on top of the meat for the last 2 minutes of grilling.

2 beef T-bone or porterhouse
    steaks, cut 1 inch thick

3 tablespoons olive oil

2 tablespoons snipped fresh
    flat-leaf parsley

1 tablespoon snipped fresh
    oregano or 1 teaspoon dried
    oregano, crushed

2 or 3 cloves garlic, minced

¼ teaspoon salt

¼ teaspoon cayenne pepper

1g carbs   **0**g fiber   **1**g net carbs

Nutrition Facts per serving: 332 cal., 20 g total fat (5 g sat. fat), 75 mg chol., 227 mg sodium, 1 g carbo., 0 g fiber, 35 g pro.

Olive-Stuffed Steaks

Prep: 20 minutes Grill: 22 minutes Makes: 4 servings

½ cup pimiento-stuffed
  green olives

3 cloves garlic, chopped

1 tablespoon capers

1½ teaspoons finely shredded
  orange peel

½ teaspoon black pepper

2 ribeye steaks, cut 1¼ to
  1½ inches thick

1. In a blender container or food processor bowl combine olives, garlic, capers, orange peel, and pepper. Cover and blend or process until mixture is chunky.

2. Cut each steak in half crosswise. Cut a horizontal pocket in each steak piece by cutting from one side almost to, but not through, the other side. Spoon about 1 tablespoon of the olive mixture into each pocket. Spoon remaining mixture over meat; rub in with your fingers.

3. For a charcoal grill, arrange medium coals around a drip pan. Test for medium heat above the pan. Place meat on the grill rack over the pan. Cover and grill until desired doneness. Allow 22 to 25 minutes for medium-rare (145°F) or 25 to 28 minutes for medium doneness (160°F). (For a gas grill, preheat grill. Reduce heat to medium. Adjust for indirect cooking. Place meat on grill rack. Cover and grill as above.)

2 g carbs   0 g fiber   2 g net carbs

Nutrition Facts per serving: 278 cal., 13 g total fat (4 g sat. fat),
81 mg chol., 533 mg sodium, 2 g carbo., 0 g fiber, 38 g pro.

Steak with Roasted Garlic & Herbs

Prep: 15 minutes Grill: 30 minutes Makes: 6 servings

1. Prepare garlic packet using the method described on page 93.

2. For a charcoal grill, grill garlic packet on the rack of an uncovered grill directly over medium coals for 30 minutes or until garlic cloves are soft. Remove bulbs from foil packet, reserving herb-oil mixture. Let cool slightly.

3. Meanwhile, in a small bowl combine pepper and salt; rub onto both sides of meat with your fingers. Grill meat next to the garlic packet to desired doneness, turning once halfway through grilling. Allow 14 to 18 minutes for medium-rare (145°F) or 18 to 22 minutes for medium doneness (160°F). (For a gas grill, preheat grill. Reduce heat to medium. Place meat on grill rack over heat. Cover and grill as above.)

4. To serve, cut meat into pieces. Carefully squeeze the pulp from the garlic cloves onto meat. Mash pulp slightly with a fork; spread over meat. Drizzle meat with the herb-oil mixture. If desired, garnish with oregano sprigs.

1 or 2 whole garlic bulbs

3 teaspoons snipped fresh basil or 1 teaspoon dried basil, crushed

1 tablespoon snipped fresh rosemary or 1 teaspoon dried rosemary, crushed

2 tablespoons olive oil or cooking oil

1 to 2 teaspoons cracked black pepper

½ teaspoon salt

1 boneless beef sirloin steak, cut 1 inch thick

Fresh oregano sprigs (optional)

2 g carbs   **0** g fiber   **2** g net carbs

Nutrition Facts per serving: 251 cal., 15 g total fat (5 g sat. fat), 76 mg chol., 235 mg sodium, 2 g carbo., 0 g fiber, 26 g pro.

T-Bone Steaks with Herb Butter

Prep: 15 minutes Freeze: 30 minutes Grill: 10 minutes Makes: 4 servings

¼ cup butter, softened

1 teaspoon snipped

    fresh parsley

1 teaspoon snipped fresh

    thyme or tarragon

4 beef T-bone steaks, cut

    1 inch thick

½ teaspoon salt

¼ teaspoon freshly ground

    black pepper

1. For herb butter, in a medium bowl combine butter, parsley, and thyme; beat until blended. Shape into a 3-×1-inch log on a 12-inch square of plastic wrap. (If butter is too soft to shape, chill in freezer for 5 minutes.) Wrap in the plastic wrap and freeze for 30 minutes.

2. Season steaks on both sides with salt and pepper. For a charcoal grill, grill meat on the rack of an uncovered grill directly over medium coals for 10 to 12 minutes for medium-rare (145°F) or 12 to 15 minutes for medium doneness (160°F), turning once halfway through grilling. (For a gas grill, preheat grill. Reduce heat to medium. Place meat on grill rack over heat. Cover and grill as above.)

3. Cut herb butter into 8 slices; place 2 slices on top of each steak.

0_g carbs 0_g fiber 0_g net carbs

Nutrition Facts per serving: 407 cal., 22 g total fat (10 g sat. fat), 122 mg chol., 491 mg sodium, 0 g carbo., 0 g fiber, 50 g pro.

Spicy Sirloin Steaks

Prep: 20 minutes Chill: 2 hours Grill: 14 minutes Makes: 8 servings

1. Chop garlic with 1 teaspoon salt on a cutting board; press with side of large knife to form a chunky paste. In a small bowl combine garlic paste, chili powder, five-spice powder, ginger, and pepper; set aside.

2. Sprinkle garlic mixture over both sides of steaks; rub in with your fingers. Place meat in a large self-sealing plastic bag; seal bag. Chill for 2 hours.

3. For a charcoal grill, grill meat on the rack of an uncovered grill directly over medium coals for 14 to 18 minutes for medium-rare (145°F) or 18 to 22 minutes for medium doneness (160°F), turning once halfway through grilling. (For a gas grill, preheat grill. Reduce heat to medium. Place meat on grill rack over heat. Cover and grill as above.)

8 cloves garlic, peeled

1 teaspoon salt

1 tablespoon chili powder

1 tablespoon five-spice powder

2 teaspoons ground ginger

1 teaspoon freshly ground
   black pepper

2 boneless beef top sirloin
   steaks, cut 1 inch thick

3g carbs **1**g fiber **2**g net carbs

Nutrition Facts per serving: 220 cal., 6 g total fat (2 g sat. fat), 103 mg chol., 386 mg sodium, 3 g carbo., 1 g fiber, 37 g pro.

Herbed Steak with Balsamic Sauce

Start to Finish: 20 minutes Makes: 4 servings

1 teaspoon cracked

    black pepper

2 teaspoons dried Italian

    seasoning, crushed

1 teaspoon garlic powder

¼ teaspoon salt

2 boneless beef top loin (strip)

    steaks, cut ¾ inch thick

1 tablespoon olive oil

½ cup beef broth

1 tablespoon balsamic vinegar

1 tablespoon butter

2 tablespoons snipped fresh

    flat-leaf parsley

1. In a small bowl combine pepper, Italian seasoning, garlic powder, and salt. Sprinkle over both sides of steaks; rub in with your fingers.

2. In a large, heavy skillet cook meat in hot oil over medium-low to medium heat until desired doneness, turning once halfway through cooking. Allow 10 to 13 minutes for medium-rare (145°F) and 12 to 15 minutes for medium doneness (160°F). Remove meat from skillet, reserving drippings in the skillet. Keep meat warm.

3. For sauce, carefully add broth and vinegar to the skillet, stirring to loosen any brown bits in bottom of skillet. Bring to boiling. Boil gently, uncovered, about 4 minutes or until sauce is reduced by half. Remove from heat; stir in butter.

4. Divide sauce among 4 dinner plates. Cut each steak in half. Place a piece of meat on top of sauce on each plate; sprinkle with parsley.

2 g carbs   **0** g fiber   **2** g net carbs

Nutrition Facts per serving: 217 cal., 11 g total fat (4 g sat. fat), 75 mg chol., 338 mg sodium, 2 g carbo., 0 g fiber, 25 g pro.

Spice-Rubbed Ribeyes

Prep: 5 minutes Grill: 10 minutes Makes: 4 servings

1. For rub, in a small nonstick skillet cook and stir chili powder, coriander, cumin seeds, and pepper over medium heat for 1 minute; cool. Sprinkle spice mixture over both sides of steaks; rub in with your fingers.

2. For a charcoal grill, grill meat on the rack of an uncovered grill directly over medium coals until desired doneness, turning once halfway through grilling. Allow 10 to 12 minutes for medium-rare (145°F) and 12 to 15 minutes for medium doneness (160°F). (For a gas grill, preheat grill. Reduce heat to medium. Place meat on grill rack over heat. Cover and grill as above.)

4 teaspoons chili powder

1 teaspoon ground coriander

1 teaspoon cumin seeds

½ teaspoon black pepper

4 boneless beef ribeye steaks, cut 1 inch thick

2g carbs   **1**g fiber   **1**g net carbs

Nutrition Facts per serving: 267 cal., 11 g total fat (4 g sat. fat), 81 mg chol., 115 mg sodium, 2 g carbo., 1 g fiber, 38 g pro.

Garlicky Steak & Asparagus

Prep: 15 minutes Broil: 8 minutes Makes: 2 servings

1 or 2 large cloves garlic,

    coarsely chopped

½ teaspoon cracked or coarsely

    ground black pepper

¼ teaspoon salt

1 boneless beef top loin steak,

    cut about ¾ inch thick

8 to 10 thin asparagus spears,

    trimmed (6 ounces)

2 teaspoons garlic-flavored olive

    oil or olive oil

½ cup beef broth

1 tablespoon dry white wine

¼ teaspoon Dijon-style mustard

1. For rub, in a small bowl combine garlic, pepper, and salt. Sprinkle over both sides of meat; rub in with your fingers. Place asparagus in a shallow dish and drizzle with oil. For sauce, in a medium skillet stir together broth and wine. Cook over high heat for 4 to 5 minutes or until mixture is reduced to ¼ cup. Whisk in mustard; keep warm.

2. Preheat broiler. Place meat on the unheated rack of a broiler pan. Broil 3 to 4 inches from the heat until desired doneness. Allow 8 to 10 minutes for medium-rare (145°F) or 10 to 12 minutes for medium doneness (160°F), turning once. Add asparagus the last 2 minutes of broiling.*

3. Spoon sauce on serving plate. Cut steak in half crosswise. Serve meat on sauce with asparagus.

*__Note:__ The asparagus cooking time will vary with the size of asparagus. If there is no room on the broiler pan, broil the asparagus after the steak.

See photo, page 105.

3g carbs   **1**g fiber   **2**g net carbs

Nutrition Facts per serving: 458 cal., 32 g total fat (11 g sat. fat), 110 mg chol., 549 mg sodium, 3 g carbo., 1 g fiber, 37 g pro.

Garlicky
Steak &
Asparagus
p. 104

Steak au
Poivre
p. 90

Steaks with
Blue Cheese
Butter
p. 91

Mediterranean
Beef Salad
p. 116

Beef with
Cucumber
Raita
p. 117

Veal Chops with Pesto-Stuffed Mushrooms p. 121

Lamb
Patties with
Feta & Mint
p. 132

Pepper
of a
Steak
p. 113

Pepper of a Steak

Prep: 10 minutes Broil: 12 minutes Makes: 4 servings

1. Sprinkle meat lightly with salt. Press pepper onto meat.

2. Preheat broiler. Place meat on the unheated rack of a broiler pan. Broil 3 to 4 inches from the heat to desired doneness, turning once halfway through broiling. Allow 12 to 14 minutes for medium-rare (145°F) or 15 to 18 minutes for medium doneness (160°F).

3. Meanwhile, in a large skillet cook sweet pepper strips and garlic in hot butter until tender. Stir in oregano. Spoon sweet pepper mixture over meat.

See photo, page 112.

4 boneless beef top loin steaks,
   cut 1 inch thick

Salt

½ teaspoon cracked black pepper

1 cup red, green, and/or yellow
   sweet pepper strips

1 clove garlic, minced

1 tablespoon butter

1 to 1½ teaspoons snipped fresh
   oregano or ¼ teaspoon dried
   oregano, crushed

3 g carbs   **1** g fiber   **2** g net carbs

Nutrition Facts per serving: 186 cal., 8 g total fat (3 g sat. fat), 75 mg chol., 225 mg sodium, 3 g carbo., 1 g fiber, 25 g pro.

Steaks with Horseradish-Cream Sauce

Start to Finish: 25 minutes Oven: 400°F Makes: 2 to 4 servings

1 tablespoon olive oil

2 1½-inch-thick beef tenderloin

   steaks (8 to 10 ounces

   each)

   Salt

   Freshly ground black pepper

½ cup whipping cream

3 tablespoons horseradish

   mustard

1. In a large skillet heat oil over medium heat. Sprinkle both sides of steaks with salt and freshly ground pepper; add to hot skillet. Cook about 4 minutes or until browned, turning once. Transfer to a 2-quart square baking dish. Bake the steaks, uncovered, in a 400° oven for 10 to 13 minutes or until medium-rare doneness (145°F).

2. Meanwhile, in a medium mixing bowl beat the whipping cream with an electric mixer on medium speed until soft peaks form. Fold in horseradish mustard. Serve with steak.

4g
carbs

0g
fiber

4g
net carbs

Nutrition Facts per serving: 641 cal., 47 g total fat (21 g sat. fat), 221 mg chol., 620 mg sodium, 4 g carbo., 0 g dietary fiber, 50 g protein.

Garlic-Mustard Steak

Prep: 10 minutes Broil: 15 minutes Makes: 4 to 6 servings

1. Score meat on both sides by making shallow diagonal cuts at 1-inch intervals in a diamond pattern. In a small bowl combine mustard, marjoram, garlic, and pepper. Brush both sides of the meat with mustard mixture.

2. Preheat broiler. Place meat on the unheated rack of a broiler pan. Broil 3 to 4 inches from the heat for 15 to 18 minutes for medium doneness (160°F), turning once halfway through broiling. Thinly slice meat diagonally across the grain.

1 1- to 1½-pound beef flank steak

2 tablespoons Dijon-style mustard

½ teaspoon dried marjoram or thyme, crushed

½ teaspoon bottled minced garlic or 1 clove garlic, minced

¼ teaspoon coarsely ground black pepper

2g carbs   **0**g fiber   **2**g net carbs

Nutrition Facts per serving: 186 cal., 8 g total fat (3 g sat. fat), 46 mg chol., 240 mg sodium, 2 g carbo., 0 g fiber, 26 g pro.

Mediterranean Beef Salad

Prep: 15 minutes Grill: 14 minutes Makes: 6 servings

1½ teaspoons dried oregano,
    crushed

½ teaspoon salt

½ teaspoon black pepper

¼ cup olive oil

¼ cup red wine vinegar

1 clove garlic, minced

1 1½-pound boneless beef top
    sirloin steak, cut 1 inch thick

1 10-ounce package torn
    romaine lettuce

⅓ cup thinly sliced cucumber

¼ cup thinly sliced red onion

½ cup crumbled garlic and herb
    feta cheese

1. Combine oregano, salt, and pepper. For dressing, in a small bowl stir together ½ teaspoon of the oregano mixture, olive oil, vinegar, and garlic; set aside. Sprinkle remaining oregano mixture evenly onto both sides of meat; rub in with your fingers.

2. For a charcoal grill, grill meat on the rack of an uncovered grill directly over medium coals to desired doneness, turning once halfway through grilling. Allow 14 to 18 minutes for medium-rare (145°F) and 18 to 22 minutes for medium doneness (160°F). (For a gas grill, preheat grill. Reduce heat to medium. Place meat on grill rack over heat. Cover and grill as above.)

3. Meanwhile, toss together romaine, cucumber, and onion. Divide romaine mixture among 6 plates. Thinly slice meat across the grain; arrange meat on romaine mixture. Whisk dressing and drizzle over salads. Sprinkle with feta.

See photo, page 108.

3g carbs   **1**g fiber   **2**g net carbs

Nutrition Facts per serving: 256 cal., 15 g total fat (4 g sat. fat),
77 mg chol., 359 mg sodium, 3 g carbo., 1 g fiber, 26 g pro.

Beef with Cucumber Raita

Prep: 10 minutes Broil: 15 minutes Makes: 4 servings

1. Preheat broiler. Sprinkle meat with salt and pepper. Place meat on the unheated rack of a broiler pan. Broil 3 to 4 inches from the heat until desired doneness, turning once halfway through broiling. Allow 15 to 17 minutes for medium-rare (145°F) or 20 to 22 minutes for medium doneness (160°F).

2. Meanwhile, for raita, in a small bowl stir together sour cream, cucumber, green onion, and mint. Season to taste with salt and pepper.

3. Thinly slice meat across the grain. Serve with raita and if desired, garnish with mint sprigs.

See photo, page 109.

1 boneless beef sirloin steak, cut
  1 inch thick
Salt and black pepper
1 8-ounce carton dairy sour
  cream
¼ cup coarsely shredded, seeded
  cucumber
2 tablespoons sliced green onion
1 tablespoon snipped fresh mint
Salt and black pepper
Fresh mint sprigs (optional)

3g carbs   **0**g fiber   **3**g net carbs

Nutrition Facts per serving: 268 cal., 16 g total fat (9 g sat. fat), 94 mg chol., 232 mg sodium, 3 g carbo., 0 g fiber, 26 g pro.

Tex-Mex Smoked Short Ribs

Prep: 20 minutes Cook: 1½ hours Soak: 1 hour Grill: 20 minutes Makes: 6 servings

4 pounds beef short ribs

4 cups hickory chips

1 tablespoon cooking oil

1½ teaspoons chili powder

1 teaspoon dry mustard

½ teaspoon ground cumin

⅛ teaspoon garlic powder

½ cup hot picante sauce

¼ teaspoon bottled hot

   pepper sauce

1. Cut ribs into serving-size pieces. Place in a 4- to 6-quart Dutch oven. Add enough water to cover meat. Bring to boiling; reduce heat. Simmer, covered, about 1½ hours or until tender. Drain meat.

2. At least 1 hour before grilling, soak wood chips in enough water to cover. For sauce, in a saucepan combine oil, chili powder, dry mustard, cumin, and garlic powder. Cook and stir over medium heat until bubbly. Remove from heat. Stir in picante and hot pepper sauces. Set aside.

3. Drain wood chips. For a charcoal grill, arrange medium-low coals around a drip pan. Pour 1 inch of water into drip pan. Test for low heat above the pan. Sprinkle half of the wood chips over the coals. Place ribs, bone sides down, on grill rack over drip pan. Brush meat with some of the sauce. Cover and grill for 20 to 30 minutes or until browned, brushing occasionally with sauce. Add the remaining wood chips halfway through grilling. (For a gas grill, preheat grill. Reduce heat to low. Adjust for indirect cooking. Add wood chips according to manufacturer's directions. Grill as above.) To serve, reheat the sauce and pass with meat.

2 g carbs   **0** g fiber   **2** g net carbs

Nutrition Facts per serving: 474 cal., 30 g total fat (12 g sat. fat), 139 mg chol., 242 mg sodium, 2 g carbo., 0 g fiber, 46 g pro.

Spicy Grilled Brisket

Prep: 25 minutes Grill: 3 hours Stand: 10 minutes Makes: 15 servings

1. At least 1 hour before grilling, soak wood chunks in enough water to cover.

2. Make several slits in surface of the brisket. Insert a sliver of garlic into each slit. Brush meat with oil. In a small bowl stir together salt, paprika, black pepper, cayenne pepper, and thyme. Sprinkle mixture evenly over both sides of meat; rub in with your fingers.

3. Drain wood chunks. For a charcoal grill, arrange medium coals around a drip pan. Test for medium-low heat above pan. Sprinkle about half of the drained wood chunks over the coals. Place meat, fat side up, on grill rack over drip pan. Cover and grill for 3 to 3¾ hours or until brisket is tender. Add more wood chunks as necessary. (For a gas grill, preheat grill. Reduce heat to low. Adjust for indirect cooking. Add wood chips according to manufacturer's directions. Grill as above, except place meat, fat side up, on a rack in a roasting pan.)

4. Let stand 10 minutes before slicing. Thinly slice meat across the grain.

1½ **pounds mesquite wood chunks**

1 **5- to 6-pound fresh beef brisket**

3 **cloves garlic, cut into slivers**

2 **tablespoons cooking oil**

2 **tablespoons coarse salt**

2 **tablespoons paprika**

1 **tablespoon black pepper**

1 **teaspoon cayenne pepper**

1 **teaspoon dried thyme, crushed**

1g carbs   **1**g fiber   **0**g net carbs

Nutrition Facts per serving: 240 cal., 11 g total fat (3 g sat. fat), 88 mg chol., 868 mg sodium, 1 g carbo., 1 g fiber, 33 g pro.

Garlic & Spice Brisket

Prep: 15 minutes Bake: 3½ hours Oven: 325°F Makes: 10 servings

1 3- to 3½-pound fresh

   beef brisket

¾ cup water

2 tablespoons cider vinegar

1 tablespoon Worcestershire

   sauce

2 teaspoons celery seeds

1 teaspoon black pepper

1 teaspoon onion salt

3 cloves garlic, minced

1. Place meat in a 13×9×2-inch baking pan. In a small bowl combine water, vinegar, Worcestershire sauce, celery seeds, pepper, onion salt, and garlic. Pour mixture over meat.

2. Cover with foil and bake in a 325° oven for 3½ to 4 hours or until tender. Slice meat across the grain to serve. If desired, spoon cooking juices over meat.

1 g carbs   **0** g fiber   **1** g net carbs

Nutrition Facts per serving: 192 cal., 7 g total fat (2 g sat. fat), 78 mg chol., 281 mg sodium, 1 g carbo., 0 g fiber, 29 g pro.

Veal Chops with Pesto-Stuffed Mushrooms

Prep: 10 minutes Marinate: 30 minutes Grill: 11 minutes Makes: 4 servings

1. For marinade, in a small bowl combine wine, sage, Worcestershire sauce, oil, and garlic. Place meat in a self-sealing plastic bag set in a shallow dish. Pour marinade over meat; seal bag. Marinate in the refrigerator for 30 minutes to 24 hours, turning bag occasionally.

2. Drain meat, reserving marinade. Sprinkle meat with pepper. For a charcoal grill, grill meat on the rack of an uncovered grill directly over medium coals for 11 to 13 minutes for medium doneness (160°F), turning once halfway through grilling and brushing with reserved marinade during the first 5 minutes of grilling.

3. Meanwhile, carefully remove stems from mushrooms; chop stems for another use or discard. Brush mushroom caps with reserved marinade. Discard any remaining marinade. Place mushrooms, stem sides down, on grill rack. Grill for 4 minutes. Turn stem sides up; spoon some pesto into each. Grill about 4 minutes more or until heated through. (For a gas grill, preheat grill. Reduce heat to medium. Place meat and mushrooms on grill rack over heat. Cover and grill as above.) Serve mushrooms with meat.

See photo, page 110.

¼ cup dry white wine

1 tablespoon snipped fresh sage

 or snipped fresh thyme

1 tablespoon Worcestershire

 sauce for chicken

1 tablespoon olive oil

1½ teaspoons bottled minced

 garlic (3 cloves)

4 veal loin chops, cut ¾ inch thick

 Black pepper

8 large fresh mushrooms

 (2 inches in diameter)

2 to 3 tablespoons purchased

 pesto

4g carbs **1**g fiber **3**g net carbs

Nutrition Facts per serving: 285 cal., 16 g total fat (2 g sat. fat), 100 mg chol., 157 mg sodium, 4 g carbo., 1 g fiber, 28 g pro.

Lemon-Mustard Veal Chops

Prep: 10 minutes Grill: 12 minutes Makes: 4 servings

1 tablespoon snipped fresh
   thyme or 1 teaspoon dried
   thyme, crushed

1 tablespoon country Dijon-style
   mustard

2 teaspoons lemon juice

1 teaspoon lemon-pepper
   seasoning

1 teaspoon garlic-pepper
   seasoning

4 veal rib or loin chops, cut
   1 inch thick

1. For sauce, in a small bowl combine thyme, mustard, lemon juice, lemon-pepper seasoning, and garlic-pepper seasoning.

2. For a charcoal grill, grill meat on the rack of an uncovered grill directly over medium coals for 12 to 15 minutes for medium doneness (160°F), turning once and brushing occasionally with sauce during the last 5 minutes of grilling. (For a gas grill, preheat grill. Reduce heat to medium. Place meat on grill rack over heat. Cover and grill as above.)

1g carbs   **0**g fiber   **1**g net carbs

Nutrition Facts per serving: 189 cal., 8 g total fat (2 g sat. fat),
116 mg chol., 460 mg sodium, 1 g carbo., 0 g fiber, 26 g pro.

Veal Rolls Stuffed with Herb Cheese

Prep: 25 minutes Grill: 20 minutes Makes: 4 servings

1. Cut meat into 4 serving-size pieces. Place each piece between 2 pieces of plastic wrap. Using the flat side of a meat mallet, lightly pound meat to $1/4$-inch thickness. Remove plastic wrap.

2. Trim haricot verts and cook, covered, in boiling lightly salted water for 4 minutes. Drain.

3. Spread each meat piece with cheese. Top with one-fourth of the beans and a slice of prosciutto (trim haricot verts and fold prosciutto if necessary to fit). Fold in sides; roll up meat. Seal edges with small metal skewers. Brush rolls with melted butter.

4. For a charcoal grill, arrange medium-hot coals around a drip pan. Test for medium heat above pan. Place meat rolls on grill rack over drip pan. Cover and grill for 20 to 24 minutes or until meat is no longer pink, turning once. (For a gas grill, preheat grill. Reduce heat to medium. Adjust for indirect cooking. Grill as above.)

5. Remove skewers from rolls. Place rolls on serving platter. If desired, sprinkle with fresh herbs.

1 pound boneless veal
  round steak

4 ounces haricot verts or tiny
  young green beans

4 tablespoons semisoft cheese
  with garlic and herb

4 slices proscuitto
  (about $2\frac{1}{2}$ ounces)

2 tablespoons butter or
  margarine, melted

Chopped fresh herbs (optional)

2g carbs   **1**g fiber   **1**g net carbs

Nutrition Facts per serving: 245 cal., 12 g total fat (7 g sat. fat), 117 mg chol., 641 mg sodium, 2 g carbo., 1 g fiber, 30 g pro.

Mediterranean Veal Brochettes

Prep: 20 minutes Marinate: 1 hour Grill: 10 minutes Makes: 6 servings

1½ pounds boneless veal,
    trimmed and cut into
    1½-inch cubes

3 green onions, sliced

¼ cup olive oil

3 tablespoons lemon juice

2 teaspoons dried tarragon,
   crushed

1½ teaspoons bottled minced
    garlic (3 cloves)

½ teaspoon dried oregano,
   crushed

¼ teaspoon freshly ground black
   pepper

1. Place meat in a self-sealing plastic bag set in a shallow dish. For marinade, in a small bowl combine green onions, oil, lemon juice, tarragon, garlic, oregano, and pepper. Pour over meat; seal bag. Marinate in the refrigerator for 1 to 4 hours, turning bag occasionally.

2. Drain meat, discarding marinade. Thread meat on six 12-inch metal skewers, leaving a ¼-inch space between pieces. For a charcoal grill, grill skewers on the rack of an uncovered grill directly over medium coals for 10 to 14 minutes for medium doneness (160°F), turning occasionally. (For a gas grill, preheat grill. Reduce heat to medium. Place skewers on grill rack over heat. Cover and grill as above.)

1 g carbs 0 g fiber 1 g net carbs

Nutrition Facts per serving: 164 cal., 6 g total fat (1 g sat. fat),
88 mg chol., 62 mg sodium, 1 g carbo., 0 g fiber, 24 g pro.

124

Bacon-Tarragon Veal Brochettes

Prep: 15 minutes Marinate: 2 hours Grill: 10 minutes Makes: 4 to 6 servings

1. Cut meat into 1-inch cubes. Place meat in a self-sealing plastic bag set in a shallow dish. For marinade, combine wine, tarragon, oil, lemon juice, salt, and pepper. Pour over meat; seal bag. Marinate in the refrigerator for 2 hours, turning bag occasionally. Drain meat, reserving marinade.

2. In a large skillet cook bacon over medium heat just until brown but still soft. Drain on paper towels. On 10- to 12-inch metal skewers, alternately thread meat and bacon, weaving bacon between and around meat in an "S" fashion.

3. For a charcoal grill, grill skewers on the rack of an uncovered grill directly over medium coals for 10 to 14 minutes for medium doneness (160°F), turning once and brushing occasionally with reserved marinade up to the last 5 minutes of grilling. (For a gas grill, preheat grill. Reduce heat to medium. Place skewers on grill rack over heat. Cover and grill as above.)

2 pounds boneless veal

3 tablespoons dry white wine

2 tablespoons snipped
   fresh tarragon

2 tablespoons olive oil

2 tablespoons lemon juice

½ teaspoon salt

½ teaspoon black pepper

8 slices bacon

1 g carbs **0** g fiber **1** g net carbs

Nutrition Facts per serving: 429 cal., 21 g total fat (6 g sat. fat), 196 mg chol., 591 mg sodium, 1 g carbo., 0 g fiber, 54 g pro.

Garlic-Studded Veal Chops with Asparagus

Prep: 15 minutes Marinate: 30 minutes Grill: 10 minutes Makes: 4 servings

12 ounces asparagus spears

2 tablespoons dry sherry

2 tablespoons olive oil

1 clove garlic, minced

4 boneless veal top loin chops,
    cut ¾ inch thick

3 or 4 cloves garlic, cut into
    thin slivers

1 tablespoon snipped fresh
    thyme or 1 teaspoon dried
    thyme, crushed

⅛ teaspoon salt

⅛ teaspoon black pepper

1. Snap off and discard woody stems from asparagus. In a medium skillet bring a small amount of water to boiling; add asparagus. Simmer, covered, 3 minutes or until crisp-tender; drain. Place asparagus in a self-sealing plastic bag; add sherry, 1 tablespoon of the oil, and minced garlic. Marinate at room temperature 30 minutes, turning occasionally.

2. Meanwhile, with the tip of a sharp knife, make a few small slits in each chop; insert garlic slivers. Combine remaining 1 tablespoon oil, thyme, salt, and pepper; brush over meat.

3. For a charcoal grill, grill meat on the rack of an uncovered grill directly over medium coals for 10 to 13 minutes for medium doneness (160°F), turning once halfway through grilling. Add asparagus spears to grill (lay spears perpendicular to wires on grill rack so they won't fall into coals). Grill for 3 to 4 minutes or until crisp-tender and lightly browned, turning occasionally. (For a gas grill, preheat grill. Reduce heat to medium. Place meat and asparagus spears on grill rack over medium heat. Cover and grill as above.)

3g carbs   **1**g fiber   **2**g net carbs

Nutrition Facts per serving: 240 cal., 11 g total fat (2 g sat. fat), 105 mg chol., 183 mg sodium, 3 g carbo., 1 g fiber, 28 g pro.

Roast Rack of Lamb

Prep: 25 minutes Roast: 45 minutes Stand: 15 minutes
Oven: 325°F Makes: 6 servings

1. Sprinkle meat with salt and pepper. In a small bowl stir together mustard, vinegar, water, and parsley. Set aside 1 tablespoon of the mustard mixture; brush remaining mustard mixture onto meat.

2. Place meat on a rack in a shallow roasting pan. Insert a meat thermometer into center of roast, not touching bone. Roast, uncovered, in a 325° oven until desired doneness. Allow 45 minutes to 1 hour for medium-rare (135°F) or 1 to 1½ hours for medium doneness (150°F). Cover meat with foil and let stand for 15 minutes. (The meat's temperature will rise 10°F during standing.)

3. In a small saucepan combine sour cream, whipping cream, and the 1 tablespoon reserved mustard mixture. Cook and stir over low heat until hot (do not boil). Season to taste with additional salt and pepper. Serve with meat.

2 1- to 1½-pound lamb rib roasts
   (6 to 8 ribs each), with or
   without backbone
   Salt and freshly ground
   black pepper
¼ cup stone-ground mustard
1 tablespoon white wine vinegar
1 tablespoon water
1 tablespoon snipped fresh
   flat-leaf parsley
½ cup dairy sour cream
¼ cup whipping cream
   Salt and black pepper

2g carbs **0**g fiber **2**g net carbs

Nutrition Facts per serving: 200 cal., 14 g total fat (6 g sat. fat), 63 mg chol., 101 mg sodium, 2 g carbo., 0 g fiber, 15 g pro.

Lamb Chops with Garlic Mushrooms

Start to Finish: 30 minutes Makes: 4 servings

2 tablespoons olive oil

2 teaspoons snipped fresh

    oregano or thyme

¼ teaspoon salt

¼ teaspoon freshly ground

    black pepper

8 lamb loin chops, cut 1 inch thick

1 medium shallot, thinly sliced

2 cups sliced fresh mushrooms

2 cloves garlic, minced

2 tablespoons dry white wine

Salt and freshly ground

    black pepper

Snipped fresh oregano or

    thyme (optional)

1. In a small bowl combine 1 tablespoon of the oil, 2 teaspoons oregano, ¼ teaspoon salt, and ¼ teaspoon pepper. Brush mixture onto one side of chops. In a large skillet heat remaining 1 tablespoon oil over medium-high heat. Add meat; cook until desired doneness, turning once halfway through cooking. Allow 9 to 11 minutes for medium-rare (145°F) to medium doneness (160°F). Transfer meat to a serving platter; keep warm.

2. Stir shallot into drippings in skillet. Cook and stir for 30 seconds. Stir in mushrooms and garlic. Cook and stir for 3 minutes or until mushrooms are tender. Remove from heat; let cool for 30 seconds. Carefully add wine to skillet. Return to heat and bring to boiling. Cook until most of the wine has evaporated. Season mushroom mixture to taste with salt and pepper. Spoon mushroom mixture over meat. If desired, sprinkle with additional oregano.

3g carbs   **0**g fiber   **3**g net carbs

Nutrition Facts per serving: 256 cal., 14 g total fat (3 g sat. fat), 80 mg chol., 255 mg sodium, 3 g carbo., 0 g fiber, 27 g pro.

Herbed Lamb Chops

Prep: 15 minutes Marinate: 4 hours Grill: 12 minutes Makes: 4 servings

1. Place meat in a self-sealing plastic bag set in a shallow dish. For marinade, in a small bowl combine wine, 2 tablespoons herb, oil, salt, pepper, and garlic. Pour over meat; seal bag. Marinate in the refrigerator for 4 to 24 hours, turning bag occasionally.

2. Drain meat, discarding marinade. For a charcoal grill, grill meat on the rack of an uncovered grill directly over medium coals until desired doneness, turning once halfway through grilling. Allow 12 to 14 minutes for medium-rare (145°F) or 15 to 17 minutes for medium doneness (160°F). (For a gas grill, preheat grill. Reduce heat to medium. Place meat on grill rack over heat. Cover and grill as above.)

3. Transfer meat to a serving platter. If desired, sprinkle with additional fresh herbs.

8 lamb rib chops, cut 1 inch thick

½ cup dry white wine

2 tablespoons snipped fresh
　　oregano, basil, and/or thyme

2 tablespoons olive oil

½ teaspoon salt

¼ teaspoon freshly ground
　　black pepper

2 cloves garlic, minced

　Snipped fresh herbs (optional)

0 g carbs　0 g fiber　0 g net carbs

Nutrition Facts per serving: 107 cal., 6 g total fat (2 g sat. fat), 32 mg chol., 124 mg sodium, 0 g carbo., 0 g fiber, 10 g pro.

Ginger-Marinated Lamb Chops

Prep: 20 minutes Marinate: 4 hours Grill: 12 minutes Makes: 4 servings

8 lamb rib chops, cut

   1 inch thick

3 tablespoons soy sauce

2 tablespoons rice vinegar

2 tablespoons cooking oil

2 tablespoons grated

   fresh ginger

¼ teaspoon salt

⅛ teaspoon crushed

   red pepper

1 green onion, chopped

1 clove garlic, minced

1. Place meat in a self-sealing plastic bag set in a shallow dish. For marinade, in a small bowl combine soy sauce, vinegar, oil, ginger, salt, crushed red pepper, green onion, and garlic. Pour over meat; seal bag. Marinate in the refrigerator for 4 to 24 hours, turning bag occasionally.

2. Drain meat, discarding marinade. For a charcoal grill, grill meat on the rack of an uncovered grill directly over medium coals until desired doneness, turning once halfway through grilling. Allow 12 to 14 minutes for medium-rare (145°F) or 15 to 17 minutes for medium doneness (160°F). (For a gas grill, preheat grill. Reduce heat to medium. Place meat on grill rack over heat. Cover and grill as above.)

1g carbs   0g fiber   1g net carbs

Nutrition Facts per serving: 350 cal., 20 g total fat (6 g sat. fat), 124 mg chol., 535 mg sodium, 1 g carbo., 0 g fiber, 39 g pro.

Lamb Chops with Rosemary

Prep: 10 minutes Marinate: 2 hours Grill: 12 minutes Makes: 4 servings

1. Place meat in a self-sealing plastic bag set in a shallow dish. For marinade, in a small bowl combine wine, lemon juice, oil, rosemary, salt, and pepper. Pour over meat; seal bag. Marinate in the refrigerator for 2 to 4 hours, turning bag occasionally. Drain meat, discarding marinade.

2. For a charcoal grill, grill meat on the rack of an uncovered grill directly over medium coals until desired doneness, turning once halfway through grilling. Allow 12 to 14 minutes for medium-rare (145°F) or 15 to 17 minutes for medium doneness (160°F). (For a gas grill, preheat grill. Reduce heat to medium. Place meat on grill rack. Cover and grill as above.) If desired, garnish with fresh rosemary.

8 lamb loin chops, cut
   1 inch thick

⅓ cup dry white wine

⅓ cup lemon juice

3 tablespoons olive oil or
   cooking oil

1 tablespoon snipped fresh
   rosemary or 1 teaspoon dried
   rosemary, crushed

½ teaspoon salt

¼ teaspoon black pepper

   Fresh rosemary sprigs
   (optional)

0_g carbs 0_g fiber 0_g net carbs

Nutrition Facts per serving: 193 cal., 9 g total fat (3 g sat. fat), 80 mg chol., 133 mg sodium, 0 g carbo., 0 g fiber, 26 g pro.

Lamb Patties with Feta & Mint

Prep: 15 minutes Grill: 14 minutes Makes: 4 servings

1 pound lean ground lamb

   or beef

2 teaspoons freshly ground

   black pepper

4 lettuce leaves

½ cup crumbled feta cheese

   (2 ounces)

4 tomato slices

1 tablespoon snipped

   fresh mint

1. Form meat into four ³/₄-inch-thick patties. Press pepper evenly into patties. For a charcoal grill, grill patties on the rack of an uncovered grill directly over medium coals for 14 to 18 minutes or until patties are no longer pink (160°F), turning once. (For a gas grill, preheat grill. Reduce heat to medium. Place patties on grill rack over heat. Cover and grill as above.)

2. Serve patties with lettuce, feta cheese, tomato slices, and mint.

See photo, page 111.

2 g carbs

0 g fiber

2 g net carbs

Nutrition Facts per serving: 181 cal., 7 g total fat (4 g sat. fat),
84 mg chol., 211 mg sodium, 2 g carbo., 0 g fiber, 26 g pro.

Rosemary-&-Garlic-Crusted Lamb

Prep: 30 minutes Grill: 1½ hours Stand: 15 minutes Makes: 6 to 8 servings

1. For rub, in a small bowl combine rosemary, pepper, and garlic. Sprinkle mixture evenly over meat; rub in with your fingers.

2. To mount on a spit rod, place one holding fork on the rod, tines toward point. Insert rod through meat, pressing tines of holding fork firmly into meat. Adjust forks and tighten screws. Test the balance and adjust, if necessary.

3. For a charcoal grill, arrange medium coals around a drip pan. Test for medium-low heat above pan. Attach spit; insert an instant-read thermometer. Turn on the motor and lower grill hood. Let the meat rotate over drip pan until desired doneness. Allow 1½ to 2¼ for medium-rare (140°F) or 1¾ to 2½ hours for medium doneness (155°F). (For a gas grill, preheat grill. Reduce heat to medium. Adjust for indirect cooking. Grill as above.)

4. Remove meat from spit. Cover with foil and let stand for 15 minutes before carving. (The meat's temperature will rise 5°F during standing.) To serve, remove strings and thinly slice meat.

2 tablespoons snipped
   fresh rosemary

2 to 3 teaspoons coarsely ground
   black pepper

2 to 3 cloves garlic, minced

1 3½- to 4-pound boneless
   leg of lamb, rolled and tied

1 g carbs   0 g fiber   1 g net carbs

Nutrition Facts per serving: 291 cal., 12 g total fat (4 g sat. fat), 134 mg chol., 103 mg sodium, 1 g carbo., 0 g fiber, 43 g pro.

133

Lemon-Rosemary Lamb Kabobs

Prep: 15 minutes Marinate: 2 hours Grill: 8 minutes Makes: 4 servings

1 pound lean boneless

   leg of lamb

¼ cup olive oil

1 teaspoon finely shredded

   lemon peel

3 tablespoons lemon juice

1 tablespoon snipped

   fresh rosemary

2 cloves garlic, minced

½ teaspoon ground cumin

½ teaspoon freshly ground

   black pepper

¼ teaspoon salt

2 small onions, each cut into

   8 wedges

1. Cut meat into 1½-inch pieces. Place meat in a self-sealing plastic bag set in a shallow dish. For marinade, in a small bowl combine oil, lemon peel, lemon juice, rosemary, garlic, cumin, pepper, and salt. Pour over meat; seal bag. Marinate in the refrigerator for 2 to 6 hours, turning bag occasionally.

2. In a medium covered saucepan cook onions in a small amount of boiling water for 3 minutes; drain onions. Drain meat, reserving marinade. Onto 8 rosemary branches or metal skewers, alternately thread meat and onion wedges, leaving a ¼-inch space between pieces. Brush onions with some of the marinade.

3. For a charcoal grill, grill skewers on the rack of an uncovered grill directly over medium coals for 8 to 12 minutes for medium-rare (145°F), turning and brushing once with marinade halfway through grilling. (For a gas grill, preheat grill. Reduce heat to medium. Place skewers on grill rack over heat. Grill as above.)

4g carbs   **1**g fiber   **3**g net carbs

Nutrition Facts per serving: 277 cal., 18 g total fat (4 g sat. fat), 72 mg chol., 200 mg sodium, 4 g carbo., 1 g fiber, 24 g pro.

Dijon-Crusted Lamb Rib Roast

Prep: 10 minutes Grill: 1 hour Stand: 15 minutes Makes: 4 servings

1. In a bowl stir together mustard, oil, garlic, thyme, salt, and pepper. Set aside 2 tablespoons of the mixture; cover and chill. Brush meat with remaining mixture. Insert a meat thermometer into roast not touching bone.

2. For a charcoal grill, arrange medium-hot coals around a drip pan. Test for medium heat above pan. Place meat, bone side down, on grill rack over drip pan. Cover and grill until meat thermometer registers desired doneness. Allow 1 to 1 1/4 hours for medium-rare (140°F) or 1 1/4 to 1 1/2 hours for medium doneness (155°F). (For a gas grill, preheat grill. Reduce heat to medium. Adjust for indirect cooking. Grill as above, except place meat, bone side down, into a roasting pan.)

3. Remove meat from grill. Cover with foil; let stand for 15 minutes before carving. (The meat's temperature will rise 5°F during standing.)

4. Meanwhile, for sauce, in a bowl stir together sour cream and reserved mustard mixture. To serve, cut meat into four 2-rib portions. Pass sauce with meat.

3 tablespoons Dijon-style mustard

1 tablespoon olive oil

2 cloves garlic, minced

1 teaspoon snipped fresh thyme or 1/2 teaspoon dried thyme, crushed

1/4 teaspoon salt

1/4 teaspoon black pepper

1 2 1/2-pound lamb rib roast (8 ribs)

1/4 cup dairy sour cream

2g carbs   **0**g fiber   **2**g net carbs

Nutrition Facts per serving: 404 cal., 26 g total fat (9 g sat. fat), 126 mg chol., 539 mg sodium, 2 g carbo., 0 g fiber, 38 g pro.

Quick and Easy Cooking Methods for Beef, Lamb, and Veal

Indoor Electric Grills

Preheat grill. Place meat on grill rack. If using a grill with a cover, close the lid. Grill for the time given below or until done. If using a grill without a cover, turn food once halfway through grilling. The following timings should be used as general guidelines. Test for doneness using a meat thermometer. Refer to your owner's manual for preheating directions, suggested cuts, and recommended grilling times.

Cut or Type	Thickness, Weight, or Size	Covered Grilling Time	Uncovered Grilling Time	Doneness
Beef				
Boneless steak (ribeye, tenderloin, top loin)	1 inch	4 to 6 minutes 6 to 8 minutes	8 to 12 minutes 12 to 15 minutes	145°F medium rare 160°F medium
Boneless top sirloin steak	1 inch	5 to 7 minutes 7 to 9 minutes	12 to 15 minutes 15 to 18 minutes	145°F medium rare 160°F medium
Flank steak	¾ to 1 inch	7 to 9 minutes	12 to 14 minutes	160°F medium
Ground meat patties	½ to ¾ inch	5 to 7 minutes	14 to 18 minutes	160°F medium
Sausages, cooked (frankfurters, smoked bratwurst, etc.)	6 per pound	2½ to 3 minutes	5 to 6 minutes	140°F heated through
Steak with bone (porterhouse, rib, T-bone)	1 inch	Not recommended Not recommended	8 to 12 minutes 12 to 15 minutes	145°F medium rare 160°F medium
Lamb Chop (loin or rib)	1 inch	6 to 8 minutes	12 to 15 minutes	160°F medium
Veal Chop (boneless loin)	¾ inch	4 to 5 minutes	7 to 9 minutes	160°F medium

Indirect-Grilling Meat

For a charcoal grill, arrange medium-hot coals around a drip pan. Test for medium heat above pan, unless chart says otherwise. Place meat, fat side up, on grill rack over drip pan. Cover and grill for the time given below or to desired temperature, adding more charcoal to maintain heat as necessary. For a gas grill, preheat grill. Reduce heat to medium. Adjust heat for indirect cooking.

Test for doneness using a meat thermometer. (Use an instant-read thermometer to test smaller portions.) Thermometer should register the "final grilling temperature." Remove meat from grill. For larger cuts, such as roasts, cover with foil and let stand 15 minutes before carving. The meat's temperature will rise 5°F to 10°F during the time it stands. Thinner cuts, such as steaks, do not have to stand.

Cut	Thickness/ Weight	Approximate Indirect-Grilling Time	Final Grilling Temperature (when to remove from grill)	Final Doneness Temperature (after 15 minutes standing)
Beef Boneless top sirloin steak	1 inch 1½ inches	22 to 26 minutes 26 to 30 minutes 32 to 36 minutes 36 to 40 minutes	145°F medium rare 160°F medium 145°F medium rare 160°F medium	No standing time No standing time No standing time No standing time
Steak (porterhouse, rib, ribeye, T-bone, tenderloin, top loin)	1 inch 1½ inches	16 to 20 minutes 20 to 24 minutes 22 to 25 minutes 25 to 28 minutes	145°F medium rare 160°F medium 145°F medium rare 160°F medium	No standing time No standing time No standing time No standing time
Tenderloin roast (medium-high heat)	2 to 3 pounds	¾ to 1 hour	135°F	145°F medium rare
Beef, Lamb, Pork, or Veal Ground meat patties	½ inch ¾ inch	15 to 18 minutes 20 to 24 minutes	160°F medium 160°F medium	No standing time No standing time

Direct-Grilling Meat

For a charcoal grill, place meat on grill rack directly over medium coals. Grill, uncovered, for the time given below or to desired doneness, turning once halfway through grilling. For a gas grill, preheat grill. Reduce heat to medium. Place meat on grill rack over heat. Cover the grill. Test for doneness using a meat thermometer.

Cut	Thickness/ Weight	Grilling Temperature	Approximate Direct-Grilling Time	Doneness
Beef				
Boneless steak (ribeye, tenderloin, top loin)	1 inch	Medium	11 to 15 minutes 14 to 18 minutes	145°F medium rare 160°F medium
	1½ inches	Medium	15 to 19 minutes 18 to 23 minutes	145°F medium rare 160°F medium
Boneless top sirloin steak	1 inch	Medium	14 to 18 minutes 18 to 22 minutes	145°F medium rare 160°F medium
	1½ inches	Medium	20 to 24 minutes 24 to 28 minutes	145°F medium rare 160°F medium
Boneless tri-tip steak (bottom sirloin)	¾ inch	Medium	9 to 11 minutes 11 to 13 minutes	145°F medium rare 160°F medium
	1 inch	Medium	13 to 15 minutes 15 to 17 minutes	145°F medium rare 160°F medium
Flank steak	1¼ to 1¾ pounds	Medium	17 to 21 minutes	160°F medium
Steak with bone (porterhouse, rib, T-bone)	1 inch	Medium	11 to 14 minutes 13 to 16 minutes	145°F medium rare 160°F medium
	1½ inches	Medium	18 to 21 minutes 22 to 25 minutes	145°F medium rare 160°F medium
Beef, Lamb, Pork, or Veal Ground Meat Patties	½ inch ¾ inch	Medium Medium	10 to 13 minutes 14 to 18 minutes	160°F medium 160°F medium
Lamb Chop (loin or rib)	1 inch	Medium	12 to 14 minutes 15 to 17 minutes	145°F medium rare 160°F medium
Chop (sirloin)	¾ to 1 inch	Medium	14 to 17 minutes	160°F medium
Veal Chop (loin or rib)	1 inch	Medium	12 to 15 minutes	160°F medium

Pork Chops, Ribs & More

Succulent, easy-to-prepare pork is naturally low in carbs and pairs well with an array of tasty seasonings. These recipes for chops rubbed with Cajun seasoning, smoked pork roast with rosemary and garlic, juicy pork tenderloin stuffed with jalapeño peppers, and others are soon-to-be-favorite main dishes.

Peppery Pork Chops

Prep: 15 minutes Marinate: 6 hours Grill: 11 minutes Makes: 4 servings

4 center-cut loin pork chops,
    cut 1 inch thick

¼ cup dry sherry

2 tablespoons soy sauce

2 tablespoons cooking oil

2 tablespoons grated
    fresh ginger

1 tablespoon rice vinegar or
    lemon juice

1 large clove garlic, minced

¾ teaspoon coarsely ground
    black pepper

1. Place meat in a self-sealing plastic bag set in a shallow dish. For marinade, in a small bowl stir together sherry, soy sauce, oil, ginger, vinegar, garlic, and pepper. Pour over meat; seal bag. Marinate in the refrigerator 6 to 24 hours, turning bag occasionally. Drain meat, discarding marinade.

2. For a charcoal grill, grill meat on the rack of an uncovered grill directly over medium coals for 11 to 14 minutes or until done (160°F) and juices run clear, turning once halfway through grilling. (For a gas grill, preheat grill. Reduce heat to medium. Place meat on grill rack. Cover and grill as above.)

1 g carbs   0 g fiber   1 g net carbs

Nutrition Facts per serving: 269 cal., 11 g total fat (3 g sat. fat),
92 mg chol., 184 mg sodium, 1 g carbo., 0 g fiber, 38 g pro.

Cajun-Style Pork Chops

Prep: 15 minutes Broil: 9 minutes Makes: 4 servings

1. In a small bowl combine oregano, onion powder, paprika, salt, cayenne pepper, and black pepper. For sauce, stir together ¼ teaspoon of the seasoning mixture, sour cream, and green onion. Cover and chill until serving time. Stir garlic and oil into remaining seasoning mixture. Sprinkle over both sides of chops; rub in with your fingers.

2. Preheat broiler. Place meat on the unheated rack of a broiler pan. Broil 3 to 4 inches from heat for 9 to 12 minutes or until done (160°F) and juices run clear, turning once halfway through broiling. Serve with sauce.

1   teasoon dried oregano, crushed

1   teaspoon onion powder

1   teaspoon paprika

½   teaspoon salt

¼   teaspoon cayenne pepper

¼   teaspoon black pepper

½   cup dairy sour cream

1   green onion, chopped

2   cloves garlic, minced

1   tablespoon cooking oil

4   pork loin or rib chops,

    cut ¾ to 1 inch thick

3g carbs   **1**g fiber   **2**g net carbs

Nutrition Facts per serving: 481 cal., 24 g total fat (9 g sat. fat), 155 mg chol., 413 mg sodium, 3 g carbo., 1 g fiber, 59 g pro.

Rosemary Pork Chops

Prep: 10 minutes Marinate: 2 hours Grill: 20 minutes Makes: 4 servings

4 pork chops, cut ¾ inch thick

2 tablespoons Dijon-style

   mustard

2 tablespoons balsamic vinegar

2 tablespoons lemon juice

2 tablespoons olive oil

3 cloves garlic, minced

4 teaspoons snipped fresh

   rosemary or 1 teaspoon

   dried rosemary, crushed

½ teaspoon salt

½ teaspoon black pepper

1. Place meat in a self-sealing plastic bag set in a shallow dish. For marinade, in a small bowl whisk together mustard, vinegar, lemon juice, oil, garlic, rosemary, salt, and pepper. Pour marinade over meat; seal bag. Marinate in the refrigerator for 2 to 4 hours, turning bag occasionally.

2. Drain meat, discarding marinade. For a charcoal grill, arrange medium-hot coals around a drip pan. Test for medium heat above pan. Place meat on grill rack over drip pan. Cover and grill 20 to 24 minutes or until done (160°F) and juices run clear. (For a gas grill, preheat grill. Reduce heat to medium. Adjust for indirect cooking. Grill as above.)

2g carbs   **0**g fiber   **2**g net carbs

Nutrition Facts per serving: 300 cal., 14 g total fat (4 g sat. fat),
105 mg chol., 244 mg sodium, 2 g carbo., 0 g fiber, 39 g pro.

Pork Chops Dijon

Start to Finish: 30 minutes Makes: 4 servings

1. In a large skillet cook meat in hot oil over medium-high heat for 5 minutes or just until brown, turning once. Remove meat from skillet. In a small bowl combine mustard, Italian dressing, and pepper; set aside.

2. Add onion to skillet. Cook and stir over medium heat for 5 minutes. Push onion aside; return meat to skillet. Spread mustard mixture over meat. Cover and cook over medium-low heat for 10 minutes or until done (160°F) and juices run clear. Serve onion over meat.

4 pork loin chops, cut
½ inch thick

1 tablespoon cooking oil

3 tablespoons Dijon-style
mustard

2 tablespoons bottled low-carb
Italian salad dressing
(no sugar added)

¼ teaspoon black pepper

1 medium onion, halved
and sliced

4 g carbs   0 g fiber   4 g net carbs

Nutrition Facts per serving: 360 cal., 17 g total fat (5 g sat. fat), 108 mg chol., 439 mg sodium, 4 g carbo., 0 g fiber, 46 g pro.

Pork Diane

Start to Finish: 30 minutes Makes: 4 servings

2 tablespoons water

2 tablespoons Worcestershire

   sauce for chicken

2 teaspoons lemon juice

2 teaspoons Dijon-style mustard

1 pound boneless pork loin

   roast, cut into four ¾- to

   1-inch slices

1 teaspoon lemon-pepper

   seasoning

2 tablespoons butter

1 tablespoon snipped fresh

   chives or parsley

1. For sauce, in a small bowl stir together water, Worcestershire sauce, lemon juice, and mustard; set aside.

2. Sprinkle both sides of each piece of meat with lemon-pepper seasoning. In a 10-inch skillet cook meat in hot butter over medium heat for 6 to 10 minutes or until done (160°F) and juices run clear, turning once. Transfer meat to platter; cover to keep warm. Remove skillet from heat.

3. Add sauce to skillet. Stir until well blended. Pour sauce over meat; sprinkle with chives.

See photo, page 145.

2g carbs   **0**g fiber   **2**g net carbs

Nutrition Facts per serving: 233 cal., 13 g total fat (5 g sat. fat),
78 mg chol., 518 mg sodium, 2 g carbo., 0 g fiber, 25 g pro.

Pork Diane
p. 144

Pork Chops
with Grilled
Vegetables
p. 159

Chili-Lime
Pork Salad
p. 187

Smoked
Pork Salad
p. 190

Italian
Pork Burgers
p. 192

Ham, Sweet
Pepper &
Zucchini
Soup
p. 198

Spicy
Sausage
Soup
p. 203

Pork au
Poivre with
Mustard &
Sage
p. 153

Pork au Poivre with Mustard & Sage

Prep: 15 minutes Cook: 14 minutes Makes: 4 servings

1. Coarsely crack black, pink, and white peppercorns; stir together. Generously coat one side of each pork chop with peppercorn mixture; press in with your fingers.

2. In a 12-inch skillet cook meat, peppered sides down, over medium-high heat for 6 minutes. Turn meat and cook about 6 minutes more or until done (160°F) and juices run clear (if meat browns too quickly, reduce heat slightly). Transfer meat to a serving platter; keep warm. Scrape any burnt peppercorns from skillet and discard.

3. For sauce, add cream, wine, mustard, sage, and drained green peppercorns to skillet. Bring to boiling; reduce heat. Simmer, uncovered, for 2 minutes or until reduced to about $1/2$ cup. Serve over meat.

See photo, page 152.

1 to 2 teaspoons whole black peppercorns

1 to 2 teaspoons whole pink peppercorns

1 to 2 teaspoons whole white peppercorns

4 boneless pork loin chops, butterflied

$2/3$ cup whipping cream

3 tablespoons dry white wine

2 tablespoons Dijon-style mustard

2 tablespoons snipped fresh sage

1 tablespoon green peppercorns in brine, drained and rinsed

4g carbs   **1**g fiber   **3**g net carbs

Nutrition Facts per serving: 416 cal., 25 g total fat (13 g sat. fat), 148 mg chol., 128 mg sodium, 4 g carbo., 1 g fiber, 39 g pro.

Lemon-&-Herb-Rubbed Pork Chops

Prep: 15 minutes Grill: 35 minutes Makes: 4 servings

4 teaspoons bottled minced

   garlic (8 cloves)

1½ teaspoons finely shredded

   lemon peel

1 teaspoon dried rosemary,

   crushed

½ teaspoon salt

½ teaspoon dried sage, crushed

½ teaspoon black pepper

4 pork loin chops, cut

   1¼ inches thick

1. For rub, in a small bowl combine garlic, lemon peel, rosemary, salt, sage, and pepper. Sprinkle rub over both sides of each chop; rub in with your fingers.

2. For a charcoal grill, arrange medium-hot coals around a drip pan. Test for medium heat above pan. Place meat on grill rack over drip pan. Cover and grill for 35 to 40 minutes or until done (160°F) and juices run clear, turning once halfway through grilling. (For a gas grill, preheat grill. Reduce heat to medium. Adjust for indirect cooking. Grill as above.)

3g carbs **0**g fiber **3**g net carbs

Nutrition Facts per serving: 351 cal., 19 g total fat (7 g sat. fat), 116 mg chol., 374 mg sodium, 3 g carbo., 0 g fiber, 41 g pro.

Curried Mustard Pork Chops

Prep: 10 minutes Marinate: 6 hours Grill: 20 minutes Makes: 4 servings

1. For marinade, stir together brown mustard, wine, curry powder, oil, crushed red pepper, green onion, and garlic. Place meat in a self-sealing plastic bag set in a shallow dish. Pour marinade over meat; seal bag. Marinate in the refrigerator for 6 to 24 hours, turning bag occasionally.

2. Drain meat, reserving marinade. For a charcoal grill, arrange medium-hot coals around a drip pan. Test for medium heat above pan. Place meat on grill rack over drip pan. Cover and grill for 20 to 24 minutes or until done (160°F) and juices run clear, turning once and brushing with marinade halfway through grilling. (For a gas grill, preheat grill. Reduce heat to medium. Adjust for indirect cooking. Grill as above.) Discard any remaining marinade.

½ cup spicy brown mustard

¼ cup dry white wine

1 tablespoon curry powder

1 tablespoon olive oil

¼ to ½ teaspoon crushed
  red pepper

1 green onion, sliced

1 clove garlic, minced

4 boneless pork loin chops, cut
  1 inch thick

2g carbs **1**g fiber **1**g net carbs

Nutrition Facts per serving: 191 cal., 12 g total fat (3 g sat. fat),
51 mg chol., 343 mg sodium, 2 g carbo., 1 g fiber, 18 g pro.

Balsamic Pork Chops

Start to Finish: 25 minutes Makes: 4 servings

4 pork loin chops, cut 1 inch thick

Salt and black pepper

1 tablespoon olive oil

1 medium shallot, minced

½ cup chicken broth

1 tablespoon balsamic vinegar

¼ teaspoon dried thyme, crushed

1 tablespoon butter

1. Sprinkle meat with salt and pepper. In a large skillet cook chops in hot oil over medium heat for 8 to 12 minutes or until done (160°F) and juices run clear, turning chops occasionally. (If meat browns too quickly, reduce heat to medium-low.) Transfer to a serving platter; cover and keep warm.

2. Add shallot to skillet; cook and stir for 1 minute. Add broth, vinegar, and thyme. Bring to boiling; reduce heat. Simmer, uncovered, for 2 minutes or until reduced to about ⅓ cup. Remove from heat; stir in butter. Pour over meat.

2g carbs   **0**g fiber   **0**g net carbs

Nutrition Facts per serving: 345 cal., 15 g total fat (5 g sat. fat), 135 mg chol., 411 mg sodium, 2 g carbo., 0 g fiber, 45 g pro.

Asian-Style Pork Steaks

Prep: 15 minutes Marinate: 4 hours Grill: 12 minutes Makes: 4 servings

1. Place meat in a self-sealing plastic bag set in a shallow dish. For the marinade, in a small bowl stir together soy sauce, wine, lemon juice, onion, ginger, garlic, and pepper. Pour over meat; seal bag. Marinate in the refrigerator for 4 to 24 hours, turning bag occasionally.

2. Drain meat, discarding marinade. For a charcoal grill, grill meat on the rack of an uncovered grill directly over medium coals for 12 to 15 minutes or until done (160°F) and juices run clear, turning once halfway through grilling. (For a gas grill, preheat grill. Reduce heat to medium. Place meat on grill rack over heat. Cover and grill as above.) Cut steaks in half.

2 pork shoulder steaks,
   cut ¾ inch thick

¼ cup soy sauce

¼ cup dry red wine

¼ cup lemon juice

1 tablespoon chopped onion

1½ teaspoons grated fresh ginger

2 cloves garlic, minced

¼ teaspoon black pepper

1 g carbs   0 g fiber   1 g net carbs

Nutrition Facts per serving: 317 cal., 12 g total fat (4 g sat. fat), 146 mg chol., 462 mg sodium, 1 g carbo., 0 g fiber, 46 g pro.

Lemon-Garlic Pork Chops

Prep: 5 minutes Grill: 12 minutes Makes: 4 servings

8 boneless pork loin chops,
  cut ¾ inch thick

¼ cup olive oil

¼ cup lemon juice

1 tablespoon snipped fresh
  tarragon or 1 teaspoon dried
  tarragon, crushed

2 teaspoons bottled minced
  garlic

1 teaspoon finely shredded
  lemon peel

½ teaspoon coarsely ground
  black pepper

1. Place meat in a self-sealing plastic bag set in a shallow dish. For marinade, combine oil, lemon juice, tarragon, garlic, lemon peel, and pepper. Pour over meat; close bag. Marinate in the refrigerator for 30 minutes, turning bag occasionally.

2. Drain meat, reserving marinade. For a charcoal grill, grill meat on the rack of an uncovered grill directly over medium coals for 12 to 15 minutes or until done (160°F) and juices run clear, turning once and brushing with reserved marinade. (For a gas grill, preheat grill. Reduce heat to medium. Place meat on grill rack over heat. Cover and grill as above.) Discard any remaining marinade.

1 g carbs   0 g fiber   1 g net carbs

Nutrition Facts per serving: 196 cal., 9 g total fat (3 g sat. fat),
62 mg chol., 46 mg sodium, 1 g carbo., 0 g fiber, 25 g pro.

Pork Chops with Grilled Vegetables

Prep: 20 minutes Grill: 35 minutes Makes: 4 servings

1. Brush 2 teaspoons oil over both sides of chops; sprinkle with lemon-pepper seasoning. In a small bowl combine sour cream, ³/₄ teaspoon of the thyme, ¹/₈ teaspoon of the salt, and ¹/₈ teaspoon of the black pepper. Cover and chill.

2. For a charcoal grill, arrange medium-hot coals around a drip pan. Test for medium heat above pan. Place meat on grill rack over drip pan. Cover and grill for 35 to 40 minutes or until done (160°F) and juices run clear, turning once halfway through grilling. Place sweet pepper and tomatoes directly over coals for the last 5 to 8 minutes of grilling or until peppers are crisp-tender and tomatoes begin to soften, turning once. (For a gas grill, preheat grill. Reduce heat to medium. Adjust for indirect cooking. Grill as above.)

3. Meanwhile, in a large bowl combine vinegar, 1 tablespoon oil, remaining ¹/₂ teaspoon thyme, remaining ¹/₈ teaspoon salt, and remaining ¹/₈ teaspoon black pepper. Add vegetables; toss gently to coat. Spoon vegetables over meat. Serve with sour cream mixture.

See photo, page 146.

2   teaspoons olive oil

4   pork loin chops, cut 1¼ inches thick

1   teaspoon lemon-pepper seasoning
      or garlic-pepper seasoning

¹/₃ cup dairy sour cream

1¼ teaspoons snipped fresh thyme
      or rosemary

¹/₄ teaspoon salt

¹/₄ teaspoon black pepper

1   green or yellow sweet pepper,
      seeded and cut into quarters

2   Roma tomatoes, halved lengthwise

1   tablespoon balsamic vinegar

1   tablespoon olive oil

5g carbs   **1**g fiber   **4**g net carbs

Nutrition Facts per serving: 449 cal., 24 g total fat (8 g sat. fat), 132 mg chol., 531 mg sodium, 5 g carbo., 1 g fiber, 51 g pro.

Chipotle Ribs with Vinegar Mop

Prep: 30 minutes Grill: 1½ hours Makes: 4 servings

3 pounds pork loin back ribs
   or meaty spareribs

1 small dried chipotle pepper,
   seeded and finely crushed
   (see note, page 51)

1 teaspoon dry mustard

1 teaspoon chili powder

½ teaspoon onion salt

½ teaspoon celery seeds

¼ cup cider vinegar

1 tablespoon Worcestershire
   sauce

¼ teaspoon bottled hot
   pepper sauce

1. Cut ribs into serving-size pieces. For rub, in a small bowl combine chipotle, ½ teaspoon of the dry mustard, chili powder, onion salt, and celery seeds. Sprinkle over ribs; rub in with your fingers. Set aside.

2. For vinegar mop, in a small bowl combine vinegar, Worcestershire sauce, remaining ½ teaspoon dry mustard, and bottled hot pepper sauce. Set aside.

3. For a charcoal grill, arrange medium-hot coals around a drip pan. Test for medium heat above the pan. Place ribs, bone sides down, on grill rack over drip pan. Cover; grill for 1½ to 1¾ hours or until ribs are tender, brushing occasionally with the vinegar mop during the last 15 minutes of grilling. (For a gas grill, preheat grill. Reduce heat to medium. Adjust for indirect cooking. Grill as above.)

3 g carbs   **0** g fiber   **3** g net carbs

Nutrition Facts per serving: 348 cal., 15 g total fat (5 g sat. fat), 100 mg chol., 344 mg sodium, 3 g carbo., 0 g fiber, 47 g pro.

Barbecued Ribs

Prep: 20 minutes Bake: 1½ hours Oven: 350°F Makes: 4 servings

1. In a small bowl combine chili powder, garlic powder, onion powder, salt, cayenne pepper, and black pepper. Sprinkle mixture over both sides of ribs; rub in with your fingers. Place meat, bone sides down, in a large shallow roasting pan. Bake, covered, in a 350° oven for 1¼ hours. Carefully drain off liquid in roasting pan.

2. Brush barbecue sauce over meat. Bake, uncovered, for 15 minutes more or until ribs are tender.

- 1 tablespoon chili powder
- 1½ teaspoons garlic powder
- 1½ teaspoons onion powder
- ½ teaspoon salt
- ¼ teaspoon cayenne pepper
- ¼ teaspoon black pepper
- 3 to 3½ pounds pork loin back ribs
- ½ cup bottled low-carb barbecue sauce

6g carbs **1**g fiber **5**g net carbs

Nutrition Facts per serving: 360 cal., 15 g total fat (5 g sat. fat), 101 mg chol., 728 mg sodium, 6 g carbo., 1 g fiber, 47 g pro.

Marinated Ribs

Prep: 15 minutes Marinate: 6 hours Roast: 1½ hours
Oven: 450°F/350°F Makes: 4 servings

3 pounds meaty pork spareribs,
   cut into serving-size pieces

⅔ cup water

½ cup cider vinegar

2 teaspoons garlic salt

2 teaspoons ground cumin

1 teaspoon crushed red pepper

1. Cut ribs into serving-size pieces. Place ribs in a large self-sealing plastic bag set in a shallow dish. In a medium bowl combine water, vinegar, 1 teaspoon of the garlic salt, 1 teaspoon of the cumin and crushed red pepper. Pour over ribs; close bag. Marinate in the refrigerator for 6 hours or overnight, turning bag occasionally. Drain ribs, discarding the marinade.

2. Place ribs, bone sides down, in a deep roasting pan. Sprinkle ribs with remaining garlic salt and cumin. Roast, uncovered, in a 450° oven for 30 minutes. Carefully drain fat. Reduce oven temperature to 350°. Roast, covered, for 45 minutes. Uncover and roast 15 minutes more or until ribs are tender.

1g carbs   0g fiber   1g net carbs

Nutrition Facts per serving: 599 cal., 43 g total fat (17 g sat. fat),
173 mg chol., 311 mg sodium, 1 g carbo., 0 g fiber, 47 g pro.

Ribs with Peanut Sauce

Prep: 30 minutes Grill: 1½ hours Makes: 8 servings

1. Cut ribs into serving-size pieces. For a charcoal grill, arrange medium-hot coals around a drip pan. Test for medium heat above pan. Place ribs on grill rack over drip pan. Cover and grill for 1½ to 1¾ hours or until ribs are tender. (For a gas grill, preheat grill. Reduce heat to medium. Adjust for indirect cooking. Grill as above.)

2. Meanwhile, for sauce, in a small saucepan gradually whisk hot water into peanut spread. Stir in lime juice, green onion, ginger, and cayenne pepper. Cook and stir over low heat until heated through. Just before serving, brush ribs with sauce. Pass any remaining sauce.

4 pounds meaty pork spareribs
 or pork loin back ribs

¼ cup hot water

¼ cup low-carb creamy peanut
 spread

2 tablespoons lime juice

2 tablespoons sliced green onion

½ teaspoon grated fresh ginger
 or ¼ teaspoon ground ginger

¼ to ½ teaspoon cayenne pepper

2g carbs   **1**g fiber   **1**g net carbs

Nutrition Facts per serving: 439 cal., 32 g total fat (12 g sat. fat), 114 mg chol., 152 mg sodium, 2 g carbo., 1 g fiber, 33 g pro.

Shredded Savory Pork

Prep: 15 minutes Roast: 2½ hours Oven: 325°F Makes: 12 servings

8 cloves garlic, minced

2 teaspoons ground coriander

2 teaspoons ground cumin

2 teaspoons dried oregano,
　　crushed

1 teaspoon onion powder

½ teaspoon salt

½ teaspoon black pepper

½ teaspoon cayenne pepper

1 3-pound boneless pork
　　shoulder blade roast

1 cup beef broth

1. In a small bowl combine garlic, coriander, cumin, oregano, onion powder, salt, and peppers; rub into meat. Place meat in a roasting pan with a cover; add beef broth. Cover and roast in a 325° oven for 2½ to 3 hours or until very tender.

2. Remove meat from liquid with a slotted spoon; discard excess fat from cooking liquid and reserve the liquid. When meat is cool enough to handle, shred the meat, pulling through it with two forks in opposite directions. Stir in enough reserved liquid to moisten.

Slow-cooker directions: Prepare roast as above. Place roast in a 3½- to 5-quart slow cooker; add beef broth. Cover and cook on low-heat setting for 8 to 10 hours or on high-heat setting for 4 to 5 hours. Continue as above.

1_g carbs 0_g fiber 1_g net carbs

Nutrition Facts per serving: 182 cal., 9 g total fat (3 g sat. fat),
77 mg chol., 246 mg sodium, 1 g carbo., 0 g fiber, 22 g pro.

Porketta Roast

Prep: 25 minutes Grill: 1½ hours
Stand: 15 minutes Makes: 10 to 12 servings

1. In a small bowl combine parsley, garlic, pepper, fennel seeds, and salt; set aside.

2. Untie roast. Using a sharp knife, cut several 1-inch slits all over the meat. Using your fingers, press some of the parsley mixture into the slits. Sprinkle remaining mixture evenly over the entire surface of the meat; rub in with your fingers. Insert a meat thermometer into the center of the roast. Tie roast with 100-percent-cotton string, if necessary.

3. For a charcoal grill, arrange medium-hot coals around a drip pan. Test for medium heat above pan. Place meat on grill rack over drip pan. Cover and grill for 1½ to 2¼ hours or until thermometer registers 155°F. (For a gas grill, preheat grill. Reduce heat to medium. Adjust for indirect cooking. Grill as above, except place meat on a rack in roasting pan.)

4. Remove meat from grill. Cover with foil and let stand 15 minutes before carving. (The meat's temperature will rise 5°F during standing.) Thinly slice meat.

½ cup snipped fresh flat-leaf parsley or 1 tablespoon dried parsley flakes

2 cloves garlic, minced

1½ teaspoons coarsely ground black pepper

1½ teaspoons fennel seeds, crushed

¾ teaspoon salt

1 3- to 4-pound boneless pork shoulder blade Boston roast (Boston butt roast or butt roast), rolled and tied

1g carbs   **0**g fiber   **1**g net carbs

Nutrition Facts per serving: 208 cal., 10 g total fat (3 g sat. fat), 92 mg chol., 253 mg sodium, 1 g carbo., 0 g fiber, 27 g pro.

German-Style Pork Roast

Prep: 30 minutes Cook: 7 hours (low) or 3½ hours (high) Makes: 8 servings

1 2½- to 3-pound boneless pork

shoulder roast

1 tablespoon caraway seeds

1½ teaspoons dried marjoram,

crushed

1 teaspoon salt

½ teaspoon black pepper

1 tablespoon olive oil

½ cup water

2 tablespoons white

wine vinegar

1 8-ounce carton dairy

sour cream

4 teaspoons arrowroot

1. If necessary, cut meat to fit into a 3½- or 4-quart slow cooker. For rub, in a bowl combine caraway seeds, marjoram, salt, and pepper. Sprinkle mixture over all sides of meat. Rub in with your fingers.

2. In a large skillet brown meat on all sides in hot oil. Drain off fat. Place meat in slow cooker. Add water to skillet; bring to boiling, stirring to loosen browned bits from bottom of skillet. Pour skillet juices and vinegar into cooker.

3. Cover and cook on low-heat setting for 7 to 9 hours or on high-heat setting for 3½ to 4½ hours. Remove meat from cooker; keep warm.

4. For gravy, skim fat from juices; measure 1¼ cups juices (add water, if necessary to make 1¼ cups). Pour juices into a small saucepan; bring to boiling. In a medium bowl combine sour cream and arrowroot. Stir hot juices into sour cream mixture; return to saucepan. Cook and stir over medium heat until mixture is thickened (do not boil). Slice meat and serve with gravy.

2g carbs   **0**g fiber   **2**g net carbs

Nutrition Facts per serving: 277 cal., 16 g total fat (7 g sat. fat),
104 mg chol., 423 mg sodium, 2 g carbo., 0 g fiber, 29 g pro.

Seeded Pork Roast

Prep: 20 minutes Cook: 7 to 9 hours (low) or
3½ to 4½ hours (high) Makes: 8 servings

1. Remove netting from roast, if present. If necessary, cut roast to fit into a 3½- or 4-quart slow cooker. Brush soy sauce over surface of meat. On a large piece of foil combine caraway seeds, dillseeds, and celery seeds. Roll roast in seeds to coat evenly.

2. Place meat in cooker. Pour broth around meat. Cover and cook on low-heat setting for 7 to 9 hours or on high-heat setting for 3½ to 4½ hours.

3. Transfer meat to a serving platter. Skim fat from cooking juices. Serve juices with meat.

1 2½- to 3-pound boneless pork
   shoulder roast

1 tablespoon soy sauce

1 teaspoon caraway seeds,
   crushed

1 teaspoon dillseeds, crushed

1 teaspoon celery seeds, crushed

1¼ cups beef broth

0_g carbs 0_g fiber 0_g net carbs

Nutrition Facts per serving: 201 cal., 8 g total fat (3 g sat. fat), 92 mg chol., 371 mg sodium, 0 g carbo., 0 g fiber, 29 g pro.

Chipotle Pork Roast

Prep: 30 minutes Marinate: 4 hours Roast: 1¼ hours
Stand: 15 minutes Oven: 325°F Makes: 6 to 8 servings

1 2- to 3-pound boneless pork
   top loin roast (single loin)

3 tablespoons lime juice

3 tablespoons chipotle peppers
   in adobo sauce

2 tablespoons olive oil

2 cloves garlic, minced

¼ teaspoon salt

1 recipe Avocado-Tomato Salsa

1. Place meat in a large self-sealing plastic bag set in a shallow dish. For marinade, in a blender container combine lime juice, chipotle peppers in adobo sauce, oil, garlic, and salt. Cover and blend until smooth. Pour marinade over meat; seal bag. Marinate in the refrigerator for 4 hours or overnight, turning bag occasionally.

2. Drain meat, discarding marinade. Place meat on a rack in a shallow roasting pan. Insert a meat thermometer into center of roast. Roast in a 325° oven for 1¼ to 1¾ hours or until thermometer registers 155°F. Cover meat and let stand for 15 minutes before slicing. (The meat's temperature will rise 5°F during standing.) Serve with Avocado-Tomato Salsa.

Avocado-Tomato Salsa: In a small bowl stir together 1 medium ripe avocado, halved, seeded, peeled, and coarsely chopped; 2 Roma tomatoes, seeded and coarsely chopped; 1 tablespoon snipped fresh cilantro; and 1 tablespoon lime juice. Season to taste with salt.

4g carbs **2**g fiber **2**g net carbs

Nutrition Facts per serving: 294 cal., 15 g total fat (4 g sat. fat), 82 mg chol., 101 mg sodium, 4 g carbo., 2 g fiber, 34 g pro.

Five-Spice Pork

Prep: 10 minutes Grill: 30 minutes Stand: 45 minutes Makes: 4 servings

1. For spice mixture, in a blender combine container cinnamon, anise seeds, peppercorns, fennel seeds, and cloves. Blend until powdery. If desired, cut random slits about ½ inch deep in tenderloin; insert garlic slices into slits. Brush meat with oil; rub about 1 tablespoon of the spice mixture over meat. Cover meat and let stand for 30 minutes. Insert a meat thermometer in thickest part of tenderloin.

2. For a charcoal grill, arrange medium-hot coals around a drip pan. Test for medium heat above pan. Place meat on grill rack over drip pan. Cover and grill for 30 to 35 minutes or until thermometer registers 155°F. (For a gas grill, preheat grill. Reduce heat to medium. Adjust for indirect cooking. Grill as above.)

3. Remove meat from grill. Cover with foil and let stand 15 minutes before slicing. (The meat's temperature will rise 5°F during standing.)

3 tablespoons ground cinnamon

2 teaspoons anise seeds

1½ teaspoons whole black
   peppercorns

1 teaspoon fennel seeds

½ teaspoon ground cloves

1 12-ounce pork tenderloin

3 cloves garlic, quartered
   (optional)

Cooking oil

Nutrition Facts per serving: 133 cal., 6 g total fat (1 g sat. fat), 60 mg chol., 44 mg sodium, 1 g carbo., 0 g fiber, 19 g pro.

Caper-Sauced Pork Medallions

Start to Finish: 30 minutes Makes: 4 servings

1 **pound pork tenderloin**

¼ **teaspoon salt**

¼ **teaspoon black pepper**

¼ **teaspoon ground sage**

1 **tablespoon olive oil**

⅔ **cup whipping cream**

1 **tablespoon capers, drained**

   Salt and black pepper

1. Slice meat crosswise into ¼-inch slices. For rub, in a small bowl combine ¼ teaspoon salt, ¼ teaspoon pepper, and sage. Sprinkle on slices; rub in with your fingers.

2. In a large skillet cook meat, half at a time, in hot oil over medium heat for 3 to 4 minutes or until juices run clear, turning once. Remove meat from skillet; remove skillet from heat. Carefully add whipping cream and capers to hot skillet. Cook and stir over low heat for 1 to 2 minutes or until slightly thickened. Season to taste with salt and pepper.

3. Serve sauce over meat.

1g carbs   0g fiber   1g net carbs

Nutrition Facts per serving: 301 cal., 21 g total fat (11 g sat. fat), 128 mg chol., 300 mg sodium, 1 g carbo., 0 g fiber, 25 g pro.

Prosciutto-Stuffed Pork Loin Roast

Prep: 15 minutes Grill: 1 hour Stand: 15 minutes Makes: 6 servings

1. Butterfly meat by making a lengthwise cut down the center, cutting to within 1/2 inch of the other side. Spread open. Cut from the center, horizontally, to within 1/2 inch of the outside side of meat. Repeat on opposite side of center. Spread open.

2. Rub top of meat with 2 tablespoons olive oil. Sprinkle with rosemary. Arrange prosciutto on top to cover completely. Arrange fresh spinach over prosciutto to cover completely.

3. Beginning at a short side, roll up meat. Tie in three or four places with 100-percent-cotton string. If desired, brush with additional olive oil and sprinkle with peppercorns. Insert a meat thermometer into center of meat.

4. For a charcoal grill, arrange medium-hot coals around a drip pan. Test for medium heat above pan. Place meat on grill rack over drip pan. Cover and grill for 1 to 1 1/4 hours or until thermometer registers 155°F.

5. Remove meat from the grill. Cover and let stand for 15 minutes before serving. (The meat's temperature will rise 5°F during standing.) Remove string; slice meat.

1 1½- to 2-pound pork loin roast (single loin)

2 tablespoons olive oil

1 to 2 tablespoons snipped fresh rosemary or 1 to 2 teaspoons dried rosemary, crushed

3 ounces thinly sliced prosciutto or dried beef

3 cups fresh spinach leaves, stems removed

   Olive oil (optional)

2 teaspoons crushed peppercorns (optional)

1 g carbs   **1** g fiber   **0** g net carbs

Nutrition Facts per serving: 209 cal., 10 g total fat (3 g sat. fat), 69 mg chol., 342 mg sodium, 1 g carbo., 1 g fiber, 28 g pro.

Herb & Garlic Pork

Prep: 10 minutes Marinate: 2 hours Grill: 1½ hours
Stand: 15 minutes Makes: 12 servings

1 3- to 4-pound boneless pork
   top loin roast (double loin,
   tied)

¼ cup olive oil

6 cloves garlic, minced

2 tablespoons snipped
   fresh basil

2 tablespoons snipped fresh
   chives or chopped
   green onion

2 teaspoons chili powder or
   ¼ teaspoon cayenne pepper

1 teaspoon snipped fresh sage
   or oregano

1 teaspoon salt

½ teaspoon black pepper

1. Place meat in a large self-sealing plastic bag set in a shallow dish. For marinade, in a small bowl combine oil, garlic, basil, chives, chili powder, sage, salt, and pepper. Pour marinade over meat; close bag. Marinate in the refrigerator for 2 to 24 hours, turning bag occasionally.

2. Drain meat, discarding marinade. Insert a meat thermometer into center of roast.

3. For a charcoal grill, arrange medium coals around a drip pan. Test for medium-low heat above pan. Place meat on grill rack over drip pan. Cover and grill for 1½ to 2¼ hours or until thermometer registers 155°F. (For a gas grill, preheat grill. Reduce heat to medium-low. Adjust for indirect cooking. Grill as above.)

4. Remove meat from the grill. Cover with foil and let stand for 15 minutes before carving. (The meat's temperature will rise 5°F during standing.) Remove strings; slice meat.

1 g carbs 0 g fiber 1 g net carbs

Nutrition Facts per serving: 181 cal., 8 g total fat (2 g sat. fat), 62 mg chol., 239 mg sodium, 1 g carbo., 0 g fiber, 25 g pro.

Rosemary & Garlic Smoked Pork Roast

Prep: 15 minutes Soak: 1 hour Grill: 1 hour Stand: 15 minutes Makes: 8 to 10 servings

1. At least 1 hour before grilling, soak wood chips in enough water to cover.

2. For rub, combine snipped rosemary, oil, garlic, pepper, and salt. Sprinkle rub evenly over meat; rub in with your fingers. Insert a meat thermometer into center of roast. Drain wood chips.

3. For a charcoal grill, arrange medium coals around a drip pan. Pour 1 inch of water into drip pan. Test for medium-low heat above the pan. Sprinkle half of the wood chips over the coals; sprinkle rosemary sprigs over chips. Place meat on grill rack over drip pan. Cover; grill for 1 to 1½ hours or until thermometer registers 155°F. Add remaining wood chips halfway through grilling. (For a gas grill, preheat grill. Reduce heat to medium-low. Adjust for indirect cooking. Grill as above, except place meat on a rack in a roasting pan.)

4. Remove meat from grill. Squeeze juice from lemon over meat. Cover with foil and let stand for 15 minutes before carving. (The meat's temperature will rise 5°F during standing.)

4 cups apple or hickory
    wood chips

2 tablespoons snipped
    fresh rosemary

1 tablespoon olive oil

4 cloves garlic, minced

½ teaspoon black pepper

¼ teaspoon salt

1 2- to 3-pound boneless pork
    top loin roast (single loin)

4 fresh rosemary sprigs

½ of a lemon or lime

1 g carbs **0** g fiber **1** g net carbs

Nutrition Facts per serving: 174 cal., 7 g total fat (2 g sat. fat), 62 mg chol., 114 mg sodium, 1 g carbo., 0 g fiber, 25 g pro.

Marinated Pork Roast

Prep: 10 minutes Marinate: 4 hours Roast: 1¼ hours
Stand: 15 minutes Oven: 325°F Makes: 6 to 8 servings

1 2- to 3-pound boneless

pork top loin roast

(single loin)

¼ cup dry white wine

3 tablespoons olive oil

1 tablespoon Dijon-style

mustard

2 cloves garlic, minced

1 tablespoon snipped fresh

sage or 1 teaspoon dried

sage, crushed

¼ teaspoon salt

¼ teaspoon black pepper

1. Place meat in a large self-sealing plastic bag set in a shallow dish. For marinade, combine wine, oil, mustard, garlic, sage, salt, and pepper. Pour over meat; seal bag. Marinate in the refrigerator for 4 hours or overnight, turning bag several times.

2. Drain meat, discarding marinade. Place meat on a rack in a shallow roasting pan. Insert a meat thermometer into center of roast. Roast in a 325° oven for 1¼ to 1¾ hours or until thermometer registers 155°F. Cover meat with foil; let stand for 15 minutes before slicing. (The meat's temperature will rise 5°F during standing.)

0 g carbs   0 g fiber   0 g net carbs

Nutrition Facts per serving: 248 cal., 11 g total fat (3 g sat. fat),
82 mg chol., 106 mg sodium, 0 g carbo., 0 g fiber, 33 g pro.

174

Apple-Smoked Pork Loin

Prep: 10 minutes Soak: 1 hour Grill: 1 hour
Stand: 15 minutes Makes: 8 servings

1. At least 1 hour before cooking, soak wood chips or chunks in enough water to cover.

2. Meanwhile, place meat in a shallow dish. In a small bowl stir together oregano, salt, pepper, and garlic. Sprinkle evenly over all sides of meat; rub in with your fingers. Insert a meat thermometer into center of roast.

3. Drain wood chips. For a charcoal grill, arrange medium coals around a drip pan. Test for medium-low heat above pan. Sprinkle half of the drained wood chips over the coals. Place meat on grill rack over drip pan. Cover and grill for 1 to 1½ hours or until thermometer registers (155°F). Add more coals and wood chips as needed during grilling.

4. Remove meat from grill. Cover with foil and let stand for 15 minutes. (The meat's temperature will rise 5°F during standing.)

3 **cups apple wood or orange wood chips or 6 to 8 apple wood or orange wood chunks**

1 **2- to 2½-pound boneless pork top loin pork roast (single loin)**

2 **teaspoons dried oregano, crushed**

½ **teaspoon salt**

½ **teaspoon coarsely ground black pepper**

4 **cloves garlic, minced**

1g carbs   **0**g fiber   **1**g net carbs

Nutrition Facts per serving: 163 cal., 6 g total fat (2 g sat. fat), 66 mg chol., 193 mg sodium, 1 g carbo., 0 g fiber, 24 g pro.

Peppercorn Pork with Creamy Sauce

Prep: 15 minutes Roast: 35 minutes Stand: 15 minutes
Oven: 425°F Makes: 4 servings

1 1- to 1½-pound peppercorn-marinated pork tenderloin

½ cup chicken broth with roasted garlic

1 teaspoon Worcestershire sauce

⅓ cup dairy sour cream

1 teaspoon Dijon-style mustard

1. Place meat on a rack in a shallow roasting pan. Insert a meat thermometer into thickest part of tenderloin. Roast in a 425° oven for 35 to 45 minutes or until thermometer registers 155°F. Cover with foil and let stand for 15 minutes. (The meat's temperature will rise 5°F during standing.)

2. Meanwhile, for sauce, in a small saucepan combine chicken broth and Worcestershire sauce. Bring to boiling; reduce heat. Simmer, uncovered, about 5 minutes or until reduced by half. Whisk in sour cream and mustard. Cook and stir until heated through (do not boil). Serve with meat.

3g carbs   **0**g fiber   **3**g net carbs

Nutrition Facts per serving: 159 cal., 7 g total fat (4 g sat. fat), 57 mg chol., 786 mg sodium, 3 g carbo., 0 g fiber, 19 g pro.

Lemony Herbed Pork Roast

Prep: 20 minutes Marinate: 2 hours Roast: 1¼ hours
Stand: 15 minutes Oven: 325°F Makes: 6 to 8 servings

1. Place meat in a large self-sealing plastic bag set in a shallow dish. For marinade, combine lemon peel, lemon juice, oil, garlic, oregano, salt, and pepper. Pour marinade over meat; seal bag. Marinate in the refrigerator for 2 to 4 hours, turning bag occasionally.

2. Drain meat, discarding marinade. Place meat on a rack in a shallow roasting pan. Insert a meat thermometer into center of roast. Roast in a 325° oven for 1¼ to 1¾ hours or until thermometer registers 155°F. Cover meat and let stand for 15 minutes before slicing. (The meat's temperature will rise 5°F during standing.)

1 2- to 3-pound boneless pork
   top loin roast (single loin)
2 teaspoons finely shredded
   lemon peel
3 tablespoons lemon juice
2 tablespoons olive oil
2 cloves garlic, minced
1 tablespoon snipped fresh
   oregano or thyme or
   1 teaspoon dried oregano
   or thyme, crushed
¼ teaspoon salt
¼ teaspoon black pepper

1g carbs   **0**g fiber   **1**g net carbs

Nutrition Facts per serving: 269 cal., 14 g total fat (4 g sat. fat), 82 mg chol., 152 mg sodium, 1 g carbo., 0 g fiber, 33 g pro.

Pork Loin with Curry-Horseradish Sauce

Prep: 25 minutes Roast: 1¼ hours Stand: 15 minutes
Oven: 325°F Makes: 8 servings

2½ teaspoons curry powder

¾ teaspoon salt

¼ teaspoon black pepper

1 2- to 3-pound boneless pork

   top loin roast (single loin)

1 8-ounce carton dairy

   sour cream

1 teaspoon prepared

   horseradish

1. In a shallow dish combine 1½ teaspoons of the curry powder, salt, and pepper. Roll meat in curry mixture to coat.

2. Place meat on a rack in a shallow roasting pan. Insert a meat thermometer into the center of the roast. Roast in a 325° oven for 1¼ to 1¾ hours or until meat thermometer registers 155°F. Cover meat with foil and let stand for 15 minutes. (The meat's temperature will rise 5°F during standing time.)

3. Meanwhile, in a small saucepan combine sour cream, horseradish, and remaining 1 teaspoon curry powder. Cook and stir over low heat until heated through (do not boil). Serve sauce with meat.

2g carbs   **0**g fiber   **2**g net carbs

Nutrition Facts per serving: 229 cal., 12 g total fat (6 g sat. fat),
74 mg chol., 276 mg sodium, 2 g carbo., 0 g fiber, 26 g pro.

Herbed Pork Tenderloins

Prep: 15 minutes Marinate: 2 hours Roast: 25 minutes
Stand: 15 minutes Oven: 425°F Makes: 8 servings

1. For marinade, in a small bowl stir together vinegar, sherry (if desired), pepper, olive oil, soy sauce, rosemary, marjoram, thyme, and garlic. Place meat in a large self-sealing plastic bag set in a shallow dish. Pour marinade over meat; close bag. Marinate in the refrigerator for 2 to 4 hours, turning bag occasionally.

2. Drain meat, reserving marinade. Sprinkle meat lightly with salt. In a large skillet brown meat quickly on all sides in hot cooking oil (about 5 minutes.)

3. Place meat in a shallow roasting pan. Pour marinade over meat. Insert a meat thermometer into the thickest portion of one of the tenderloins. Roast, uncovered, in a 425° oven for 15 minutes. Spoon pan juices over meat. Roast for 10 to 15 minutes more or until thermometer registers 155°F. Cover meat with foil and let stand for 15 minutes. (The meat's temperature will rise 5°F during standing.)

4. Transfer meat to a serving platter, reserving pan juices. Strain juices and pour over meat.

2 tablespoons balsamic vinegar

2 tablespoons dry sherry
   (optional)

1 tablespoon cracked
   black pepper

1 tablespoon olive oil

1 tablespoon soy sauce

2 3-inch fresh rosemary sprigs

2 3-inch fresh marjoram sprigs

2 3-inch fresh thyme sprigs

2 cloves garlic, minced

2 12-ounce pork tenderloins

Salt

2 tablespoons cooking oil

2g carbs   **0**g fiber   **2**g net carbs

Nutrition Facts per serving: 156 cal., 8 g total fat (2 g sat. fat), 55 mg chol., 159 mg sodium, 2 g carbo., 0 g fiber, 18 g pro.

Herb-Cured Pork

Prep: 15 minutes Chill: 24 hours Grill: 1 hour
Stand: 15 minutes Makes: 6 servings

1 tablespoon snipped fresh
   thyme or ¾ teaspoon dried
   thyme, crushed

1 tablespoon snipped fresh
   sage or ¾ teaspoon dried
   sage, crushed

1 tablespoon snipped fresh
   rosemary or ¾ teaspoon
   dried rosemary, crushed

2 cloves garlic, minced

1½ teaspoons coarsely ground
   black pepper

1 to 1½ teaspoons coarse salt

½ teaspoon crushed red pepper

1 2- to 3-pound boneless pork
   top loin roast (single loin)

1. For rub, in a small bowl combine thyme, sage, rosemary, garlic, black pepper, salt, and crushed red pepper. Sprinkle rub over all sides of meat; rub in with your fingers. Place meat in a baking dish. Cover tightly and chill for 24 hours.

2. For a charcoal grill, arrange medium coals around a drip pan. Test for medium-low heat above pan. Insert a meat thermometer into center of the roast. Place meat on grill rack. Cover; grill for 1 to 1½ hours or until thermometer registers 155°F. (For a gas grill, preheat grill. Reduce heat to medium. Adjust for indirect cooking. Grill as above.)

3. Remove meat from grill. Cover with foil; let stand for 15 minutes before carving. (The meat's temperature will rise 5°F during standing.)

1g carbs   **0**g fiber   **1**g net carbs

Nutrition Facts per serving: 225 cal., 8 g total fat (3 g sat. fat),
82 mg chol., 376 mg sodium, 1 g carbo., 0 g fiber, 34 g pro.

Pork Tenderloin with Green Olive Tapenade

Prep: 20 minutes Chill: 4 hours Grill: 1 hour
Stand: 15 minutes Makes: 6 servings

1. For tapenade, in a food processor bowl combine olives, capers, mustard, oil, lemon juice, anchovy paste, thyme, and garlic. Cover; process until smooth, scraping down sides as necessary. Cover and chill for 4 to 24 hours.

2. Split each tenderloin lengthwise, cutting to but not through the opposite side. Spread tenderloin open. Place meat between two pieces of plastic wrap overlapping one long side of each tenderloin about 2 inches. Using the flat side of a meat mallet and working from the center to the edges, pound meat into a 10×12-inch rectangle. Remove plastic wrap. Spread tapenade over meat to within 1 inch of edges. Fold in long sides just to cover edge of stuffing. Starting at one of the short sides, roll up. Tie with 100-percent-cotton string at 1-inch intervals. Insert a meat thermometer into center of meat.

3. For a charcoal grill, arrange medium-hot coals around a drip pan. Test for medium heat above pan. Place meat on grill rack over drip pan. Cover; grill for 1 to 1 1/4 hours or until thermometer registers (155°F). (For a gas grill, preheat grill. Reduce heat to medium. Adjust for indirect cooking. Grill as above, but place meat on a rack in a roasting pan.)

4. Remove meat from grill. Cover with foil and let stand for 15 minutes. (The meat's temperature will rise 5°F during standing.) Remove strings and slice.

1 cup pitted green olives, drained

1 tablespoon capers, drained

1 tablespoon Dijon-style mustard

1 tablespoon olive oil

1 tablespoon lemon juice

2 teaspoons anchovy paste

1 teaspoon snipped fresh thyme

1 small clove garlic, minced

2 ¾-pound pork tenderloins

1 g carbs   0 g fiber   1 g net carbs

Nutrition Facts per serving: 201 cal., 10 g total fat (2 g sat. fat), 83 mg chol., 347 mg sodium, 1 g carbo., 0 g fiber, 27 g pro.

Marinated Pork Tenderloins

Prep: 15 minutes Marinate: 2 hours Grill: 30 minutes
Stand: 15 minutes Makes: 10 servings

3 tablespoons dried oregano,
   crushed

½ teaspoon salt

½ teaspoon freshly ground
   black pepper

2 ¾- to 1-pound pork
   tenderloins

1 cup olive oil

½ cup lemon juice

½ cup soy sauce

1. In a small bowl combine oregano, salt, and pepper. Sprinkle mixture evenly over both sides of meat; rub in with your fingers. Place meat in a self-sealing plastic bag set in a shallow dish.

2. For marinade, in a small bowl combine oil, lemon juice, and soy sauce. Pour over meat; seal bag. Marinate in the refrigerator for 2 hours, turning bag occasionally. Drain meat; discard marinade. Insert a meat thermometer into thickest part of one tenderloin.

3. For a charcoal grill, arrange hot coals around a drip pan. Test for medium-high heat above pan. Place meat on grill rack over drip pan. Cover and grill for 30 to 35 minutes or until thermometer registers 155°F. (For a gas grill, preheat grill. Reduce heat to medium-high. Adjust for indirect cooking. Grill as above, except place meat on a rack in a roasting pan.)

4. Remove meat from grill. Cover with foil and let stand for 15 minutes. (The meat's temperature will rise 5°F during standing.)

2g carbs   **1**g fiber   **1**g net carbs

Nutrition Facts per serving: 148 cal., 8 g total fat (2 g sat. fat),
51 mg chol., 355 mg sodium, 2 g carbo., 1 g fiber, 17 g pro.

Jalapeño-Stuffed Pork Tenderloin

Prep: 30 minutes Chill: 8 hours Grill: 35 minutes
Stand: 15 minutes Makes: 4 to 6 servings

1. Butterfly meat by making a lengthwise cut down the center, cutting to within $1/2$ inch of the other side. Spread open. Cut from the center, horizontally, to within $1/2$ inch of the outside edge. Repeat on the opposite side of center. Spread open. Cover with plastic wrap. Using the flat side of a meat mallet and working from the center to the edges, pound meat to $1/2$-inch thickness. Remove plastic wrap.

2. In a small bowl combine half of the jalapeño peppers, tomato, cilantro, lime juice, garlic, and $1/4$ teaspoon of the salt. Sprinkle over meat. Starting from a long side, roll up into a spiral, tucking in ends. Tie at 1-inch intervals with 100-percent-cotton string; place in a shallow dish. Cover and chill for 8 to 24 hours. Cover and refrigerate remaining jalapeño peppers.

3. In a small bowl combine butter, remaining jalapeño peppers, and $1/4$ teaspoon salt. Insert a meat thermometer into thickest part of meat. For a charcoal grill, arrange medium-hot coals around a drip pan. Test for medium heat above pan. Place meat on grill rack over drip pan. Cover and grill for 35 to 45 minutes or until thermometer registers 155°F, brushing occasionally with butter mixture the first 20 minutes of grilling. Discard any remaining butter mixture.

4. Remove meat from grill. Cover with foil and let stand 15 minutes. (The meat's temperature will rise 5°F during standing.) Remove string; slice meat.

1 1- to 1¼-pound pork tenderloin

6 fresh jalapeño peppers, seeded and
   chopped (see note, page 51)

1 Roma tomato, chopped

2 tablespoons snipped fresh cilantro

2 tablespoons lime juice

5 cloves garlic, minced

½ teaspoon salt

¼ cup butter, melted

4g carbs   **1**g fiber   **3**g net carbs

Nutrition Facts per serving: 260 cal., 16 g total fat (9 g sat. fat),
106 mg chol., 543 mg sodium, 4 g carbo., 1 g fiber, 25 g pro.

Chili-Coated Pork Tenderloin

Prep: 10 minutes Roast: 25 minutes Stand: 15 minutes
Oven: 425°F Makes: 6 servings

1 tablespoon chili powder

1 teaspoon salt

1 teaspoon dried oregano,
crushed

½ teaspoon freshly ground
black pepper

½ teaspoon ground cumin

¼ teaspoon cayenne pepper

2 ¾- to 1-pound pork
tenderloins

1. For rub, in a small bowl combine chili powder, salt, oregano, black pepper, cumin, and cayenne pepper. Sprinkle rub over all sides of meat; rub in with your fingers. Insert a meat thermometer into thickest part of one tenderloin. Place meat on a rack in a shallow roasting pan. Roast in a 425° oven for 25 to 35 minutes or until thermometer registers 155°F. Cover meat with foil and let stand for 15 minutes. (The meat's temperature will rise 5°F during standing.)

1 g carbs   **1** g fiber   **0** g net carbs

Nutrition Facts per serving: 138 cal., 3 g total fat (1 g sat. fat),
73 mg chol., 446 mg sodium, 1 g carbo., 1 g fiber, 24 g pro.

Sausage-Stuffed Tenderloin

Prep: 30 minutes Roast: 50 minutes Stand: 15 minutes
Oven: 375°F Makes: 6 servings

1. Split meat lengthwise, cutting to, but not through, opposite side. Open flat. Place meat between two pieces of plastic wrap. Working from center to edges, pound meat with flat side of a meat mallet to about a 10×6-inch rectangle.

2. Arrange prosciutto evenly over meat. Remove sausage from casing, if present. Arrange sausage in a strip lengthwise down the center of the meat. Roll up from long side; tie with 100–percent-cotton string. Place on a rack in a shallow roasting pan. Brush with oil. In a small bowl combine Italian seasoning, garlic salt, and pepper. Sprinkle evenly over meat; rub in with your fingers. Insert a meat thermometer into thickest part of tenderloin.

3. Roast, uncovered, in a 375° oven for 50 to 60 minutes or until thermometer registers 155°F. Cover meat with foil and let stand for 15 minutes. (The meat's temperature will rise 5°F during standing.) Remove string; slice meat.

1 1-pound pork tenderloin

2 ounces thinly sliced prosciutto

6 ounces uncooked sweet
   Italian sausage

2 teaspoons olive oil

1 teaspoon dried Italian
   seasoning, crushed

¼ teaspoon garlic salt

¼ teaspoon black pepper

0 g carbs   0 g fiber   0 g net carbs

Nutrition Facts per serving: 219 cal., 13 g total fat (4 g sat. fat), 77 mg chol., 532 mg sodium, 0 g carbo., 0 g fiber, 23 g pro.

Parsleyed Pinwheels

Prep: 25 minutes Grill: 12 minutes Makes: 4 servings

1 1-pound pork tenderloin

 Salt and black pepper

1 tablespoon butter, softened

½ cup grated Romano cheese

⅓ cup snipped fresh parsley

1. Split meat lengthwise, cutting to, but not through, opposite side. Open flat. Place meat between two pieces of plastic wrap. Using the flat side of a meat mallet and working from center to edges, lightly pound meat to about a 12×6-inch rectangle. Sprinkle with salt and pepper. Spread with butter. In a small bowl combine cheese and parsley; sprinkle over tenderloin. Press parsley mixture lightly into meat. Roll up, starting from a long side. Secure at 1-inch intervals with wooden toothpicks. Slice between toothpicks to form 1-inch pinwheels.

2. For a charcoal grill, grill pinwheels, cut sides up, on the rack of an uncovered grill directly over medium coals for 12 to 14 minutes or until done (160°F) and juices run clear, turning once. (For a gas grill, preheat grill. Reduce heat to medium. Place pinwheels on grill rack over heat. Cover and grill as above.) Remove toothpicks before serving.

To broil: Preheat broiler. Place pinwheels, cut sides up, on the greased unheated rack of a broiler pan. Broil 4 inches from the heat for 12 to 14 minutes or until done (160°F) and juices run clear, turning once.

1 g carbs 0 g fiber 1 g net carbs

Nutrition Facts per serving: 206 cal., 9 g total fat (4 g sat. fat), 87 mg chol., 370 mg sodium, 1 g carbo., 0 g fiber, 28 g pro.

Chili-Lime Pork Salad

Prep: 25 minutes Roast: 25 minutes Stand: 15 minutes
Oven: 425°F Makes: 4 servings

1. Sprinkle meat with salt and pepper. Sprinkle chili powder over meat; rub in with your fingers. Insert a meat thermometer into thickest part of tenderloin. Place meat on a rack in a shallow roasting pan. Roast in a 425° oven for 25 to 35 minutes or until thermometer registers 155°F. Cover meat with foil and let stand 15 minutes. (The meat's temperature will rise 5°F during standing.)

2. Meanwhile, for dressing, in a screw-top jar combine oil, lime juice, cilantro, vinegar, ¼ teaspoon salt, and dash pepper. Cover; shake well. Arrange lettuce on 4 salad plates. Top with tomatoes and avocado. Thinly slice meat; arrange slices on salads. Serve with dressing.

See photo, page 147.

1 ¾- to 1-pound pork tenderloin

Salt and black pepper

2 teaspoons chili powder

¼ cup olive oil or salad oil

3 tablespoons lime juice

2 tablespoons snipped
    fresh cilantro

1 tablespoon white wine vinegar

¼ teaspoon salt

Dash black pepper

6 cups torn romaine lettuce

8 cherry tomatoes, quartered

½ of a medium avocado, pitted,
    peeled, and coarsely chopped

8g carbs **4**g fiber **4**g net carbs

Nutrition Facts per serving: 284 cal., 20 g total fat (3 g sat. fat), 55 mg chol., 278 mg sodium, 8 g carbo., 4 g fiber, 20 g pro.

Italian Pork Salad

Prep: 20 minutes Roast: 25 minutes Stand: 15 minutes
Oven: 425°F Makes: 4 servings

1- to 1¾-pound pork tenderloin

Salt and black pepper

⅔ cup bottled low-carb Italian

salad dressing

8 cups mixed Italian salad

greens (romaine and

radicchio)

½ cup very thinly sliced

fennel bulb

½ cup thinly sliced yellow

sweet pepper

1 ounce Parmesan cheese

1. Place meat on a rack in a shallow roasting pan. Sprinkle with salt and pepper. Insert a meat thermometer into thickest portion of tenderloin. Brush meat with 2 tablespoons of the salad dressing. Roast in a 425° oven for 25 to 35 minutes or until thermometer registers 155°F. Cover with foil and let stand for 15 minutes before slicing. (The meat's temperature will rise 5°F during standing.)

2. Meanwhile, arrange salad greens on 4 salad plates. Top with fennel and sweet pepper. Use a vegetable peeler to shave thin pieces of Parmesan cheese on top of salads. Thinly slice meat; arrange slices on salads. Serve with remaining salad dressing.

5g carbs   **2**g fiber   **3**g net carbs

Nutrition Facts per serving: 243 cal., 15 g total fat (3 g sat. fat), 60 mg chol., 712 mg sodium, 5 g carbo., 2 g fiber, 22 g pro.

Pork with Cabbage Slaw

Prep: 25 minutes   Broil: 9 minutes   Makes: 4 servings

1. Stir together soy sauce and ginger. Brush soy sauce mixture onto both sides of each chop.

2. Preheat broiler. Place meat on the unheated rack of a broiler pan. Broil 3 to 4 inches from the heat for 9 to 11 minutes or until done (160°F) and juices run clear, turning once halfway through broiling.

3. Meanwhile, for dressing, in a screw-top jar combine vinegar, salad oil, sesame oil, salt, and crushed red pepper. Cover; shake well. In a large bowl combine cabbage, cucumber, and radishes. Add dressing; toss to coat. Transfer salad to a serving platter. Slice meat and serve with salad.

- 1 tablespoon soy sauce
- 2 teaspoons grated fresh ginger
- 4 boneless pork loin chops, cut ¾ inch thick
- 3 tablespoons rice vinegar
- 2 tablespoons salad oil
- 1 teaspoon toasted sesame oil
- ⅛ teaspoon salt
- ⅛ teaspoon crushed red pepper
- 4 cups finely shredded Chinese (Napa) cabbage
- ½ cup cucumber cut into matchstick pieces
- ¼ cup radishes cut into matchstick pieces

4g carbs   **2**g fiber   **2**g net carbs

Nutrition Facts per serving: 350 cal., 18 g total fat (5 g sat. fat), 92 mg chol., 386 mg sodium, 4 g carbo., 2 g fiber, 40 g pro.

Smoked Pork Salad

Prep: 15 minutes Cook: 8 minutes Makes: 4 servings

4   boneless cooked smoked
    pork chops, cut ¾ inch thick

1   tablespoon cooking oil

6   cups torn Boston or
    bibb lettuce

8   pear or grape tomatoes,
    halved

2   ounces Gouda or white
    cheddar cheese, cut into
    bite-size pieces

½   bottled low-carb oil-and-
    vinegar salad dressing

2   teaspoons Dijon-style mustard

1   teaspoon snipped fresh thyme

1. In a large skillet cook meat in hot oil for 8 to 10 minutes or until hot, turning once.

2. Meanwhile, divide lettuce, tomatoes, and cheese among 4 salad plates. In a small bowl whisk together salad dressing, mustard, and thyme. Drizzle some of the dressing over salads. Thinly slice meat; arrange slices on top of salads. Serve with remaining dressing.

See photo, page 148.

5g carbs   **1**g fiber   **4**g net carbs

Nutrition Facts per serving: 386 cal., 29 g total fat (8 g sat. fat), 77 mg chol., 1,629 mg sodium, 5 g carbo., 1 g fiber, 26 g pro.

Asian Pork Soup

Start to Finish: 20 minutes Makes: 6 servings

1. In a large saucepan cook pork in hot oil for 2 to 3 minutes or until slightly pink in center. Remove from pan; set aside. Add mushrooms and garlic to saucepan; cook until tender.

2. Stir in broth, sherry, soy sauce, ginger, and crushed red pepper. Bring to boiling. Stir in meat, cabbage, and green onion; heat through.

12 ounces lean boneless pork, cut into thin bite-size strips

1 tablespoon cooking oil

2 cups sliced fresh shiitake mushrooms

2 cloves garlic, minced

3 14-ounce cans reduced-sodium chicken broth

2 tablespoons dry sherry

2 tablespoons reduced-sodium soy sauce

2 teaspoons grated fresh ginger or ½ teaspoon ground ginger

¼ teaspoon crushed red pepper

2 cups thinly sliced Chinese (Napa) cabbage

1 green onion, thinly sliced

4g carbs **1**g fiber **3**g net carbs

Nutrition Facts per serving: 142 cal., 6 g total fat (2 g sat. fat), 31 mg chol., 690 mg sodium, 4 g carbo., 1 g fiber, 16 g pro.

Italian Pork Burgers

Prep: 15 minutes Grill: 15 minutes Makes: 4 servings

1 pound ground pork

1¼ teaspoons dried Italian

seasoning, crushed

¼ teaspoon salt

¼ teaspoon black pepper

2 ounces Italian fontina or

mozzarella cheese,

thinly sliced

½ cup pitted green olives,

coarsely chopped

1 teaspoon olive oil

Dash crushed red pepper

1. In a large bowl combine ground pork, 1 teaspoon of the Italian seasoning, salt, and black pepper; mix well. Form mixture into four ³/₄-inch-thick patties.

2. For a charcoal grill, grill patties on the rack of an uncovered grill directly over medium coals for 14 to 18 minutes or until done (160°F) and juices run clear, turning once halfway through grilling. Top each burger with cheese. Grill 1 to 2 minutes more until cheese begins to melt. (For a gas grill, preheat grill. Reduce heat to medium. Place patties on grill rack over heat. Cover and grill as above.)

3. Meanwhile, in a small bowl combine olives, oil, crushed red pepper, and remaining ¼ teaspoon Italian seasoning. Top burgers with olive mixture.

See photo, page 149.

1_g carbs

0_g fiber

1_g net carbs

Nutrition Facts per serving: 219 cal., 16 g total fat (7 g sat. fat), 69 mg chol., 706 mg sodium, 1 g carbo., 0 g fiber, 18 g pro.

Pork Mini Loaves

Prep: 20 minutes Bake: 15 minutes Oven: 350°F Makes: 4 servings

1. In a large bowl combine egg, pork rinds, sour cream, 2 tablespoons barbecue sauce, mustard, sage, salt, and pepper. Add ground pork; mix well. Divide pork mixture into twelve 2¹⁄₂-inch muffin cups, lightly patting into cups.

2. Bake in a 350° oven for 15 to 20 minutes or until done (160°F) and juices run clear. Run a knife around the edge of each muffin cup. Remove mini loaves from cups. Brush tops with remaining 2 tablespoons barbecue sauce.

1 beaten egg

¹⁄₃ cup finely crushed fried pork rinds

¹⁄₄ cup dairy sour cream

2 tablespoons low-carb original barbecue sauce

2 teaspoons dry mustard

1 teaspoon ground sage

¹⁄₂ teaspoon salt

¹⁄₂ teaspoon black pepper

1 pound ground pork

2 tablespoons low-carb original barbecue sauce

3g carbs   **0**g fiber   **3**g net carbs

Nutrition Facts per serving: 227 cal., 15 g total fat (6 g sat. fat), 118 mg chol., 657 mg sodium, 3 g carbo., 0 g fiber, 21 g pro.

Parmesan Patties

Prep: 20 minutes Broil: 13 minutes Makes: 4 servings

1 2-ounce wedge
   Parmesan cheese

1 pound ground pork

½ teaspoon black pepper

½ teaspoon garlic salt

¼ teaspoon dried oregano,
   crushed

1 large Roma tomato,
   very thinly sliced

2 tablespoons finely shredded
   fresh basil

1. With a vegetable peeler, shave about half of the Parmesan into thin strips; set aside. Finely shred remaining Parmesan (should yield about ¼ cup).

2. In a large bowl combine ground pork, finely shredded Parmesan, pepper, garlic salt, and oregano. Form mixture into four ¾-inch-thick patties.

3. Preheat broiler. Place patties on the unheated rack of a broiler pan. Broil 3 to 4 inches from heat for 12 to 14 minutes or until done (160°F) and juices run clear, turning once halfway through broiling. Top each patty with tomato slices and strips of Parmesan. Broil 1 minute more. Top patties with basil.

2 g carbs **0** g fiber **2** g net carbs

Nutrition Facts per serving: 199 cal., 12 g total fat (6 g sat. fat), 63 mg chol., 404 mg sodium, 2 g carbo., 0 g fiber, 20 g pro.

Swedish-Style Meatballs

Prep: 25 minutes Bake: 18 minutes Oven: 350°F Makes: 4 servings

1. In a large bowl combine egg yolk, onion, 1/2 teaspoon salt, 1/4 teaspoon nutmeg, and 1/8 teaspoon pepper; add pork rinds and ground pork. Mix well. Shape into twenty 1-inch meatballs; place in a 15×10×1-inch baking pan.

2. Bake in a 350° oven for 18 to 20 minutes or until juices run clear.

3. Meanwhile, for sauce, in a medium saucepan combine whipping cream, mustard, and 1/8 teaspoon nutmeg. Bring just to boiling; reduce heat and simmer, uncovered, about 5 minutes or until reduced to 2/3 cup. Season to taste with salt and pepper.

4. Transfer meatballs to a serving dish; pour sauce over meatballs.

1 slightly beaten egg yolk

1 tablespoon finely chopped onion

1/2 teaspoon salt

1/4 teaspoon ground nutmeg

1/8 teaspoon black pepper

1/4 cup finely crushed fried pork rinds (about 1/2 ounce)

1 pound ground pork

1 cup whipping cream

2 teaspoons Dijon-style mustard

1/8 teaspoon ground nutmeg

Salt and black pepper

3g carbs   **0**g fiber   **3**g net carbs

Nutrition Facts per serving: 405 cal., 35 g total fat (19 g sat. fat), 292 mg chol., 487 mg sodium, 3 g carbo., 0 g fiber, 20 g pro.

Ham Salad

Prep: 15 minutes Chill: 1 hour Makes: 4 servings

3 tablespoons mayonnaise

2 tablespoons dairy sour cream

1 tablespoon Dijon-style

   mustard

1 teaspoon snipped fresh sage

   or thyme or ¼ teaspoon

   dried sage or thyme,

   crushed

1½ cups diced cooked ham

¼ cup thinly sliced green onions

4 cups torn salad greens

1. In a medium bowl combine mayonnaise, sour cream, mustard, and sage. Add ham and green onions; stir gently to coat. Cover and chill for 1 to 4 hours. Serve ham salad over greens.

Cheese-&-Pepper Ham Salad: In a medium bowl combine 1½ cups diced cooked ham, ¼ cup crumbled white cheddar cheese, and ¼ cup chopped red sweet pepper. Add ⅓ cup bottled low-carb ranch salad dressing; stir gently to coat. Cover and chill for 1 to 4 hours. Serve ham salad over greens. Makes 4 servings.

4g carbs **1**g fiber **3**g net carbs

Nutrition Facts per serving: 222 cal., 18 g total fat (5 g sat. fat), 44 mg chol., 855 mg sodium, 4 g carbo., 1 g fiber, 11 g protein.

Ham-&-Salad Spirals

Prep: 20 minutes Chill: 1 hour Makes: 4 servings

1. In a medium bowl stir together mayonnaise, vinegar, dill, salt, and pepper. Add cabbage and broccoli; toss to coat. Cover and chill for 1 to 4 hours.

2. Place a cheese slice on top of each ham slice. Spoon about 2 tablespoons cabbage mixture onto center of each cheese slice. Roll up; secure with toothpicks.

⅓ cup mayonnaise

1 teaspoon white wine vinegar

¼ teaspoon dried dill

⅛ teaspoon salt

Dash black pepper

1½ cups shredded cabbage

½ cup chopped broccoli or chopped zucchini

8 thin slices provolone or Swiss cheese (about 8 ounces)

8 thin slices cooked ham (about 8 ounces)

6g carbs   **2**g fiber   **4**g net carbs

Nutrition Facts per servings: 432 cal., 34 g total fat (13 g sat. fat), 84 mg chol., 1,423 mg sodium, 6 g carbo., 2 g fiber, 24 g pro.

Ham, Sweet Pepper & Zucchini Soup

Prep: 20 minutes Cook: 5 minutes Makes: 6 servings

1 medium zucchini,

    coarsely chopped

1 medium yellow sweet pepper,

    coarsely chopped

2 cloves garlic, minced

1 tablespoon butter

3 14-ounce cans chicken broth

1 pound cooked boneless ham,

    coarsely chopped

2 tablespoons snipped

    fresh basil

1. In a large saucepan cook zucchini, sweet pepper, and garlic in hot butter until tender. Add broth. Bring to boiling; reduce heat. Simmer, covered, for 5 minutes. Stir in ham; heat through. Stir in basil.

See photo, page 150.

7 g
carbs

2 g
fiber

5 g
net carbs

Nutrition Facts per serving: 167 cal., 9 g total fat (3 g sat. fat), 51 mg chol., 1,814 mg sodium, 7 g carbo., 2 g fiber, 15 g pro.

Ham Soup with Mustard Greens

Prep: 20 minutes Cook: 10 minutes Makes: 6 servings

1. In a large saucepan cook sweet pepper, onion, and garlic in hot butter until tender. Add broth and crushed red pepper. Bring to boiling; reduce heat. Simmer, covered, for 5 minutes. Stir in ham; heat through. Stir in mustard greens; cook 2 to 3 minutes or just until wilted.

½ cup chopped red sweet pepper

¼ cup chopped onion

3 cloves garlic, minced

1 tablespoon butter

3 14-ounce cans chicken broth

⅛ teaspoon crushed red pepper

12 ounces cooked boneless ham, coarsely chopped

4 cups coarsely chopped fresh mustard greens

7g carbs   **2**g fiber   **5**g net carbs

Nutrition Facts per serving: 141 cal., 7 g total fat (3 g sat. fat), 40 mg chol., 1,574 mg sodium, 7 g carbo., 2 g fiber, 12 g pro.

Ham Slice with Mustard Sauce

Start to Finish: 20 minutes Makes: 4 servings

1 1- to 1¼-pound cooked
   boneless center-cut ham
   slice, cut 1 inch thick

1 tablespoon butter

¼ cup chicken broth

¼ cup dairy sour cream

2 tablespoons horseradish
   mustard or Dijon-style
   mustard

1 tablespoon chopped
   green onion

1. In a large skillet cook ham in hot butter over medium heat for 14 to 16 minutes or until ham is heated through, turning once halfway through cooking. Transfer to a serving platter; keep warm.

2. Reduce heat to low. Add broth to skillet. Cook until bubbly, stirring to loosen any brown bits in bottom of skillet. Add sour cream, mustard, and green onion to skillet. Cook and stir over low heat until heated through (do not boil). Serve sauce with ham.

6g carbs   **2**g fiber   **4**g net carbs

Nutrition Facts per serving: 246 cal., 16 g total fat (6 g sat. fat), 78 mg chol., 1,636 mg sodium, 6 g carbo., 2 g fiber, 20 g pro.

Homemade Pork Sausage

Prep: 15 minutes Grill: 14 minutes Makes: 4 servings

1. In a large bowl combine basil, garlic, fennel seeds, crushed red pepper, salt, and black pepper. Add ground pork; mix well. Divide pork mixture into 4 equal portions. Shape each portion into a 6-inch log around a flat-sided metal skewer.

2. For a charcoal grill, grill meat on the rack of an uncovered grill directly over medium coals for 14 to 18 minutes or until juices run clear, turning once halfway through grilling. (For a gas grill, preheat grill. Reduce heat to medium. Place meat on grill rack over heat. Cover and grill as above.)

3. To serve, use a fork to slide the meat from skewers.

3 tablespoons finely snipped
   fresh basil

2 cloves garlic, minced

1 teaspoon fennel seeds

1 teaspoon crushed red pepper

¾ teaspoon salt

½ teaspoon black pepper

1½ pounds ground pork

1g carbs **0**g fiber **1**g net carbs

Nutrition Facts per serving: 422 cal., 35 g total fat (13 g sat. fat), 121 mg chol., 532 mg sodium, 1 g carbo., 0 g fiber, 30 g pro.

Sausage Quiche Cups

Prep: 20 minutes Bake: 30 minutes Cool: 5 minutes
Oven: 325°F Makes: 4 servings

8 ounces bulk pork sausage

4 beaten eggs

½ cup whipping cream

¾ cup shredded mozzarella

   cheese (3 ounces)

2 tablespoons grated

   Parmesan cheese

2 green onions, thinly sliced

¼ teaspoon dried thyme,

   crushed

⅛ teaspoon black pepper

1. In a medium skillet, cook sausage until brown. Drain fat. Divide sausage among 4 greased 6-ounce custard cups.

2. In a bowl combine eggs, whipping cream, mozzarella cheese, Parmesan cheese, green onions, thyme, and pepper; divide evenly among the cups.

3. Bake in a 325° oven about 30 minutes or until puffed and set. Cool 5 minutes on wire rack before serving.

3g carbs

0g fiber

3g net carbs

Nutrition Facts per serving: 390 cal., 31 g total fat (15 g sat. fat), 305 mg chol., 521 mg sodium, 3 g carbo., 0 g fiber, 22 g pro.

Spicy Sausage Soup

Start to Finish: 25 minutes Makes: 6 servings

1. In a Dutch oven cook sausage, onion, and garlic until sausage is brown; drain off fat. Stir in broth and Italian seasoning. Bring to boiling; reduce heat. Stir in Swiss chard; cook until just wilted. Stir in tomato; cook 1 minute more. If desired, top each serving with Parmesan Cheese Crisps.

Parmesan Cheese Crisps: Preheat oven to 400°F. Coarsely shred 6 ounces Parmesan cheese. Line a baking sheet with parchment paper or nonstick foil. Place about 1 tablespoon cheese on prepared sheet; pat into a 2-inch circle. Repeat with remaining cheese, allowing 2 inches between circles. Bake for 7 to 8 minutes or until bubbly and lightly golden. Let stand on sheets for 1 to 2 minutes. Transfer to a wire rack; cool completely.

See photo, page 151.

1 pound bulk hot or mild
  pork sausage

¼ cup chopped onion

2 cloves garlic, minced

3 14-ounce cans chicken broth

½ teaspoon dried Italian
  seasoning, crushed

4 cups coarsely chopped Swiss
  chard leaves

1 Roma tomato, chopped

1 recipe Parmesan Cheese
  Crisps (optional)

6g carbs   **1**g fiber   **5**g net carbs

Nutrition Facts per serving: 227 cal., 16 g total fat (6 g sat. fat), 48 mg chol., 1,258 mg sodium, 6 g carbo., 1 g fiber, 11 g pro.

Brats with Onion-Pepper Relish

Prep: 15 minutes Cook: 15 minutes Makes: 4 servings

4   uncooked bratwurst

½   cup water

1   small onion, thinly sliced

1   small red or green sweet

    pepper, cut into thin strips

¼   teaspoon black pepper

⅛   teaspoon salt

1   tablespoon butter or

    margarine

2   tablespoons spicy

    brown mustard

1. In a large nonstick skillet cook bratwurst over medium heat about 5 minutes or until brown, turning frequently. Carefully add water. Bring to boiling; reduce heat. Simmer, covered, for 15 to 20 minutes or until done (160°F). Drain on paper towels.

2. Meanwhile, for onion-pepper relish, in a covered medium saucepan cook onion, sweet pepper, black pepper, and salt in hot butter for 6 to 7 minutes or until onion is golden, stirring once.

3. Spread bratwurst with mustard and top with relish.

5g carbs   **1**g fiber   **4**g net carbs

Nutrition Facts per serving: 306 cal., 25 g total fat (12 g sat. fat), 58 mg chol., 872 mg sodium, 5 g carbo., 1 g fiber, 17 g pro.

Cheese-Stuffed Bratwurst

Prep: 20 minutes Grill: 8 minutes Makes: 8 servings

1. Cut a lengthwise slit in each bratwurst about ¹/₂ inch deep. Cut cheese into eight thin 2¹/₂-inch-long strips. Insert a cheese strip and some green onion into each bratwurst.

2. For a charcoal grill, arrange medium-hot coals around a drip pan. Test for medium heat above pan. Place bratwurst, cheese side up, on the grill rack over drip pan. Cover and grill for 8 to 10 minutes or until cheese melts and bratwurst are heated through. (For a gas grill, preheat grill. Reduce heat to medium. Adjust for indirect cooking. Grill as above.) If desired, serve bratwurst with mustard.

8 cooked bratwurst or cooked
   smoked Polish sausages
3 ounces Monterey Jack cheese
¹/₃ cup thinly sliced green onions
   Mustard (optional)

2 g carbs   **0** g fiber   **2** g net carbs

Nutrition Facts per serving: 222 cal., 17 g total fat (7 g sat. fat), 54 mg chol., 469 mg sodium, 2 g carbo., 0 g fiber, 13 g pro.

Quick and Easy Cooking Methods for Pork

Indoor Grilling Pork

Preheat grill. Place pork on grill rack. If using a grill with a cover, close the lid. Grill for the time given below or until done. If using a grill without a cover, turn food once halfway through grilling. The following timings should be used as general guidelines. Test for doneness using a meat thermometer. Refer to your owner's manual for preheating directions, suggested cuts, and recommended grilling times.

Cut or Type	Thickness, Weight, or Size	Covered Grilling Time	Uncovered Grilling Time	Doneness
Chop (boneless top loin)	¾ inch	6 to 8 minutes	12 to 15 minutes	160°F medium

Direct Grilling Pork

For a charcoal grill, place meat on grill rack directly over medium coals. Grill, uncovered, for the time given below or to desired doneness, turning once halfway through grilling. (For a gas grill, preheat grill. Reduce heat to medium. Place meat on grill rack over heat. Cover and grill as above.) Test for doneness using a meat thermometer.

Cut or Type	Thickness, Weight, or Size	Grilling Temperature	Approximate Grilling Time	Doneness
Chop with bone (loin or rib)	¾ to 1 inch 1¼ to 1½ inch	medium medium	11 to 14 minutes 18 to 22 minutes	160°F medium 160°F medium
Chop (boneless top loin)	¾ to 1 inch 1¼ to 1½ inch	medium medium	12 to 15 minutes 17 to 21 minutes	160°F medium 160°F medium
Sausages (frankfurters, smoked bratwurst, etc.)		medium	3 to 7 minutes	Heated through

Indirect-Grilling Pork

For a charcoal grill, arrange medium-hot coals around a drip pan. Test for medium heat above pan, unless chart says otherwise. Place meat, fat side up, on grill rack over drip pan. Cover and grill for the time given below or to desired temperature, adding more charcoal to maintain heat as necessary. For a gas grill, preheat grill. Reduce heat to medium. Adjust heat for indirect cooking.

Test for doneness using a meat thermometer. (Use an instant-read thermometer to test smaller portions.) Thermometer should register the "final grilling temperature." Remove meat from grill. For larger cuts, such as roasts, cover with foil and let stand 15 minutes before carving. The meat's temperature will rise 5°F to 10°F during the time it stands. Thinner cuts, such as steaks, do not have to stand.

Cut	Thickness/ Weight	Approximate Indirect-Grilling Time	Final Grilling Temperature (when to remove from grill)	Final Doneness Temperature (after 15 minutes standing)
Pork				
Boneless sirloin roast	1½ to 2 pounds	1 to 1½ hours	155°F	160°F medium
Boneless top loin roast (single)	2 to 3 pounds	1 to 1½ hours	155°F	160°F medium
(double loin, tied)	3 to 5 pounds	1½ to 2¼ hours	155°F	160°F medium
Chop (boneless top loin)	¾ to 1 inch	20 to 24 minutes	160°F medium	No standing time
	1¼ to 1½ inches	30 to 35 minutes	160°F medium	No standing time
Loin or rib	¾ to 1 inch	22 to 25 minutes	160°F medium	No standing time
	1¼ to 1½ inches	35 to 40 minutes	160°F medium	No standing time
Country-style ribs		1½ to 2 hours	Tender	No standing time
Ham, cooked (boneless)	3 to 5 pounds	1¼ to 2 hours	140°F	No standing time
	6 to 8 pounds	2 to 2¾ hours	140°F	No standing time
Ham, cooked (slice)	1 inch	20 to 24 minutes	140°F	No standing time
Loin back ribs or spareribs		1½ to 1¾ hours	Tender	No standing time
Loin center rib roast (backbone loosened)	3 to 4 pounds	1¼ to 2 hours	155°F	160°F medium
	4 to 6 pounds	2 to 2¾ hours	155°F	160°F medium
Sausages uncooked (bratwurst, Polish or Italian sausage links)	about 4 per pound	20 to 30 minutes	160°F medium	No standing time
Smoked shoulder picnic (with bone), cooked	4 to 6 pounds	1½ to 2¼ hours	140°F	No standing time
Tenderloin	¾ to 1 pound	40 to 50 minutes	160°F medium	No standing time

Skillet Cooking Pork

Select a skillet that is just large enough to fit the amount of meat you are cooking. (If the skillet is too large, the pan juices can burn.) Lightly coat a heavy skillet with nonstick cooking spray. (Or use a heavy nonstick skillet.) Preheat skillet over medium-high heat until very hot. Add meat. Do not add any liquid and do not cover the skillet. Reduce heat to medium and cook for the time given or until done, turning meat occasionally. If meat browns too quickly, reduce heat to medium-low.

Cut or Type	Thickness, Weight, or Size	Covered Grilling Time	Doneness
Pork Canadian-style bacon	¼ inch	3 to 4 minutes	Heated through
Chop (loin or rib) (with bone or boneless)	¾ to 1 inch	8 to 12 minutes	160°F medium
Cutlet	¼ inch	3 to 4 minutes	160°F medium
Ham slice, cooked	1 inch	14 to 16 minutes	140°F Heated through
Tender medallions	¼ to ½ inch	4 to 8 minutes	160°F medium

Broiling Pork

Preheat broiler. Place meat on the unheated rack of a broiler pan. For cuts less than 1½ inches thick, broil 3 to 4 inches from the heat. For 1½-inch-thick cuts, broil 4 to 5 inches from the heat. Broil for the time given or until done, turning meat over after half of the broiling time.

Cut or Type	Thickness, Weight, or Size	Grilling Temperature	Approximate Grilling Time	Doneness
Chop with bone (loin or rib)	¾ to 1 inch 1¼ to 1½ inches	160°F 160°F	9 to 12 minutes 16 to 20 minutes	medium medium
Chop with bone (sirloin)	¾ to 1 inch 1¼ to 1½ inches	160°F 160°F	10 to 13 minutes 17 to 21 minutes	medium medium
Chop (boneless top loin)	¾ to 1 inch 1¼ to 1½ inches	160°F 160°F	9 to 11 minutes 15 to 18 minutes	medium medium
Ham slice, cooked	1 inch	140°F	12 to 15 minutes	Heated through
Sausages, cooked (frankfurters, smoked bratwurst, etc.)		140°F	3 to 7 minutes	Heated through

Chicken & Turkey

Whether roasted, sautéed, or stuffed, these recipes are sure to liven up your plate and relieve chicken boredom. From Roasted Italian Chicken to Oriental Chicken Kabobs, you'll find flavor footprints from around the world. With more than 65 recipes to explore, it's easy to stay on track with your phase 1 diet.

Stuffed Chicken Breasts

Prep: 25 minutes Cook: 12 minutes Makes: 4 servings

4 skinless, boneless
    chicken breast halves
4 ounces feta cheese
    with peppercorn or
    feta cheese, crumbled
½ of a 7-ounce jar roasted red
    sweet peppers, drained and
    cut into strips (½ cup)
1 tablespoon olive oil
¼ cup chicken broth

1. Place each chicken breast half between two pieces of plastic wrap. Using the flat side of a meat mallet, pound lightly to ¼-inch thickness. Discard plastic wrap.

2. Sprinkle chicken with cheese. Place roasted pepper strips in the center of each breast. Fold in sides and roll up, pressing the edges to seal. Secure with wooden toothpicks.

3. In a large nonstick skillet cook chicken in hot oil over medium heat about 5 minutes, turning to brown all sides. Add broth. Bring to boiling; reduce heat. Simmer, covered, for 7 to 8 minutes or until chicken is no longer pink (170°F). Spoon juices over chicken.

2g carbs   **0**g fiber   **2**g net carbs

Nutrition Facts per serving: 265 cal., 11 g total fat (5 g sat. fat),
107 mg chol., 449 mg sodium, 2 g carbo., 0 g fiber, 37 g pro.

Chicken with Lemon-Thyme Pesto

Prep: 1 hour Grill: 50 minutes Makes: 6 servings

1. If desired, skin chicken. Season with salt and pepper.

2. In a food processor bowl or blender container combine lemon thyme and pistachios; cover and process or blend with several on/off turns until finely chopped. With processor or blender running, gradually drizzle in oil, stopping to scrape down sides as necessary. Stir in freshly ground black pepper. Set aside.

3. For a charcoal grill, arrange medium-hot coals around a drip pan. Test for medium heat above the pan. Place chicken pieces, bone sides down, on grill rack over drip pan. Cover and grill for 50 to 60 minutes or until chicken is no longer pink (170°F for breasts, 180°F for thighs and drumsticks), turning and brushing with half of the pesto during the last 5 minutes of grilling. Reserve remaining pesto for another use. If desired, serve with lemon wedges.

3½ pounds meaty chicken pieces
(breast halves, thighs, and drumsticks)
Salt and black pepper

1⅓ cups fresh thyme plus
2 teaspoons finely shredded lemon peel

½ cup salted pistachio nuts

½ cup olive oil

¼ teaspoon freshly ground black pepper

Lemon wedges (optional)

3g carbs   **1**g fiber   **2**g net carbs

Nutrition Facts per serving: 414 cal., 26 g total fat (6 g sat. fat), 121 mg chol., 225 mg sodium, 3 g carbo., 1 g fiber, 40 g pro.

Rosemary Chicken

Prep: 15 minutes Marinate: 6 hours Grill: 35 minutes Makes: 6 servings

2 to 2½ pounds meaty chicken
  pieces (breast halves,
  thighs, and drumsticks)

½ cup dry white wine

2 tablespoons olive oil

4 cloves garlic, minced

4 teaspoons snipped
  fresh rosemary

1 tablespoon finely shredded
  lemon peel

¼ teaspoon salt

¼ teaspoon black pepper

1. If desired, skin chicken. Place chicken in a self-sealing plastic bag set in a shallow dish.

2. For marinade, in a small bowl combine wine, oil, garlic, rosemary, lemon peel, salt, and pepper. Pour over chicken; seal bag. Marinate in the refrigerator for 6 hours or overnight, turning bag occasionally.

3. Drain chicken, discarding marinade. For a charcoal grill, grill chicken, bone sides up, on the rack of an uncovered grill directly over medium coals for 35 to 45 minutes or until chicken is no longer pink (170°F for breasts, 180°F for thighs and drumsticks), turning once halfway through grilling.

0_g carbs 0_g fiber 0_g net carbs

Nutrition Facts per serving: 192 cal., 10 g total fat (3 g sat. fat), 69 mg chol., 93 mg sodium, 0 g carbo., 0 g fiber, 22 g pro.

Chicken Stuffed with Smoked Mozzarella

Prep: 40 minutes Bake: 25 minutes Oven: 400°F Makes: 6 servings

1. Place each chicken breast half between two pieces of plastic wrap. Using the flat side of a meat mallet, pound lightly into a rectangle about ⅛ inch thick. Remove plastic wrap. Season with salt and pepper.

2. For filling, in a medium skillet cook shallots and garlic in 2 teaspoons hot oil until tender. Remove from heat; stir in spinach, nuts, and mozzarella.

3. To fill each roll, place 2 to 3 tablespoons of filling in the center of each chicken piece. Fold in bottom and sides and roll up; secure with wooden toothpicks.

4. Lightly brush each roll with the 1 tablespoon oil. Place rolls, seam sides down, in a shallow baking pan. Sprinkle with Parmesan cheese. Bake, uncovered, in a 400° oven about 25 minutes or until chicken is no longer pink (170°F). Remove toothpicks.

6 skinless, boneless
    chicken breast halves
    Salt and black pepper
¼ cup finely chopped shallots
    or onions
1 clove garlic, minced
2 teaspoons olive oil
½ of a 10-ounce package frozen
    chopped spinach, thawed and
    well-drained
3 tablespoons pine nuts
3 ounces smoked mozzarella
    cheese, shredded (¾ cup)
1 tablespoon olive oil
¼ cup grated Parmesan cheese

3 g carbs   **1** g fiber   **2** g net carbs

Nutrition Facts per serving: 291 cal., 12 g total fat (3 g sat. fat), 99 mg chol., 351 mg sodium, 3 g carbo., 1 g fiber, 42 g pro.

Thyme & Garlic Chicken

Start to Finish: 30 minutes Makes: 4 servings

4 medium skinless, boneless

    chicken breast halves

4 cloves garlic, minced

½ teaspoon dried thyme,

    crushed

¼ teaspoon salt

¼ teaspoon black pepper

2 tablespoons butter

¼ cup chicken broth

1 tablespoon balsamic vinegar

1. Place each chicken breast half between two pieces of plastic wrap. Using the flat side of a meat mallet, pound chicken lightly to ½-inch thickness. Remove plastic wrap. Set chicken breast halves aside.

2. In a small bowl combine garlic, thyme, salt, and pepper. Rub mixture over one side of each chicken breast half. In a large skillet cook chicken in hot butter over medium heat for 8 to 10 minutes or until the chicken is no longer pink (160°F), turning once. Transfer chicken to serving platter; keep warm.

3. Carefully add chicken broth to the skillet. Cook and stir for 1 minute, scraping to loosen browned bits from the pan. Remove from heat. Stir in vinegar. Pour over chicken.

2g carbs   **0**g fiber   **2**g net carbs

Nutrition Facts per serving: 227 cal., 8 g total fat (4 g sat. fat), 98 mg chol., 328 mg sodium, 2 g carbo., 0 g fiber, 33 g pro.

Marinated Chicken Breasts with Mushroom Sauce

Prep: 15 minutes Marinate: 6 hours Grill: 50 minutes Makes: 4 servings

1. If desired, skin chicken. Place chicken in a self-sealing plastic bag set in a shallow bowl. For marinade, in a small bowl combine ½ cup wine, oil, oregano, basil, and garlic. Pour over chicken; seal bag. Marinate in the refrigerator for 6 to 24 hours, turning bag occasionally. Drain chicken, discarding marinade. Season lightly with salt and pepper.

2. For a charcoal grill, arrange medium-hot coals around a drip pan. Test for medium heat above pan. Place chicken, bone sides down, on grill rack over drip pan. Cover and grill for 50 to 60 minutes or until chicken is no longer pink (170°F). (For a gas grill, preheat grill. Reduce heat to medium. Adjust for indirect cooking. Grill as above.)

3. For sauce, in a small saucepan cook mushrooms in butter until tender. Stir in ¼ cup wine. Bring to boiling; reduce heat. Simmer, uncovered, for 5 minutes. Season to taste with salt and pepper. Spoon sauce over chicken.

4 chicken breast halves

½ cup dry white wine

2 tablespoons olive oil or
   cooking oil

1 teaspoon dried oregano,
   crushed

1 teaspoon dried basil, crushed

2 cloves garlic, minced
   Salt and black pepper

1 cup sliced fresh mushrooms

1 tablespoon butter

¼ cup dry white wine
   Salt and black pepper

1g carbs   **0**g fiber   **1**g net carbs

Nutrition Facts per serving: 205 cal., 7 g total fat (2 g sat. fat), 80 mg chol., 92 mg sodium, 1 g carbo., 0 g fiber, 30 g pro.

Pesto Chicken Breasts with Summer Squash

Start to Finish: 25 minutes Makes: 4 servings

4 skinless, boneless

    chicken breast halves

    Salt and black pepper

1 tablespoon olive oil

2 cups coarsely chopped

    yellow summer squash

    and/or zucchini

1 recipe Pesto

2 tablespoons finely shredded

    Asiago or Parmesan cheese

1. Sprinkle chicken with salt and pepper. In a large nonstick skillet cook chicken in hot oil over medium heat for 8 to 10 minutes or until the chicken is no longer pink (170°F), turning once halfway through cooking. Remove chicken from skillet; keep warm.

2. Add squash to hot skillet. Cook and stir for 2 to 3 minutes or until squash is crisp-tender. Transfer chicken and squash to 4 dinner plates. Spread Pesto over chicken; sprinkle with cheese.

Pesto: In a food processor bowl or blender container combine $\frac{1}{2}$ cup packed fresh basil leaves; 2 tablespoons grated Parmesan cheese; 1 small clove garlic, quartered; and dash salt. Cover and process with several on/off turns until a paste forms, stopping the machine several times and scraping sides. With machine running, gradually add 1 tablespoon olive oil. Process until the mixture is almost smooth.

See photo, page 217.

3 g carbs   **1** g fiber   **2** g net carbs

Nutrition Facts per serving: 258 cal., 11 g total fat (3 g sat. fat), 88 mg chol., 341 mg sodium, 3 g carbo., 1 g fiber, 36 g pro.

Pesto
Chicken
Breasts with
Summer
Squash
p. 216

Chicken with
Lemon-
Mushroom
Sauce
p. 231

Lemon-Dill
Butter
Chicken &
Cucumbers
p. 238

Baked
Herbed
Chicken
p. 240

Chicken Medallions with Creamy Tarragon-Mustard Sauce
p. 245

Chicken
Alfredo
p. 246

Herbed
Mustard
Chicken
p. 254

Chicken
Breasts with
Caper
Vinaigrette
p. 225

Chicken Breasts with Caper Vinaigrette

Prep: 15 minutes Grill: 12 minutes Makes: 4 servings

1. Drain tomato strips, reserving oil. Set tomato strips aside. Brush chicken with some of the reserved oil.

2. For a charcoal grill, grill chicken on the rack of an uncovered grill directly over medium coals for 12 to 15 minutes or until chicken is no longer pink (170°F), turning once and brushing with remaining reserved oil halfway through grilling. (For a gas grill, preheat grill. Reduce heat to medium. Place chicken on grill rack over heat. Cover and grill as above.)

3. Meanwhile, for vinaigrette, in a small bowl whisk together salad dressing, capers, pepper, and garlic.

4. Diagonally slice each chicken breast. If desired, arrange chicken pieces on top of Bibb lettuce on plates. Spoon vinaigrette over chicken. Top with tomato strips.

See photo, page 224.

¼ cup oil-packed dried tomato strips

4 skinless, boneless
    chicken breast halves

¼ cup bottled low-carb Italian
    salad dressing

2 tablespoons capers, drained

¼ teaspoon black pepper

1 clove garlic, minced

    Bibb lettuce or other salad
    greens (optional)

3g carbs   **1**g fiber   **2**g net carbs

Nutrition Facts per serving: 218 cal., 4 g total fat (1 g sat. fat), 99 mg chol., 447 mg sodium, 3 g carbo., 1 g fiber, 40 g pro.

Easy Marinated Chicken Breasts

Prep: 10 minutes Marinate: 2 hours Grill: 12 minutes Makes: 8 servings

8 skinless, boneless

    chicken breast halves

½ cup bottled low-carb Italian

    salad dressing (not creamy)

3 tablespoons soy sauce

½ teaspoon ground ginger

¼ teaspoon crushed

    red pepper

1. Place chicken breasts in a self-sealing plastic bag set in a shallow dish. For marinade, in a small bowl stir together salad dressing, soy sauce, ginger, and crushed red pepper. Pour marinade over chicken; seal bag. Marinate in the refrigerator for 2 to 24 hours, turning bag occasionally. Drain chicken, discarding marinade.

2. For a charcoal grill, grill chicken on the rack of an uncovered grill directly over medium coals for 12 to 15 minutes or until chicken is no longer pink (170°F), turning once halfway through grilling. (For a gas grill, preheat grill. Reduce heat to medium. Place chicken on grill rack over heat. Cover and grill as above.

0_g carbs 0_g fiber 0_g net carbs

Nutrition Facts per serving: 181 cal., 4 g total fat (1 g sat. fat),
82 mg chol., 338 mg sodium, 0 g carbo., 0 g fiber, 33 g pro

German-Style Chicken

Prep: 10 minutes Bake: 45 minutes Oven: 375°F Makes: 4 servings

1. If desired, skin chicken. Arrange breasts in a 3-quart rectangular baking dish; set aside. In a small bowl combine mustard, sherry, and paprika. Spoon 2 tablespoons of the mustard mixture evenly over top of chicken. Sprinkle with bacon. Bake, uncovered, in a 375° oven for 45 to 55 minutes or until chicken is no longer pink (170°F). Spoon remaining mustard mixture over chicken.

4   chicken breast halves

¼   cup Dusseldorf or
      horseradish mustard

2   tablespoons dry sherry

½   teaspoon sweet Hungarian
      paprika or ¼ teaspoon hot
      Hungarian paprika

2   slices bacon, crisp-cooked,
      drained, and crumbled

2g carbs   **0**g fiber   **2**g net carbs

Nutrition Facts per serving: 192 cal., 5 g total fat (1 g sat. fat),
76 mg chol., 364 mg sodium, 2 g carbo., 0 g fiber, 31 g pro.

Vegetable-Stuffed Chicken

Prep: 25 minutes Cook: 21 minutes Makes: 4 servings

1½ cups chopped fresh
     mushrooms

1 clove garlic, minced

2 tablespoons olive oil

¼ teaspoon dried marjoram or
     thyme, crushed

4 skinless, boneless chicken
     breast halves

2 ounces Gruyère cheese,
     shredded (½ cup)

½ cup chicken broth

¼ cup dry white wine or
     chicken broth

1 tablespoon snipped
     fresh parsley

1. In a large skillet cook and stir mushrooms and garlic in 1 tablespoon hot oil over medium heat for 3 minutes or until mushrooms are tender. Stir in marjoram. Remove from heat. Transfer mushroom mixture to a small bowl to cool slightly. Meanwhile, cut a horizontal slit in the thickest portion of each chicken breast, cutting to, but not through, the other side, forming a pocket. Place 1 rounded tablespoon of cheese and 1 rounded tablespoon of mushroom mixture into each pocket. Secure with wooden toothpicks.

2. Add remaining 1 tablespoon oil to the skillet. Cook chicken in hot oil over medium heat about 6 minutes or until browned, turning once. Remove skillet from heat. Carefully pour broth and wine into skillet. Return skillet to heat. Bring to boiling; reduce heat. Simmer, covered, about 8 minutes or until chicken is no longer pink (170°F). Transfer chicken to a platter; cover to keep warm.

3. Bring pan juices to boiling over medium-high heat. Boil gently, uncovered, for 7 to 8 minutes or until mixture is lightly browned and reduced to about 2 tablespoons. Remove toothpicks from chicken. Spoon liquid over chicken. Sprinkle with parsley.

2g carbs   **0**g fiber   **2**g net carbs

Nutrition Facts per serving: 302 cal., 14 g total fat (4 g sat. fat),
98 mg chol., 250 mg sodium, 2 g carbo., 0 g fiber, 39 g pro.

Basil-&-Garlic-Stuffed Chicken Breasts

Prep: 25 minutes Grill: 25 minutes Makes: 4 servings

1. In a small bowl combine Parmesan cheese, snipped fresh basil, 1 tablespoon melted butter, and garlic; set aside.

2. Place each chicken breast half between two pieces of plastic wrap. Using the flat side of a meat mallet, pound lightly to about 1/8-inch thickness. Remove plastic wrap. Spread cheese mixture on chicken. Fold in sides of each chicken breast; roll up, pressing edges to seal. Fasten with water-soaked wooden toothpicks.

3. For sauce, in a small bowl combine lemon peel, lemon juice, and 1 tablespoon melted butter; set aside.

4. For a charcoal grill, arrange medium-hot coals around a drip pan. Test for medium heat above pan. Place chicken on the grill rack over drip pan. Cover and grill for 25 to 30 minutes or until chicken is no longer pink (170°F), brushing occasionally with sauce the last 10 minutes of grilling. (For a gas grill, preheat grill. Reduce heat to medium. Adjust grill for indirect cooking. Grill as above.)

- 1/4 cup grated Parmesan cheese
- 2 to 3 tablespoons snipped fresh basil
- 1 tablespoon butter, melted
- 2 cloves garlic, minced
- 4 skinless, boneless chicken breast halves
- 1/2 teaspoon finely shredded lemon peel
- 2 tablespoons lemon juice
- 1 tablespoon butter, melted

1g carbs **0**g fiber **1**g net carbs

Nutrition Facts per serving: 241 cal., 10 g total fat (5 g sat. fat), 103 mg chol., 197 mg sodium, 1 g carbo., 0 g fiber, 35 g pro.

Herb-Stuffed Chicken Breasts

Prep: 20 minutes Grill: 50 minutes Makes: 6 servings

1 3-ounce package cream
   cheese, softened

2 tablespoons snipped fresh
   basil leaves

1 tablespoon snipped
   fresh chives

1 clove garlic, minced
   Salt and black pepper

6 chicken breast halves
   Salt and black pepper

2 tablespoons olive oil or
   cooking oil

1 tablespoon lemon or lime
   juice

1 tablespoon water
   Fresh chives (optional)

1. For stuffing, in a small bowl stir together cream cheese, 2 tablespoons basil, 1 tablespoon chives, and garlic. Season to taste with salt and pepper.

2. If desired, skin chicken. Cut a slit horizontally in each chicken breast to make a pocket. Insert a rounded tablespoon of stuffing into each slit. Fasten slit closed with water-soaked wooden toothpicks. Sprinkle breasts with salt and pepper. In a small bowl combine oil, lemon juice, and water.

3. For a charcoal grill, arrange medium-hot coals around a drip pan. Test for medium heat above pan. Place chicken, bone side down, on grill rack over drip pan. Cover; grill for 50 to 60 minutes or until chicken is no longer pink (170°F), brushing occasionally with oil mixture. (For a gas grill, preheat grill. Reduce heat to medium. Adjust for indirect cooking. Grill as above.) If desired, garnish with chives.

1_g carbs 0_g fiber 1_g net carbs

Nutrition Facts per serving: 430 cal., 29 g total fat (9 g sat. fat),
142 mg chol., 262 mg sodium, 1 g carbo., 0 g fiber, 40 g pro.

Chicken with Lemon-Mushroom Sauce

Start to Finish: 25 minutes Makes: 4 servings

1. Place each chicken breast half between two pieces of plastic wrap. Using the flat side of a meat mallet, pound lightly to $\frac{1}{4}$-inch thickness. Sprinkle chicken with salt and pepper.

2. In a large skillet cook chicken in hot oil over medium-high heat for 5 to 6 minutes or until no longer pink (170°F), turning once. Remove chicken from skillet. Place on a serving platter; cover with foil to keep warm.

3. For sauce, in the same skillet cook mushrooms for 2 minutes; remove from heat. Stir in chicken broth and lemon juice. Return to heat. Bring to boiling. Boil gently, uncovered, for 2 minutes. Stir in parsley. Spoon over chicken. If desired, garnish with lemon slices.

See photo, page 218.

4 skinless, boneless
   chicken breast halves

$\frac{1}{4}$ teaspoon salt

$\frac{1}{8}$ teaspoon black pepper

2 tablespoons cooking oil

2 cups sliced fresh mushrooms

$\frac{1}{3}$ cup chicken broth

2 tablespoons lemon juice

1 tablespoon snipped fresh parsley

   Thin lemon slices (optional)

2g carbs **0**g fiber **2**g net carbs

Nutrition Facts per serving: 237 cal., 10 g total fat (2 g sat. fat), 82 mg chol., 306 mg sodium, 2 g carbo., 0 g fiber, 35 g pro.

Triple Cheese-Stuffed Chicken Breasts

Prep: 20 minutes Bake: 45 minutes Oven: 375°F Makes: 6 servings

6 chicken breast halves

½ cup soft goat cheese
(chèvre), crumbled

½ cup shredded mozzarella
cheese (2 ounces)

⅓ cup grated Parmesan or
Romano cheese

2 teaspoons snipped fresh basil
or ½ teaspoon dried basil,
crushed

1 teaspoon snipped fresh
oregano or ¼ teaspoon dried
oregano, crushed

¼ teaspoon black pepper

1 teaspoon olive oil

1. With your fingers, gently separate the skin from the meat along the rib edge of each breast half.

2. For stuffing, in a medium bowl combine goat cheese, mozzarella cheese, Parmesan cheese, basil, oregano, and pepper. Stuff about ¼ cup stuffing between the skin and meat of each breast. Place chicken, skin side up, in a 3-quart rectangular baking dish. Brush chicken lightly with oil. Bake in a 375° oven for 45 to 55 minutes or until chicken is no longer pink (170°F).

1 g carbs   **0** g fiber   **1** g net carbs

Nutrition Facts per serving: 366 cal., 22 g total fat (8 g sat. fat),
122 mg chol., 245 mg sodium, 1 g carbo., 0 g fiber, 39 g pro.

Cheesy Tuscan Chicken Pockets

Prep: 15 minutes   Grill: 12 minutes   Makes: 4 servings

1. Using a sharp knife, cut a pocket in the side of each chicken breast half. Spread 1 tablespoon of the cheese mixture into each pocket; top with a folded slice of prosciutto. Secure pockets with wooden toothpicks. Brush chicken with some of the salad dressing.

2. For a charcoal grill, grill chicken on the rack of uncovered grill directly over medium coals for 12 to 15 minutes or until chicken is no longer pink (170°F), turning once and brushing with remaining salad dressing halfway through grilling. (For a gas grill, preheat grill. Reduce heat to medium. Place chicken on grill rack over heat. Cover and grill as above.)

4 skinless, boneless
    chicken breast halves

¼ cup semisoft cheese with
    garlic and herbs

3 ounces thinly sliced prosciutto

⅓ cup bottled low-carb Italian
    salad dressing

2g carbs   **0**g fiber   **2**g net carbs

Nutrition Facts per serving: 312 cal., 15 g total fat (5 g sat. fat), 113 mg chol., 888 mg sodium, 2 g carbo., 0 g fiber, 40 g pro.

Easy Balsamic Chicken

Prep: 15 minutes Grill: 10 minutes Marinate: 1 hour Makes: 4 servings

4 skinless, boneless

chicken breast halves

¼ cup balsamic vinegar

¼ cup olive oil

3 cloves garlic, minced

¼ teaspoon salt

¼ teaspoon crushed red pepper

1. Place each chicken breast between two pieces of plastic wrap. Using the flat side of a meat mallet, pound lightly to ½-inch thickness. Remove plastic wrap.

2. Place chicken in a shallow dish. In a small bowl combine vinegar, oil, garlic, salt, and crushed red pepper. Pour over chicken. Cover and marinate in the refrigerator for 1 to 4 hours, turning bag occasionally. Drain, discarding marinade.

3. For a charcoal grill, grill chicken on the rack of an uncovered grill directly over medium coals for 10 to 12 minutes or until chicken is no longer pink (170°F), turning once halfway through grilling. (For a gas grill, preheat grill. Reduce heat to medium. Place chicken on grill rack over heat. Cover and grill as above.)

2 g carbs   **0** g fiber   **2** g net carbs

Nutrition Facts per serving: 177 cal., 6 g total fat (2 g sat. fat), 66 mg chol., 125 mg sodium, 2 g carbo., 0 g fiber, 26 g pro.

Chili-Spiced Grilled Chicken

Prep: 15 minutes Grill: 12 minutes Makes: 6 servings

1. In a small saucepan cook onion and garlic in hot butter over medium heat until tender. Stir in chili powder, cumin, and cayenne pepper. Cook for 1 minute; remove from heat. Sprinkle chicken breasts with salt. Brush onion mixture over chicken.

2. For a charcoal grill, grill chicken on the rack of an uncovered grill directly over medium coals for 12 to 15 minutes or until chicken is no longer pink (170°F), turning once halfway through grilling. (For a gas grill, preheat grill. Reduce heat to medium. Place chicken on grill rack over heat. Cover and grill as above.)

1 small onion, finely chopped
  (⅓ cup)

1 clove garlic, minced

2 tablespoons butter

2 teaspoons chili powder

¼ teaspoon ground cumin

¼ teaspoon cayenne pepper

6 skinless, boneless chicken
  breast halves

Salt

2g carbs   **0**g fiber   **2**g net carbs

Nutrition Facts per serving: 214 cal., 7 g total fat (3 g sat. fat),
98 mg chol., 143 mg sodium, 2 g carbo., 0 g fiber, 35 g pro.

Crab-Stuffed Chicken

Prep: 25 minutes Cook: 25 minutes Makes: 4 servings

1 teaspoon finely shredded
   orange peel

1 tablespoon light cream

½ of an 8-ounce tub
   cream cheese

⅛ teaspoon salt

⅛ teaspoon black pepper

6- to 6½-ounce can crabmeat,
   drained, flaked, and
   cartilage removed

4 skinless, boneless chicken
   breast halves

  Salt and black pepper

1 tablespoon butter

1. For filling, in a small bowl combine orange peel, cream, cream cheese, ⅛ teaspoon salt, and ⅛ teaspoon pepper. Gently stir in crabmeat; set aside.

2. Place each chicken breast half between two pieces of plastic wrap. Using the flat side of a meat mallet, pound lightly into a rectangle about ⅛ inch thick. Remove plastic wrap. Sprinkle chicken with additional salt and pepper. Spread one-fourth of the filling evenly in center of each chicken piece. Fold narrow ends over filling; fold in sides. Roll up each chicken breast from a short side. Secure with wooden toothpicks.

3. In a medium skillet cook chicken in hot butter over medium-low heat about 25 minutes or until no longer pink (170°F), turning to brown evenly.

2g carbs   **0**g fiber   **2**g net carbs

Nutrition Facts per serving: 327 cal., 15 g total fat (9 g sat. fat), 161 mg chol., 467 mg sodium, 2 g carbo., 0 g fiber, 43 g pro.

Tangy Lemon Chicken

Prep: 15 minutes Marinate: 2 hours Grill: 12 minutes Makes: 4 servings

1. Place chicken in a self-sealing plastic bag set in a shallow dish. For marinade, in a small bowl stir together salad dressing, lemon peel, lemon juice, salt, and pepper. Pour over chicken; seal bag. Marinate in the refrigerator for 2 to 4 hours, turning bag occasionally. Drain chicken, reserving marinade.

2. For a charcoal grill, grill chicken on the rack of an uncovered grill directly over medium coals for 12 to 15 minutes or until chicken is no longer pink (170°F), turning and brushing with marinade halfway through grilling. Discard remaining marinade. (For a gas grill, preheat grill. Reduce heat to medium. Place chicken on grill rack over heat. Cover and grill as above.)

3. If desired, serve grilled chicken over greens.

4 skinless, boneless
   chicken breast halves

⅓ cup low-carb creamy Italian
   salad dressing

1 tablespoon finely shredded
   lemon peel

¼ cup lemon juice

½ teaspoon salt

¼ teaspoon black pepper

   Torn mixed greens (optional)

1g carbs   **0**g fiber   **1**g net carbs

Nutrition Facts per serving: 175 cal., 4 g total fat (1 g sat. fat),
82 mg chol., 240 mg sodium, 1 g carbo., 0 g fiber, 33 g pro.

Lemon-Dill Butter Chicken & Cucumbers

Prep: 10 minutes Broil: 12 minutes Makes: 4 servings

4 skinless, boneless

   chicken breast halves

1 medium lemon

3 tablespoons butter

½ teaspoon dried dill

¼ teaspoon salt

¼ teaspoon black pepper

1½ cups coarsely chopped

   cucumber or zucchini

1. Preheat broiler. Place chicken on the unheated rack of a broiler pan. Broil 4 to 5 inches from heat for 12 to 15 minutes or until no longer pink (170°F), turning once halfway through broiling.

2. Meanwhile, finely shred ½ teaspoon peel from the lemon. Cut lemon in half; squeeze lemon to make 2 tablespoons juice.

3. In a small skillet melt butter over medium heat. Stir in lemon peel, lemon juice, dill, salt, and pepper. Stir in cucumber. Cook and stir over medium heat for 3 minutes or just until cucumber is tender. Spoon sauce over chicken.

See photo, page 219.

2g carbs

0g fiber

2g net carbs

Nutrition Facts per serving: 244 cal., 11 g total fat (6 g sat. fat), 107 mg chol., 477 mg sodium, 2 g carbo., 0 g fiber, 33 g pro.

Garlic & Mint Chicken Breasts

Prep: 15 minutes Marinate: 4 hours Grill: 12 minutes Makes: 4 servings

1. In a blender container combine mint leaves, lemon juice, oil, soy sauce, chili powder, pepper, and garlic. Cover and blend until smooth.

2. Place chicken in a self-sealing plastic bag set in a shallow dish. Pour mint mixture over chicken; seal bag. Marinate in the refrigerator for 4 to 24 hours, turning bag occasionally.

3. For a charcoal grill, grill chicken on the rack of an uncovered grill directly over medium coals for 12 to 15 minutes or until no longer pink (170°F), turning once halfway through grilling. (For a gas grill, preheat grill. Reduce heat to medium. Place chicken on grill rack over heat. Cover and grill as above.)

½ cup fresh mint leaves

1 tablespoon lemon juice

1 tablespoon olive oil

1 tablespoon reduced-sodium
   soy sauce

1 teaspoon chili powder

¼ teaspoon black pepper

4 cloves garlic

4 skinless, boneless chicken
   breast halves

2 g carbs   **0** g fiber   **2** g net carbs

Nutrition Facts per serving: 202 cal., 6 g total fat (1 g sat. fat),
82 mg chol., 228 mg sodium, 2 g carbo., 0 g fiber, 34 g pro.

Baked Herbed Chicken

Prep: 20 minutes Bake: 25 minutes Oven: 375°F Makes: 4 servings

4 skinless, boneless

  chicken breast halves

  Salt and coarsely ground

  black pepper

½ of an 8-ounce package

  cream cheese, softened

¼ cup finely chopped red or

  green sweet pepper

½ teaspoon snipped fresh

  rosemary or tarragon or

  ¼ teaspoon dried rosemary

  or tarragon, crushed

1 tablespoon olive oil

1 tablespoon snipped

  fresh chives

1. Place each chicken breast half between two pieces of plastic wrap. Using the flat side of a meat mallet, pound lightly to about ⅛-inch thickness. Remove plastic wrap.

2. Season chicken with salt and pepper. Top each chicken piece with 2 tablespoons of the cream cheese and 1 tablespoon of the sweet pepper. Sprinkle with rosemary. Fold in the sides. Roll up, pressing the edges to seal. Secure the rolls with wooden toothpicks, if necessary.

3. Cook chicken rolls in hot oil in a large skillet over medium-high heat about 4 minutes or until lightly browned, turning to brown all sides. Remove to a 2-quart square baking dish. Sprinkle with additional pepper. Bake, uncovered, in a 375° oven for 25 to 30 minutes or until chicken is no longer pink (170°F).

4. Sprinkle with snipped chives.

See photo, page 220.

1 g carbs   0 g fiber   1 g net carbs

Nutrition Facts per serving: 292 cal., 15 g total fat (7 g sat. fat), 113 mg chol., 307 mg sodium, 1 g carbo., 0 g fiber, 35 g pro.

Zesty Barbecued Chicken

Prep: 10 minutes Marinate: 1 hour Grill: 12 minutes Makes: 4 servings

1. For marinade, in a screw-top jar combine oil, lime juice, water, onion, tarragon, salt, ginger, pepper sauce, garlic powder, and black pepper. Cover and shake well.

2. Place chicken in a self-sealing plastic bag set in a shallow dish. Pour marinade over chicken; close bag. Marinate in the refrigerator for 1 to 2 hours, turning bag occasionally.

3. Drain chicken, reserving marinade. For a charcoal grill, grill chicken on the rack of an uncovered grill directly over medium coals for 12 to 15 minutes or until chicken is no longer pink (170°F), turning once and brushing with marinade halfway through grilling. Discard marinade.

¼ cup cooking oil

¼ cup lime juice

¼ cup water

2 tablespoons finely chopped onion

2 teaspoons dried tarragon, crushed

¾ teaspoon salt

½ teaspoon ground ginger

½ teaspoon bottled hot pepper sauce

¼ teaspoon garlic powder

¼ teaspoon black pepper

4 skinless, boneless chicken breast halves

1 g carbs   **0** g fiber   **1** g net carbs

Nutrition Facts per serving: 225 cal., 9 g total fat (2 g sat. fat), 82 mg chol., 297 mg sodium, 1 g carbo., 0 g fiber, 33 g pro.

Chicken & Prosciutto Roll-Ups

Prep: 25 minutes Grill: 30 minutes Makes: 4 servings

2 tablespoons dry white wine

2 teaspoons snipped fresh
   thyme or ½ teaspoon dried
   thyme, crushed

4 skinless, boneless
   chicken breast halves
   Black pepper

4 thin slices prosciutto (about
   1 ounce total)

2 ounces Italian fontina cheese,
   thinly sliced

¼ of a 7-ounce jar roasted red
   sweet peppers, cut into thin
   strips (about ¼ cup)

1. For sauce, in a small bowl combine wine and thyme. Set aside.

2. Place each chicken piece between two pieces of plastic wrap. Using the flat side of a meat mallet, pound the chicken lightly into a rectangle about ⅛ inch thick. Remove plastic wrap. Season chicken with black pepper.

3. Place a slice of prosciutto and one-fourth of the cheese on each chicken piece. Arrange one-fourth of the roasted sweet pepper strips on cheese near bottom edge of each chicken piece. Starting from bottom edge, roll up each piece into a spiral; secure with wooden toothpicks. Brush with sauce.

4. For a charcoal grill, arrange medium-hot coals around a drip pan. Test for medium heat above pan. Place chicken on grill rack over drip pan. Cover and grill for 30 minutes or until chicken is no longer pink (170°F). (For a gas grill, preheat grill. Reduce heat to medium. Adjust grill for indirect cooking. Grill as above.)

1 g carbs   **0** g fiber   **1** g net carbs

Nutrition Facts per serving: 237 cal., 7 g total fat (3 g sat. fat), 103 mg chol., 382 mg sodium, 1 g carbo., 0 g fiber, 39 g pro.

Blue Cheese-Stuffed Chicken Breasts

Prep: 25 minutes Bake: 45 minutes Oven: 350°F Makes: 4 servings

1. Place each breast half between two pieces of plastic wrap. Using the flat side of a meat mallet, pound lightly to about ¼-inch thickness. Remove plastic wrap. Season chicken with salt and pepper.

2. In a small bowl combine cream cheese, blue cheese, and pecans. Place one-fourth of the cheese mixture on each chicken breast near one of the short ends. Fold in sides; roll up. Press edges to seal. Secure with wooden toothpicks.

3. Place chicken rolls in a 2-quart square baking dish. In a small bowl combine butter and paprika. Brush chicken rolls with mixture. Bake, uncovered, in a 350° oven for 45 to 50 minutes or until chicken is no longer pink (170°F). Remove toothpicks. If desired, sprinkle with parsley.

4   skinless, boneless

    chicken breast halves

    Salt and black pepper

1   3-ounce package cream

    cheese, softened

¼   cup crumbled blue cheese

    (1 ounce)

½   cup chopped pecans, toasted

2   tablespoons butter, melted

¼   teaspoon paprika

    Snipped fresh parsley (optional)

3g carbs **1**g fiber **2**g net carbs

Nutrition Facts per serving: 262 cal., 26 g total fat (10 g sat. fat), 51 mg chol., 375 mg sodium, 3 g carbo., 1 g fiber, 7 g pro.

243

Mustard-Broiled Chicken

Prep: 15 minutes Broil: 12 minutes Makes: 4 servings

4 skinless, boneless
chicken breast halves

⅓ cup mayonnaise

1 tablespoon Dijon-style
mustard

⅛ teaspoon cayenne pepper

1. Preheat broiler. Place chicken on the unheated rack of a broiler pan. Broil 4 to 5 inches from the heat for 8 minutes. Meanwhile, in a small bowl stir together mayonnaise, mustard, and cayenne pepper. Turn chicken; spoon mayonnaise mixture over chicken. Broil for 4 to 6 minutes more or until chicken is no longer pink (170°F).

1g
carbs

0g
fiber

1g
net carbs

Nutrition Facts per serving: 297 cal., 17 g total fat (3 g sat. fat),
95 mg chol., 279 mg sodium, 1 g carbo., 0 g fiber, 34 g pro.

Chicken Medallions with Creamy Tarragon-Mustard Sauce

Start to Finish: 25 minutes Makes: 4 servings

1. Place each chicken breast half between two pieces of plastic wrap. Using the flat side of a meat mallet, pound lightly to ¹/₂-inch thickness. Remove plastic wrap. Sprinkle chicken with salt and pepper.

2. In a 12-inch skillet cook chicken breasts, two at a time, in hot oil over medium-high heat for 2 to 3 minutes or until golden, turning once. Transfer chicken to a serving platter; keep warm.

3. For sauce, remove skillet from heat. Carefully add wine to hot skillet. Return to heat. Cook and stir to loosen any brown bits in bottom of skillet. Add crème fraîche, mustard, and parsley to skillet; stir with a wire whisk until combined. Spoon sauce over chicken.

See photo, page 221.

4 skinless, boneless
    chicken breast halves
    Salt and black pepper
2 tablespoons olive oil
¹/₄ cup dry white wine or
    chicken broth
2 tablespoons crème fraîche or
    dairy sour cream
2 tablespoons tarragon mustard
    or dill mustard
2 teaspoons snipped parsley

1 g carbs   **0** g fiber   **1** g net carbs

Nutrition Facts per serving: 255 cal., 11 g total fat (3 g sat. fat), 92 mg chol., 306 mg sodium, 1 g carbo., 0 g fiber, 33 g pro.

Chicken Alfredo

Prep: 25 minutes Bake: 15 minutes Oven: 350°F Makes: 6 servings

6 medium skinless, boneless
   chicken breast halves
   Salt and black pepper
1 tablespoon cooking oil
1 cup whipping cream
4 ounces Asiago or Parmesan
   cheese, finely shredded
   (1 cup)
⅓ cup drained roasted red
   sweet peppers, cut into
   thin strips
3 tablespoons finely shredded
   fresh basil

1. Sprinkle chicken with salt and pepper. In a 12-inch skillet brown chicken breasts in hot oil about 10 minutes, turning to brown evenly. Transfer chicken to a 3-quart rectangular baking dish; set aside.

2. For sauce, in a medium saucepan beat whipping cream with a wire whisk or rotary beater for 1 to 2 minutes or until thickened. Heat over medium heat just until simmering. Reduce heat to medium-low. Gradually whisk in cheese until melted.

3. Pour sauce over chicken breasts in dish; top with sweet peppers. Bake, uncovered, in a 350° oven for 15 to 20 minutes or until chicken is no longer pink (170°F). Sprinkle with basil.

See photo, page 222.

2g carbs   **0**g fiber   **2**g net carbs

Nutrition Facts per serving: 418 cal., 27 g total fat (15 g sat. fat), 162 mg chol., 353 mg sodium, 2 g carbo., 0 g fiber, 41 g pro.

Chicken Marsala

Start to Finish: 30 minutes Makes: 4 servings

1. Place each piece of chicken between two pieces of plastic wrap. Using the flat side of a meat mallet, pound lightly to about $1/4$-inch thickness. Remove plastic wrap.

2. Heat oil in a large skillet over medium heat. Add two chicken breast halves. Cook over medium heat for 3 to 4 minutes or until no longer pink, turning once. Transfer to a platter; keep warm. Repeat with remaining chicken breast halves.

3. Carefully add mushrooms, water, and salt to skillet. Cook and stir over medium heat about 3 minutes or until mushrooms are tender and most of the liquid has evaporated. Remove skillet from heat. Add Marsala to skillet. Return to heat. Bring to boiling; reduce heat. Boil gently, uncovered, for 1 minute. Spoon mushrooms and sauce over chicken. Sprinkle with sliced green onion.

4 skinless, boneless

   chicken breast halves

1 tablespoon olive oil

$1^{1}\!/_{2}$ cups sliced fresh mushrooms

2 tablespoons water

$1\!/_4$ teaspoon salt

$1\!/_4$ cup dry Marsala or dry sherry

2 tablespoons sliced green onion

2g carbs   **0**g fiber   **2**g net carbs

Nutrition Facts per serving: 190 cal., 6 g total fat (1 g sat. fat), 66 mg chol., 210 mg sodium, 2 g carbo., 0 g fiber, 28 g pro.

Chicken Salad with Olives & Peppers

Prep: 15 minutes Chill: 2 hours Makes: 4 servings

2 cups chopped cooked chicken

¼ cup chopped roasted red
   sweet peppers

¼ cup sliced pimiento-stuffed
   green olives

½ of an 8-ounce tub cream
   cheese with chives and
   onion

   Black pepper

1. In a medium bowl combine chicken, sweet peppers, and olives. Add cream cheese, stirring until combined. Season to taste with black pepper. Cover and chill for 2 to 24 hours.

4g carbs   **1**g fiber   **3**g net carbs

Nutrition Facts per serving: 229 cal., 16 g total fat (7 g sat. fat),
61 mg chol., 501 mg sodium, 4 g carbo., 1 g fiber, 17 g pro.

Rotisserie Chicken Greek Salad

Start to Finish: 20 minutes Makes: 4 servings

1. Remove chicken meat from the bones; discard bones. Cut chicken into bite-size pieces. Place chicken in a medium bowl; set aside. In a small bowl whisk together oil, vinegar, garlic, salt, and pepper. Drizzle chicken with 2 tablespoons of the oil mixture; toss to combine. Meanwhile, in a large bowl toss romaine, mint, and oregano with remaining oil mixture. Arrange on a large serving platter.

2. Arrange chicken in center of the greens. Sprinkle salad with cheese and olives.

1 2- to 2½-pound purchased
   roasted chicken, whole or cut up

¼ cup olive oil

¼ cup red wine vinegar

1 clove garlic, minced

¼ teaspoon salt

⅛ teaspoon black pepper

6 cups torn romaine lettuce

⅓ cup small fresh mint leaves,
   lightly packed

⅓ cup small fresh oregano
   leaves, lightly packed

⅓ cup crumbled feta cheese

¼ cup kalamata olives, pitted
   and halved

5 g carbs   **2** g fiber   **3** g net carbs

Nutrition Facts per serving: 549 cal., 38 g total fat (9 g sat. fat), 145 mg chol., 508 mg sodium, 5 g carbo., 2 g fiber, 45 g pro.

Smoked Chicken

Prep: 20 minutes Chill: 1 hour Soak: 1 hour Grill: 1¼ hours
Stand: 10 minutes Makes: 8 servings

2 3-pound whole roasting chickens

1 teaspoon salt

1 teaspoon onion salt

1 teaspoon garlic salt

1 teaspoon seasoned salt

1 teaspoon paprika

1 teaspoon black pepper

¼ teaspoon cayenne pepper (optional)

4 cups hickory or mesquite wood chips

1. Rinse inside of chickens; pat dry with paper towels. In a small bowl, stir together salt, onion salt, garlic salt, seasoned salt, paprika, black pepper and if desired, cayenne pepper. Rub mixture all over chickens. Cover and refrigerate for 1 hour. Soak wood chips for 1 hour in enough water to cover; drain.

2. Twist wing tips under chicken backs. Secure legs.

3. For a charcoal grill, arrange medium-hot coals around a drip pan. Test for medium heat above pan. Sprinkle half of the drained wood chips over the coals. Place chickens, breast sides up, on grill rack over drip pan. Cover and grill for 1¼ to 1½ hours or until an instant-read thermometer inserted into center of inside thigh muscle, not touching bone, registers 180°F. Add remaining drained wood chips halfway through grilling. (For a gas grill, preheat grill. Reduce heat to medium. Adjust for indirect grilling. Add chips according to manufacturer's directions. Grill as above.)

4. Remove chickens from grill. Cover with foil and let stand for 10 minutes before carving.

0 g carbs   0 g fiber   0 g net carbs

Nutrition Facts per serving: 323 cal., 18 g total fat (5 g sat. fat), 118 mg chol., 911 mg sodium, 0 g carbo., 0 g fiber, 37 g pro.

Garlic-Grilled Whole Chicken

Prep: 25 minutes Grill: 1 hour Stand: 10 minutes Makes: 5 servings

1. Rinse inside of chicken; pat dry with paper towels. Twist wing tips under the back. Cut one of the garlic cloves lengthwise in half. Rub skin of chicken with cut edge of garlic. Place garlic halves, lemon slices, and sweet pepper slices in cavity of chicken. Mince remaining two cloves of garlic. Combine minced garlic, basil, and salt; set aside. Starting at the neck on one side of the breast, slip your fingers between skin and meat, loosening the skin as you work toward the tail end. Once your entire hand is under the skin, free the skin around the thigh and leg area up to, but not around, the tip of the drumstick. Repeat on the other side of the breast. Rub garlic mixture over entire surface under skin. Securely fasten opening with water-soaked wooden toothpicks. Stir together oil and lemon juice; brush over chicken.

2. For a charcoal grill, arrange medium-hot coals around a drip pan. Test for medium heat above pan. Place chicken, breast side up, on grill rack over drip pan. Cover and grill for 1 to 1¼ hours or until chicken is no longer pink and the drumsticks move easily in their sockets (180°F), brushing occasionally with oil-lemon mixture. (For a gas grill, preheat grill. Reduce heat to medium. Adjust for indirect cooking. Grill as above.)

3. Remove chicken from grill. Cover with foil and let stand for 10 minutes before carving.

1 2½- to 3-pound whole broiler-fryer chicken

3 cloves garlic, peeled

½ lemon, sliced

½ of a medium red sweet pepper, sliced

1 tablespoon snipped fresh basil or

   1 teaspoon dried basil, crushed

⅛ teaspoon salt

1 tablespoon olive oil or cooking oil

1 tablespoon lemon juice

2 g carbs **0** g fiber **2** g net carbs

Nutrition Facts per serving: 245 cal., 15 g total fat (4 g sat. fat), 79 mg chol., 127 mg sodium, 2 g carbo., 0 g fiber, 25 g pro.

Chicken in Saffron-Cream Sauce

Prep: 20 minutes Cook: 45 minutes Makes: 6 servings

2½ to 3 pounds meaty chicken
    pieces (breast halves,
    thighs, and drumsticks)

¼ teaspoon salt

¼ teaspoon black pepper

3 tablespoons butter

1 cup whipping cream

2 teaspoons tomato paste

¼ teaspoon dried thyme,
    crushed

1 bay leaf

Dash thread saffron

1. Sprinkle chicken pieces with salt and pepper. In a large skillet cook chicken in hot butter about 5 minutes per side or until browned. Drain off fat.

2. Meanwhile, in a small bowl stir together whipping cream, tomato paste, thyme, bay leaf, and saffron.

3. Pour cream mixture over chicken in skillet. Bring to boiling; reduce heat. Cover and simmer for 30 to 35 minutes or until chicken is no longer pink (170°F for breasts, 180°F for thighs and drumsticks). Remove chicken from skillet; keep warm. Boil sauce gently about 5 minutes or until desired consistency. Discard bay leaf. Arrange chicken on a serving platter; spoon sauce over chicken.

2g carbs   **0**g fiber   **2**g net carbs

Nutrition Facts per serving: 379 cal., 28 g total fat (14 g sat. fat), 146 mg chol., 207 mg sodium, 2 g carbo., 0 g fiber, 28 g pro.

Spicy Oven-Baked Chicken

Prep: 25 minutes Chill: 2 hours Bake: 40 minutes Oven: 400°F Makes: 4 servings

1. In a small bowl combine lemon juice, 1½ teaspoons of the turmeric, paprika, garlic, salt, garam masala, allspice, and cayenne pepper.

2. Loosen chicken skin slightly and rub spice mixture under skin. Place thighs and drumsticks, skin sides up, in a shallow roasting pan. Combine remaining turmeric and oil; brush onto chicken. Cover and chill for 2 to 4 hours.

3. Bake, uncovered, in a 400° oven for 40 to 45 minutes or until chicken is no longer pink (180°F).

2 tablespoons lemon juice

2 teaspoons ground turmeric

1½ teaspoons paprika

1 clove garlic, minced

½ teaspoon salt

½ teaspoon garam masala

¼ teaspoon ground allspice

¼ teaspoon cayenne pepper

4 chicken thighs

4 chicken drumsticks

2 teaspoons cooking oil

2 g carbs   **0** g fiber   **2** g net carbs

Nutrition Facts per serving: 367 cal., 23 g total fat (6 g sat. fat), 151 mg chol., 410 mg sodium, 2 g carbo., 0 g fiber, 34 g pro.

Herbed Mustard Chicken

Prep: 15 minutes Grill: 50 minutes Makes: 4 servings

1 tablespoon snipped
   fresh parsley

1 tablespoon water

1 tablespoon mayonnaise

1 tablespoon Dijon-style
   mustard

1 teaspoon dried oregano,
   crushed

⅛ teaspoon cayenne pepper

2½ to 3 pounds meaty chicken
   pieces (breast halves,
   thighs, and drumsticks)

Salt and black pepper

1. For sauce, in a small bowl combine parsley, water, mayonnaise, mustard, oregano, and cayenne pepper. Cover and refrigerate until ready to use. If desired, skin chicken. Sprinkle chicken with salt and pepper.

2. For a charcoal grill, arrange medium-hot coals around a drip pan. Test for medium heat above pan. Place chicken, bone side down, on grill rack over drip pan. Cover and grill for 50 to 60 minutes or until chicken is no longer pink (170°F for breasts, 180°F for thighs and drumsticks), brushing occasionally with sauce the last 10 minutes of grilling. (For a gas grill, preheat grill. Reduce heat to medium. Adjust for indirect grilling. Grill as above.)

See photo, page 223.

1 g carbs   **0** g fiber   **1** g net carbs

Nutrition Facts per serving: 352 cal., 19 g total fat (5 g sat. fat),
132 mg chol., 261 mg sodium, 1 g carbo., 0 g fiber, 43 g pro.

Chipotle-Rubbed Baked Chicken

Prep: 20 minutes Bake: 45 minutes Oven: 375°F Makes: 6 servings

1. If desired, skin chicken. Place chicken pieces, bone sides down, in a lightly greased 15×10×1-inch baking pan.

2. In a small bowl combine butter, chile powder, salt, and pepper; brush onto chicken pieces.

3. Bake in a 375° oven for 45 to 55 minutes or until chicken is no longer pink (170°F for breasts, 180°F for thighs and drumsticks). Sprinkle green onions over chicken pieces.

2½ to 3 pounds meaty chicken pieces (breast halves, thighs, and drumsticks)

2 tablespoons butter, melted

1 to 1½ teaspoons chipotle chile powder

Dash salt

Dash black pepper

¼ cup sliced green onions

1 g carbs   0 g fiber   1 g net carbs

Nutrition Facts per serving: 252 cal., 15 g total fat (5 g sat. fat), 97 mg chol., 133 mg sodium, 1 g carbo., 0 g fiber, 28 g pro.

Pecan Chicken

Prep: 30 minutes Roast: 1¼ hours Stand: 10 minutes
Oven: 375°F Makes: 4 servings

1 3- to 3½-pound whole
   broiler-fryer chicken

6 cloves garlic, thinly sliced

⅔ cup finely chopped pecans

¼ cup butter, melted

1 tablespoon snipped fresh
   thyme or 1 teaspoon dried
   thyme, crushed

½ teaspoon black pepper

¼ teaspoon salt

1. Rinse inside of chicken; pat dry with paper towels. Skewer neck skin of chicken to back; tie legs to tail. Twist wing tips under back. Using a small, sharp knife, make numerous slits about 1 inch wide and ½ inch deep in the breast portions of the chicken. Stuff garlic into slits.

2. In a small bowl combine pecans, butter, thyme, pepper, and salt. Pat mixture onto top of chicken.

3. Place chicken, breast side up, on a rack in a shallow roasting pan. If desired, insert a meat thermometer into center of an inside thigh muscle, not touching bone.

4. Roast, uncovered, in a 375° oven for 1¼ to 1½ hours or until drumsticks move easily in their sockets and chicken is no longer pink (180°F). If necessary, cover chicken loosely with foil for the last 15 minutes of roasting to prevent pecans from overbrowning. Remove chicken from oven. Cover with foil. Let stand for 10 minutes before serving.

4g carbs   **2**g fiber   **2**g net carbs

Nutrition Facts per serving: 725 cal., 59 g total fat (18 g sat. fat), 205 mg chol., 400 mg sodium, 4 g carbo., 2 g fiber, 45 g pro.

Three-Pepper Chicken

Prep: 20 minutes Bake: 45 minutes Oven: 375°F Makes: 6 servings

1. If desired, skin chicken. Place chicken pieces, bone sides up, in a lightly greased 15×10×1-inch baking pan. Bake in a 375° oven for 25 minutes.

2. Meanwhile, in a small bowl stir together butter, chile pepper, salt, black pepper, cayenne pepper, and garlic. Brush some of the pepper mixture onto chicken. Turn chicken bone sides down; brush with remaining pepper mixture. Bake for 20 to 30 minutes more or until chicken is no longer pink (170°F for breasts, 180°F for thighs and drumsticks).

2½ to 3 pounds meaty chicken
   pieces (breast halves, thighs,
   and drumsticks)

3 tablespoons butter, melted

1 fresh jalapeño chile pepper,
   seeded and finely chopped
   (see note, page 51)

¼ teaspoon salt

¼ teaspoon black pepper

¼ teaspoon cayenne pepper

4 cloves garlic, minced

1g carbs **0**g fiber **1**g net carbs

Nutrition Facts per serving: 272 cal., 17 g total fat (7 g sat. fat),
103 mg chol., 235 mg sodium, 1 g carbo., 0 g fiber, 28 g pro.

Lemon-Mustard Chicken

Prep: 10 minutes Broil: 25 minutes Makes: 6 servings

2 to 2½ pounds meaty chicken pieces (breast halves, thighs, and drumsticks)

2 tablespoons cooking oil

1 tablespoon Dijon-style mustard

1 tablespoon lemon juice

1½ teaspoons lemon-pepper seasoning

1 teaspoon dried oregano or basil, crushed

⅛ teaspoon cayenne pepper

1. If desired, skin chicken. Preheat broiler. Place chicken pieces, bone side up, on the unheated rack of a broiler pan. Broil 4 to 5 inches from the heat about 20 minutes or until lightly browned.

2. Meanwhile, for glaze, in a bowl stir together oil, mustard, lemon juice, lemon-pepper seasoning, oregano, and cayenne pepper. Brush chicken with glaze. Turn chicken; brush with remaining glaze. Broil for 5 to 15 minutes more or until chicken is no longer pink (170°F for breasts, 180°F for thighs and drumsticks).

1 g carbs   0 g fiber   1 g net carbs

Nutrition Facts per serving: 174 cal., 10 g total fat (2 g sat. fat), 61 mg chol., 390 mg sodium, 1 g carbo., 0 g fiber, 20 g pro.

Pepper-Lime Chicken

Prep: 10 minutes Broil: 25 minutes Makes: 6 servings

1. If desired, skin chicken. Preheat broiler. Place chicken pieces, bone side up, on the unheated rack of a broiler pan. Broil 4 to 5 inches from the heat about 20 minutes or until lightly browned.

2. Meanwhile, for glaze, in a bowl stir together lime peel, lime juice, oil, garlic, thyme, pepper, and salt. Brush chicken with glaze. Turn chicken; brush with more glaze. Broil for 5 to 15 minutes more or until chicken is no longer pink, (170°F for breasts, 180°F for thighs and drumsticks), brushing with glaze during the last 5 minutes of cooking.

2 to 2½ pounds meaty chicken pieces (breast halves, thighs, and drumsticks)

½ teaspoon finely shredded lime peel

¼ cup lime juice

1 tablespoon cooking oil

2 cloves garlic, minced

1 teaspoon dried thyme

½ to 1 teaspoon cracked black pepper

¼ teaspoon salt

1 g carbs   **0** g fiber   **1** g net carbs

Nutrition Facts per serving: 153 cal., 7 g total fat (2 g sat. fat), 61 mg chol., 145 mg sodium, 1 g carbo., 0 g fiber, 20 g pro.

Greek Chicken Thighs

Prep: 20 minutes Marinate: 4 hours Grill: 50 minutes
Stand: 2 minutes Makes: 4 servings

8 chicken thighs

¼ cup dry red wine

2 tablespoons olive oil

1 teaspoon finely shredded
   lemon peel

1 teaspoon snipped
   fresh rosemary

1 teaspoon snipped
   fresh oregano

1 clove garlic, minced

¼ teaspoon salt

¼ teaspoon black pepper

½ cup crumbled feta cheese

1. If desired, skin chicken. Place chicken in a self-sealing plastic bag set in a shallow dish. For marinade, in a small bowl combine wine, oil, lemon peel, rosemary, oregano, garlic, salt, and pepper. Pour over chicken; seal bag. Marinate in the refrigerator for 4 to 24 hours, turning bag occasionally. Drain chicken, discarding marinade.

2. For a charcoal grill, arrange medium-hot coals around a drip pan. Test for medium heat above pan. Place chicken thighs, bone sides down, on grill rack over drip pan. Cover and grill for 50 to 60 minutes or until chicken is no longer pink (180°F). (For a gas grill, preheat grill. Reduce heat to medium. Adjust for indirect cooking. Grill as above.) Transfer chicken to a serving platter.

3. Sprinkle chicken with feta cheese. Cover loosely with foil and let stand for 2 minutes before serving.

1 g carbs   0 g fiber   1 g net carbs

Nutrition Facts per serving: 540 cal., 40 g total fat (12 g sat. fat),
199 mg chol., 393 mg sodium, 1 g carbo., 0 g fiber, 41 g pro.

Lemon & Garlic Grilled Chicken

Prep: 30 minutes Grill: 1 hour Stand: 10 minutes Makes: 6 servings

1. Cut one of the lemons into thin slices; set aside. Finely shred 1 teaspoon lemon peel from the other lemon; set peel aside. Squeeze juice from the lemon; measure juice. If necessary, add enough water to equal 3 tablespoons. Set aside 1 tablespoon juice.

2. Stir together lemon peel, remaining 2 tablespoons lemon juice, 3 tablespoons melted butter, rosemary, salt, and pepper.

3. Rinse inside of chicken; pat dry with paper towels. Place lemon slices and garlic in chicken cavity. Twist wing tips under the back. Brush chicken with lemon mixture.

4. For a charcoal grill, arrange medium-hot coals around a drip pan. Test for medium heat above pan. Place chicken, breast side up, on grill rack above drip pan. Cover and grill for 1 to 1¼ hours or until chicken is no longer pink and drumsticks move easily in their sockets (180°F). (For a gas grill, preheat grill. Reduce heat to medium. Adjust for indirect grilling. Grill as above except place chicken on a rack in a roasting pan.) Remove chicken from grill. Cover with foil and let stand for 10 minutes before carving.

5. Meanwhile, for sauce, in a small saucepan combine reserved lemon juice and chicken broth. Bring to boiling; reduce heat. Boil gently, uncovered, for 5 minutes. Stir in 1 tablespoon butter. Serve with chicken.

2 lemons

3 tablespoons butter, melted

1 tablespoon snipped fresh
    rosemary or 1 teaspoon dried
    rosemary, crushed

¼ teaspoon salt

⅛ teaspoon black pepper

1 2½- to 3-pound whole
    broiler-fryer chicken

4 cloves garlic, halved

½ cup chicken broth

1 tablespoon butter

2 g carbs **0** g fiber **2** g net carbs

Nutrition Facts per serving: 348 cal., 27 g total fat (9 g sat. fat), 117 mg chol., 309 mg sodium, 2 g carbo., 0 g fiber, 24 g pro.

Mustard-Marinated Chicken

Prep: 25 minutes Marinate: 2 hours Grill: 50 minutes Makes: 4 servings

2 to 2½ pounds meaty chicken pieces (breast halves, thighs, and drumsticks)

⅓ cup prepared mustard

⅓ cup Dijon-style mustard

3 tablespoons white wine vinegar or rice vinegar

2 tablespoons olive oil or cooking oil

⅛ teaspoon cayenne pepper

1. If desired, skin chicken. Place chicken in a self-sealing plastic bag set in a shallow dish. For marinade, in a small bowl combine prepared mustard, Dijon-style mustard, vinegar, oil, and cayenne pepper. Pour over chicken; seal bag. Marinate in the refrigerator for 2 to 4 hours, turning bag occasionally. Drain chicken, discarding marinade.

2. For a charcoal grill, arrange medium-hot coals around a drip pan. Test for medium heat above pan. Place chicken, bone side down, on grill rack over drip pan. Cover and grill for 50 to 60 minutes or until chicken is no longer pink (170°F for breasts, 180°F for thighs and drumsticks). (For a gas grill, preheat grill. Reduce heat to medium. Adjust for indirect cooking. Grill as above.)

3g carbs   **0**g fiber   **3**g net carbs

Nutrition Facts per serving: 306 cal., 16 g total fat (4 g sat. fat), 104 mg chol., 461 mg sodium, 3 g carbo., 0 g fiber, 36 g pro.

Roasted Italian Chicken

Prep: 15 minutes Roast: 1¼ hours Stand: 10 minutes
Oven: 375°F Makes: 6 servings

1. In a small bowl whisk together vinegar, oil, lemon juice, garlic, salt, pepper, oregano, basil, and thyme. Set aside.

2. Rinse inside of chicken; pat dry with paper towels. Place chicken, breast side up, on a rack in a shallow roasting pan. Tie legs to tail. Twist wing tips under back. Slip your fingers between the skin and the breast and leg meat of the chicken, forming a pocket. Spoon herb mixture into pocket.

3. Roast, uncovered, in a 375° oven for 1¼ to 1½ hours or until drumsticks move easily in their sockets and chicken is no longer pink (180°F). Remove chicken from oven. Cover with foil and let stand for 10 minutes before carving.

2 tablespoons balsamic vinegar

2 tablespoons olive oil

1 tablespoon lemon juice

3 cloves garlic, minced

½ teaspoon salt

½ teaspoon coarsely ground black pepper

1 tablespoon snipped fresh oregano or

    1 teaspoon dried oregano, crushed

1 tablespoon snipped fresh basil or

    1 teaspoon dried basil, crushed

1½ teaspoons snipped fresh thyme or

    ½ teaspoon thyme, crushed

1 3- to 3½-pound whole broiler-fryer chicken

2 g carbs   **0** g fiber   **2** g net carbs

Nutrition Facts per serving: 266 cal., 17 g total fat (4 g sat. fat), 79 mg chol., 268 mg sodium, 2 g carbo., 0 g fiber, 25 g pro.

Chicken with Wine Sauce

Prep: 15 minutes Cook: 30 minutes Makes: 4 servings

4 chicken breast halves

1 cup sliced fresh mushrooms

1 shallot, chopped

1 teaspoon dried basil, crushed

1 clove garlic, minced

1 tablespoon olive oil

⅓ cup chicken broth

⅓ cup dry white wine

¼ teaspoon salt

¼ teaspoon black pepper

1. Skin chicken; set chicken aside.

2. In a large skillet cook mushrooms, shallot, basil, and garlic in hot oil over medium heat until shallot is tender.

3. Stir in chicken broth, wine, salt, and pepper. Arrange chicken in skillet. Bring to boiling; reduce heat. Cover and cook over low heat about 30 minutes or until chicken is no longer pink (170°F). Transfer chicken and vegetables to a serving platter. Serve pan juices over chicken.

3g carbs   **0**g fiber   **3**g net carbs

Nutrition Facts per serving: 359 cal., 19 g total fat (5 g sat. fat), 115 mg chol., 321 mg sodium, 3 g carbo., 0 g fiber, 39 g pro.

Herb-Roasted Chicken

Prep: 15 minutes Roast: 1 hour Stand: 10 minutes Oven: 375°F Makes: 6 servings

1. Rinse inside of chicken; pat dry with paper towels. Skewer neck skin of chicken to back; tie legs to tail. Twist wings under back. Place chicken, breast side up, on a rack in a shallow roasting pan. Brush with melted butter; rub garlic over bird.

2. In a small bowl stir together basil, salt, sage, thyme, and pepper; rub onto bird. If desired, insert a meat thermometer into center of an inside thigh muscle not touching bone. Roast, uncovered, in a 375° oven for 1 to 1¼ hours or until drumsticks move easily in their sockets and chicken is no longer pink (180°F). Remove chicken from oven. Cover with foil, and let stand 10 minutes before carving.

1 2½- to 3-pound whole broiler-
   fryer chicken

2 tablespoons butter, melted

2 cloves garlic, minced

1 teaspoon dried basil, crushed

½ teaspoon salt

½ teaspoon ground sage

½ teaspoon dried thyme, crushed

¼ teaspoon black pepper

1g carbs   **0**g fiber   **1**g net carbs

Nutrition Facts per serving: 210 cal., 14 g total fat (3 g sat. fat), 79 mg chol., 326 mg sodium, 1 g carbo., 0 g fiber, 20 g pro.

Curried Barbecued Chicken

Prep: 15 minutes Marinate: 4 hours Grill: 50 minutes Makes: 4 to 6 servings

2½ to 3 pounds meaty chicken
    pieces (breast halves,
    thighs, and drumsticks)

2 teaspoons finely shredded
  lime peel

⅓ cup lime juice

1 tablespoon curry powder

1 tablespoon cooking oil

2 cloves garlic, minced

½ teaspoon salt

¼ teaspoon ground cumin

¼ teaspoon ground coriander

⅛ teaspoon cayenne pepper

1. Place chicken in a self-sealing plastic bag set in a shallow dish. For marinade, stir together lime peel, lime juice, curry powder, oil, garlic, salt, cumin, coriander, and cayenne pepper. Pour over chicken; seal bag. Marinate in the refrigerator 4 to 24 hours, turning bag occasionally. Drain chicken, reserving marinade.

2. For a charcoal grill, arrange medium-hot coals around a drip pan. Test for medium heat above the pan. Place chicken pieces, bone side down, on grill rack over drip pan. Cover and grill for 50 to 60 minutes or until chicken is no longer pink (170°F for breasts, 180°F for thighs and drumsticks), brushing with some of the marinade during the first 40 minutes of grilling. Discard remaining marinade. (For a gas grill, preheat grill. Reduce heat to medium. Adjust for indirect cooking. Grill as above.)

4 g carbs

1 g fiber

3 g net carbs

Nutrition Facts per serving: 366 cal., 20 g total fat (6 g sat. fat),
130 mg chol., 382 mg sodium, 4 g carbo., 1 g fiber, 42 g pro.

Spicy Barbecued Chicken

Prep: 20 minutes Cook: 5 minutes Grill: 35 minutes Makes: 4 servings

1. For sauce, in a small saucepan combine vinegar, mustard, Worcestershire sauce, paprika, black pepper, hot pepper sauce, celery seeds, and salt. Bring to boiling; reduce heat. Simmer, uncovered, for 5 minutes, stirring occasionally.

2. If desired, skin chicken. Sprinkle chicken with salt and black pepper. Brush chicken pieces with sauce. For a charcoal grill, grill chicken pieces, bone sides up, on an uncovered grill directly over medium coals for 35 to 45 minutes or until no longer pink (170°F for breasts, 180°F for thighs and drumsticks), turning and brushing with remaining sauce halfway through grilling. (For a gas grill, preheat grill. Reduce heat to medium. Place chicken on grill rack over heat. Cover and grill as above.)

½ cup cider vinegar

2 tablespoons spicy
  brown mustard

1 tablespoon Worcestershire
  sauce or Worcestershire
  sauce for chicken

1 teaspoon paprika

½ teaspoon black pepper

¼ teaspoon bottled
  hot pepper sauce

⅛ teaspoon celery seeds

⅛ teaspoon salt

2 pounds meaty chicken pieces
  (breast halves, thighs, and
  drumsticks), skinned

Salt and black pepper

4_g carbs 0_g fiber 4_g net carbs

Nutrition Facts per serving: 211 cal., 8 g total fat (2 g sat. fat), 92 mg chol., 469 mg sodium, 4 g carbo., 0 g fiber, 30 g pro.

Mediterranean Marinated Chicken Thighs

Prep: 20 minutes Marinate: 4 hours Grill: 15 minutes Makes: 6 servings

12 skinless, boneless
    chicken thighs

1/3 cup dry red wine

3 tablespoons olive oil

1 tablespoon snipped fresh
    oregano or 1 teaspoon
    dried oregano, crushed

2 teaspoons snipped fresh
    rosemary or 1 teaspoon
    dried rosemary, crushed

1 teaspoon finely
    shredded lemon peel

2 cloves garlic, minced

1/2 teaspoon salt

1/4 teaspoon black pepper

1 medium cucumber,
    seeded and chopped

2 medium tomatoes,
    seeded and finely
    chopped

1 tablespoon white
    balsamic vinegar

1/4 teaspoon salt

1/8 teaspoon black pepper

1. Place chicken in a self-sealing plastic bag set in a shallow dish. For marinade, in a small bowl stir together wine, 2 tablespoons of the oil, 1 1/2 teaspoons of the fresh oregano or 1/2 teaspoon of the dried oregano, rosemary, lemon peel, garlic, 1/2 teaspoon salt, and 1/4 teaspoon pepper. Pour marinade over chicken; seal bag. Marinate in the refrigerator for 4 to 24 hours, turning bag occasionally.

2. For relish, in a medium bowl stir together cucumber, tomatoes, remaining 1 tablespoon oil, vinegar, remaining oregano, 1/4 teaspoon salt, and 1/8 teaspoon pepper. Cover and chill for up to 4 hours. Drain chicken, discarding marinade.

3. For a charcoal grill, grill chicken on the rack of an uncovered grill directly over medium coals for 15 to 18 minutes or until no longer pink (180°F). (For a gas grill, preheat grill. Reduce heat to medium. Place chicken on grill rack over heat. Cover and grill as above.) Serve chicken with relish.

4g carbs   **1**g fiber   **3**g net carbs

Nutrition Facts per serving: 269 cal., 10 g total fat (2 g sat. fat),
151 mg chol., 279 mg sodium, 4 g carbo., 1 g fiber, 39 g pro.

Chicken Drumsticks Extraordinaire

Prep: 15 minutes Grill: 50 minutes Makes: 4 servings

1. In a blender container or small food processor bowl combine basil, pecans, oil, garlic, salt, and pepper. Cover and blend or process until pureed, scraping down sides as needed. Divide basil mixture in half; cover and chill half of the mixture.

2. If desired, skin chicken. Brush chicken with unchilled basil mixture; discard remainder of the basil mixture used as brush-on. For a charcoal grill, arrange medium-hot coals around a drip pan. Test for medium heat above pan. Place chicken on grill rack over drip pan. Cover and grill for 50 to 60 minutes or until chicken is no longer pink (180°F), turning once halfway through grilling and brushing with the chilled basil mixture during the last 5 minutes of grilling. (For a gas grill, preheat grill. Reduce heat to medium. Adjust for indirect cooking. Grill as above.)

1 cup lightly packed fresh
    basil leaves

½ cup broken pecans

¼ cup olive oil

2 cloves garlic, minced

¼ teaspoon salt

¼ teaspoon black pepper

8 meaty chicken drumsticks

3g carbs   **2**g fiber   **1**g net carbs

Nutrition Facts per serving: 451 cal., 36 g total fat (6 g sat. fat),
118 mg chol., 243 mg sodium, 3 g carbo., 2 g fiber, 30 g pro.

Buffalo Chicken Thighs

Prep: 20 minutes Broil: 25 minutes Makes: 6 servings

12 chicken thighs

2 tablespoons butter, melted

2 tablespoons bottled

hot pepper sauce

2 teaspoons paprika

¼ teaspoon salt

¼ teaspoon cayenne pepper

1 recipe Blue Cheese Dip

1. If desired, skin chicken. In a small bowl stir together butter, hot pepper sauce, paprika, salt, and cayenne pepper. Brush over both sides of chicken thighs.

2. Preheat broiler. Arrange chicken on the unheated rack of a broiler pan. Broil 4 to 5 inches from the heat for 12 minutes. Turn chicken. Broil for 13 to 15 minutes more or until chicken is no longer pink (180°F). Serve with Blue Cheese Dip.

Blue Cheese Dip: In a blender container or food processor bowl combine ½ cup dairy sour cream; ½ cup mayonnaise; ½ cup crumbled blue cheese; 1 tablespoon white wine vinegar; and 1 clove garlic, minced. Cover and blend or process until smooth. Cover and chill for up to 1 week. If desired, top with additional crumbled blue cheese before serving.

2g carbs   **0**g fiber   **2**g net carbs

Nutrition Facts per serving: 639 cal., 54 g total fat (16 g sat. fat), 196 mg chol., 555 mg sodium, 2 g carbo., 0 g fiber, 35 g pro.

Asian Chicken Wings

Prep: 25 minutes Cook: 25 minutes Makes: 6 servings

1. Cut off and discard tips of chicken wings. If desired, cut wings at joints.

2. For sauce, in a 4-quart Dutch oven combine water, soy sauce, ginger, leek, vinegar, chile peppers, five-spice powder, and garlic. Bring to boiling. Add chicken wings. Return to boiling; reduce heat. Simmer, covered, for about 25 minutes or until chicken is no longer pink.

3. Remove chicken wings with a slotted spoon; discard cooking liquid, ginger, leek, and chile peppers. Serve wings hot.

3 **pounds chicken wings**

1½ **cups water**

⅔ **cup soy sauce**

4 **slices fresh ginger**

1 **leek, cut up**

1 **tablespoon vinegar**

2 or 3 **dried red chile peppers**

(see note, page 51)

½ **teaspoon five-spice powder**

2 **cloves garlic, minced**

0_g carbs 0_g fiber 0_g net carbs

Nutrition Facts per serving: 272 cal., 19 g total fat (5 g sat. fat), 94 mg chol., 396 mg sodium, 0 g carbo., 0 g fiber, 23 g pro.

Green Curry Chicken

Prep: 30 minutes Cook: 50 minutes Makes: 4 servings

2½ pounds meaty chicken
     pieces (breast halves,
     thighs, and drumsticks)
Salt and black pepper
2 tablespoons cooking oil
½ cup reduced-sodium
     chicken broth
1 to 2 tablespoons green
     curry paste
2 tablespoons soy sauce
½ cup whipping cream
¼ cup shredded fresh
     basil leaves

1. If desired, skin chicken. Sprinkle chicken with salt and pepper. In a large skillet cook chicken, half at a time if necessary, in hot oil over medium heat for 5 to 7 minutes or until browned, turning to brown evenly. Return all chicken to skillet.

2. In a small bowl stir together broth, curry paste, and soy sauce. Pour over chicken. Bring to boiling; reduce heat. Simmer, covered, for 45 to 50 minutes or until chicken is no longer pink (170°F for breasts, 180°F for thighs and drumsticks). Remove chicken to a serving platter; cover to keep warm.

3. Transfer liquid from skillet to a 1-cup glass measure. Skim fat from liquid; discard fat. Return remaining liquid to skillet. Stir in whipping cream. Bring to boiling; reduce heat. Boil gently, uncovered, for 3 to 5 minutes or until thickened, stirring frequently. Spoon sauce over chicken; sprinkle with fresh basil.

2g carbs   **0**g fiber   **2**g net carbs

Nutrition Facts per serving: 432 cal., 29 g total fat (11 g sat. fat), 156 mg chol., 933 mg sodium, 2 g carbo., 0 g fiber, 39 g pro.

Italian Baked Chicken Breasts

Prep: 20 minutes Marinate: 2 hours Bake: 45 minutes
Broil: 4 minutes Oven: 375°F Makes: 4 servings

1. Skin chicken, if desired. Place chicken in a self-sealing plastic bag set in a shallow bowl. For marinade, in a small bowl combine wine, oil, vinegar, water, lemon juice, Italian seasoning, garlic, $\frac{1}{4}$ teaspoon salt, and $\frac{1}{4}$ teaspoon black pepper. Pour over chicken; seal bag. Marinate in the refrigerator for 2 to 6 hours, turning bag occasionally.

2. Drain chicken, discarding marinade. Sprinkle with additional salt and pepper. Arrange chicken in a shallow baking pan. Bake, uncovered, in a 375° oven for 45 to 55 minutes or until chicken is tender and no longer pink (170°F). Sprinkle with cheese. Broil 4 to 5 inches from heat for 4 minutes or until cheese is melted and beginning to brown.

4 chicken breast halves

½ cup dry white wine

¼ cup olive oil

2 tablespoons white
wine vinegar

2 tablespoons water

1 tablespoon lemon juice

1 tablespoon dried Italian
seasoning, crushed

3 cloves garlic, minced

¼ teaspoon salt

¼ teaspoon black pepper

Salt and black pepper

⅓ cup finely shredded
Parmesan cheese

2_g carbs 0_g fiber 2_g net carbs

Nutrition Facts per serving: 688 cal., 41 g total fat (15 g sat. fat), 206 mg chol., 1,026 mg sodium, 2 g carbo., 0 g fiber, 73 g pro.

Oriental Chicken Kabobs

Prep: 25 minutes Marinate: 2 hours Grill: 12 minutes Makes: 4 servings

¼ cup water

2 tablespoons soy sauce

2 tablespoons dry sherry

1 teaspoon grated fresh ginger
   or ¼ teaspoon ground
   ginger

⅛ teaspoon crushed
   red pepper

8 skinless, boneless
   chicken thighs

1. For marinade, combine water, soy sauce, sherry, ginger, and crushed red pepper. Cut chicken into thin strips. Thread chicken, accordion-style onto metal skewers. Place kabobs in a self-sealing plastic bag set in a shallow dish. Pour marinade over chicken; seal bag. Marinate in the refrigerator for 2 to 24 hours, turning bag occasionally. Drain kabobs, discarding marinade.

2. For a charcoal grill, grill kabobs on the rack of an uncovered grill directly over medium coals for 12 to 15 minutes or until chicken is no longer pink (180°F), turning once halfway through grilling. (For a gas grill, preheat grill. Reduce heat to medium. Place kabobs on grill rack over heat. Cover and grill as above.)

1_g carbs 0_g fiber 1_g net carbs

Nutrition Facts per serving: 189 cal., 6 g total fat (1 g sat. fat),
113 mg chol., 557 mg sodium, 1 g carbo., 0 g fiber, 30 g pro.

Yakitori Chicken Skewers

Prep: 20 minutes Marinate: 1 hour Grill: 8 minutes Makes: 4 servings

1. Cut chicken breasts lengthwise into ½-inch strips. Place chicken in a self-sealing plastic bag set in a shallow dish. In a small bowl combine soy sauce, sherry, oil, garlic, and crushed red pepper. Pour over chicken; seal bag. Marinate in the refrigerator for 1 to 4 hours, turning bag occasionally.

2. Drain chicken, discarding marinade. Thread chicken strips accordion-style onto four 12-inch skewers.

3. For a charcoal grill, grill skewers on the rack of an uncovered grill directly over medium coals for 8 minutes or until chicken is no longer pink (170°F), turning occasionally to brown evenly. (For a charcoal grill, preheat grill. Reduce heat to medium. Place skewers on grill rack over heat. Cover and grill as above.)

1 **pound skinless, boneless chicken breast halves**

¼ **cup reduced-sodium soy sauce**

¼ **cup dry sherry**

2 **teaspoons toasted sesame oil**

2 **cloves garlic, minced**

¼ **teaspoon crushed red pepper**

1g carbs **0**g fiber **1**g net carbs

Nutrition Facts per serving: 147 cal., 3 g total fat (1 g sat. fat), 66 mg chol., 246 mg sodium, 1 g carbo., 0 g fiber, 27 g pro.

Chile-Lime Chicken Skewers

Prep: 20 minutes Grill: 10 minutes Makes: 4 servings

1 pound skinless, boneless
   chicken breast halves

2 limes

1½ teaspoons ground ancho
   chile pepper

1 teaspoon garlic-herb
   seasoning

1. Cut chicken into 1-inch strips. Place strips in a shallow dish; set aside. Finely shred enough peel from 1 of the limes to measure 1 teaspoon (chill lime and use for juice another time). Cut remaining lime into wedges and set aside. For rub, combine lime peel, ground chile pepper, and garlic-herb seasoning. Sprinkle over chicken; rub in with your fingers.

2. Thread chicken accordion-style onto 4 long metal skewers, leaving a ¼-inch space between pieces. For a charcoal grill, grill on the rack of an uncovered grill directly over medium coals for 10 to 12 minutes or until chicken is no longer pink (170°F), turning once. (For a gas grill, preheat grill. Reduce heat to medium. Place chicken skewers on grill rack over heat. Cover and grill as above.) Serve with lime wedges.

1g carbs   **0**g fiber   **1**g net carbs

Nutrition Facts per serving: 132 cal., 2 g total fat (0 g sat. fat),
66 mg chol., 62 mg sodium, 1 g carbo., 0 g fiber, 26 g pro.

Chicken Shish Kabobs

Prep: 15 minutes Marinate: 1 hour Broil: 10 minutes Makes: 6 to 8 servings

1. Cut chicken into 1-inch cubes. Place in a self-sealing plastic bag set in a shallow dish. In a small bowl stir together lemon juice, oil, garlic, salt, and pepper. Pour over chicken; close bag. Marinate in the refrigerator for 1 hour.

2. Drain chicken, discarding marinade. Thread chicken pieces onto six to eight 12-inch skewers. Preheat broiler. Place skewers on the unheated rack of a broiler pan. Broil 4 to 5 inches from the heat about 10 minutes or until chicken is no longer pink, turning once halfway through broiling.

2 pounds skinless, boneless
  chicken breast halves

½ cup lemon juice

⅓ cup cooking oil or olive oil

3 or 4 cloves garlic, minced

½ teaspoon salt

½ teaspoon black pepper

1g carbs **0**g fiber **1**g net carbs

Nutrition Facts per serving: 352 cal., 19 g total fat (5 g sat. fat),
143 mg chol., 261 mg sodium, 1 g carbo., 0 g fiber, 43 g pro.

Hot-off-the-Grill Chicken

Prep: 15 minutes Grill: 35 minutes Makes: 4 servings

½ cup olive oil

2 cloves garlic, minced

2 tablespoons fresh rosemary

1 tablespoon fresh oregano

1 teaspoon cracked

    black pepper

1 tablespoon snipped fresh

    garlic chives or chives

1 teaspoon salt

1 teaspoon dry mustard

1 2½- to 3-pound broiler-fryer

    chicken, cut up

1. In a blender container combine oil, garlic, rosemary, oregano, pepper, chives, salt, and dry mustard. Cover and blend until nearly smooth. Rub mixture over all surfaces of the chicken.

2. For a charcoal grill, grill chicken pieces, bone side up, on the rack of an uncovered grill directly over medium coals for 35 to 45 minutes or until no longer pink (180°F), turning halfway through grilling. (For a gas grill, preheat grill. Reduce heat to medium. Place chicken pieces on grill rack over heat. Cover and grill as above.)

1g carbs   **0**g fiber   **1**g net carbs

Nutrition Facts per serving: 515 cal., 43 g total fat (1 g sat. fat), 99 mg chol., 674 mg sodium, 1 g carbo., 0 g fiber, 21 g pro.

Chicken Liver Sauté

Start to Finish: 25 minutes Makes: 4 servings

1. Rinse chicken livers; pat dry. Set livers aside. In a large skillet cook bacon until crisp. Remove bacon from skillet, reserving 2 tablespoons of the drippings. Crumble bacon; set aside.

2. Cook onion in reserved bacon drippings until tender. Stir in chicken livers and black pepper. Cover and cook over medium heat about 5 minutes or until livers are only slightly pink in center, stirring occasionally. Stir in bacon and chicken broth. Cook and stir about 1 minute more or until heated through. Sprinkle with parsley.

1 **pound chicken livers, cut in half**

4 **slices bacon**

1 **medium onion, cut into**
    thin wedges

⅛ **teaspoon black pepper**

¼ **cup chicken broth**

1 **tablespoon snipped fresh parsley**

3g carbs   **0**g fiber   **3**g net carbs

Nutrition Facts per serving: 217 cal., 13 g total fat (5 g sat. fat), 455 mg chol., 186 mg sodium, 3 g carbo., 0 g fiber, 20 g pro.

Prosciutto-Stuffed Turkey Breast

Prep: 30 minutes Roast: 1¼ hours Stand: 10 minutes
Oven: 375°F Makes: 6 servings

1 large leek, thinly sliced (½ cup)

4 teaspoons olive oil or cooking oil

⅓ cup pine nuts, toasted

¼ cup grated Parmesan cheese

2 tablespoons snipped fresh

   sage or 2 teaspoons dried

   sage, crushed

2 tablespoons snipped

   fresh parsley

1 2- to 2½-pound turkey

   breast half

2 ounces thinly sliced prosciutto

   or cooked ham

¼ cup chicken broth

¼ cup dry white wine

1. For stuffing, cook leek in 2 teaspoons of the oil until tender. In a small bowl combine leek, nuts, Parmesan cheese, sage, and parsley. Set aside.

2. Remove skin from turkey in one piece; set aside. Remove bone. Place breast half, skinned side down, between two pieces of plastic wrap. Using the flat side of a meat mallet, pound to ½-inch thickness.

3. To stuff, arrange prosciutto on top of turkey. Spoon stuffing onto prosciutto. Starting with a short side, roll up turkey and stuffing. Wrap skin around turkey. Tie with 100-percent-cotton kitchen string. Place on a rack in a roasting pan. Brush with remaining oil. Insert a meat thermometer into center. Roast in a 375° oven for 1¼ to 1½ hours or until turkey is no longer pink (170°F). Transfer turkey to serving platter, reserving 2 tablespoons drippings. Cover turkey with foil and let stand for 10 minutes before carving.

4. For sauce, spoon reserved drippings into a small saucepan. Stir in broth and wine. Bring to boiling; reduce heat. Boil gently about 8 minutes or until reduced to about ½ cup. Serve with turkey.

3g carbs   **0**g fiber   **3**g net carbs

Nutrition Facts per serving: 323 cal., 19 g total fat (5 g sat. fat), 93 mg chol., 488 mg sodium, 3 g carbo., 0 g fiber, 34 g pro.

Best-Ever Turkey on the Grill

Prep: 20 minutes   Grill: 2½ hours   Stand: 15 minutes   Makes: 8 to 10 servings

1. Remove the neck and giblets from turkey. Rinse turkey; pat dry with paper towels. In a small bowl combine Italian seasoning, poultry seasoning, salt, and pepper. Loosen skin from both sides of breast and tops of legs. Rub seasoning mixture on poultry breast and legs under the skin. Skewer the neck skin to the back. Twist wing tips under the back. Insert a meat thermometer into the center of the inside thigh muscle, not touching bone.

2. For a charcoal grill, arrange medium-hot coals around a drip pan; test for medium heat above pan.

3. Place turkey, breast side up, on the grill rack over drip pan. Cover and grill for 2½ to 3½ hours or until meat thermometer registers 180°F and turkey is no longer pink. Add coals halfway through grilling time or as necessary to maintain heat. (For a gas grill, preheat grill. Reduce heat to medium. Adjust for indirect cooking. Grill as above.)

4. Remove turkey from grill. Cover with foil and let stand for 15 to 20 minutes before carving.

1 8- to 12-pound whole turkey

2 teaspoons dried Italian seasoning, basil, or oregano, crushed

1 teaspoon poultry seasoning

½ teaspoon salt

½ teaspoon black pepper

0_g carbs 0_g fiber 0_g net carbs

Nutrition Facts per serving: 449 cal., 14 g total fat (4 g sat. fat), 275 mg chol., 221 mg sodium, 0 g carbo., 0 g fiber, 76 g pro.

Turkey Drumsticks with Sesame Rub

Prep: 15 minutes Grill: 45 minutes Makes: 4 servings

2 turkey drumsticks

3 tablespoons thinly sliced

   green onion

1 tablespoon sesame seeds

1½ teaspoons toasted

    sesame oil

1 teaspoon grated fresh ginger

¼ teaspoon salt

   Dash cayenne pepper

1 clove garlic, minced

1. Skin drumsticks. For rub, in a small bowl combine green onion, sesame seeds, sesame oil, ginger, salt, cayenne pepper, and garlic. Spread rub mixture evenly over turkey.

2. For a charcoal grill, arrange medium-hot coals around a drip pan. Test for medium heat above pan. Place drumsticks on grill rack over drip pan. Cover and grill for 45 minutes to 1¼ hours or until turkey is no longer pink (180°F). (For a gas grill, preheat grill. Reduce heat to medium. Adjust for indirect cooking. Place drumsticks on a rack in a pan. Place pan on grill rack. Grill as above.)

Chicken Drumsticks with Sesame Rub: Prepare as above, except substitute 8 chicken drumsticks for turkey drumsticks. Place on grill rack and grill, covered, for 35 to 40 minutes or until chicken is no longer pink (180°F).

1 g carbs 0 g fiber 1 g net carbs

Nutrition Facts per serving: 130 cal., 6 g total fat (1 g sat. fat), 69 mg chol., 186 mg sodium, 1 g carbo., 0 g fiber, 16 g pro.

Herbed-Lemon Turkey with Wild Mushroom Gravy

Prep: 20 minutes Roast: 1½ hours Stand: 10 minutes
Oven: 325°F Makes: 6 to 8 servings

1. In a small bowl stir together 2 tablespoons of the oil, rosemary, sage, and thyme; set aside.

2. Lift the skin on the turkey breast and using a spatula, spread herb mixture over turkey breast meat. Place turkey breast on a rack in a shallow roasting pan, spreading lemon and onion underneath. Insert a meat thermometer into the breast, not touching bone. Brush with remaining oil.

3. Roast, uncovered, in a 325° oven for 1½ to 2¼ hours or until thermometer registers 170°F, covering with foil the last 45 minutes of roasting to prevent overbrowning. Cover with foil and let stand for 10 minutes before carving.

4. Meanwhile, place mushrooms in a small bowl and cover with the boiling water. Let stand 10 minutes. Drain mushrooms, reserving liquid. Strain mushroom-soaking liquid through a sieve lined with a coffee filter. Reserve liquid. Rinse and drain mushrooms a second time; chop mushrooms and set aside.

5. Pour pan drippings from turkey into a large measuring cup. Skim and discard fat from drippings. Add enough mushroom liquid and broth to remaining drippings to equal 1⅓ cups. In a medium saucepan stir together arrowroot and 2 tablespoons more broth until smooth; stir in mushroom liquid mixture, cream, and sherry. Cook and stir just until thickened (do not boil). Stir in mushrooms. Season to taste with salt and pepper. Serve with turkey.

3 tablespoons olive oil

1 tablespoon snipped fresh rosemary

1½ teaspoons snipped fresh sage

1 teaspoon snipped fresh thyme

1 4½-pound whole turkey breast with bone

1 lemon, quartered

1 medium onion, quartered

½ cup dried porcini or shiitake mushrooms

1 cup boiling water

Chicken broth

2 tablespoons arrowroot

½ cup whipping cream

2 tablespoons dry sherry

Salt and black pepper

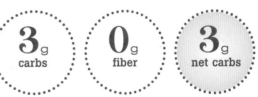

3g carbs   **0**g fiber   **3**g net carbs

Nutrition Facts per serving: 605 cal., 35 g total fat (11 g sat. fat), 215 mg chol., 186 mg sodium, 3 g carbo., 0 g fiber, 63 g pro.

Asparagus-Stuffed Turkey Rolls

Prep: 20 minutes Cook: 10 minutes Makes: 4 servings

2 turkey breast tenderloins

16 thin asparagus spears

1 tablespoon cooking oil

½ cup chicken broth

2 tablespoons lemon juice

¼ teaspoon salt

⅛ teaspoon black pepper

Lemon peel strips (optional)

1. Halve turkey tenderloins horizontally forming four turkey steaks. Place each steak between two pieces of plastic wrap. Using the flat side of a meat mallet, lightly pound to ¼-inch thickness. Trim asparagus spears, breaking off the woody ends. Arrange four asparagus spears on the short end of each turkey piece. Roll up turkey; secure with wooden toothpicks, if necessary.

2. Cook turkey rolls in hot oil in a large skillet over medium heat until browned on all sides. Add broth, lemon juice, salt, and pepper. Bring to boiling; reduce heat. Cover and simmer for 8 to 10 minutes or until turkey is no longer pink (170°F).

3. Transfer turkey to a serving platter; discard toothpicks. Cover and keep warm. Boil liquid in skillet, uncovered, for 2 to 3 minutes or until reduced to ½ cup. Spoon over turkey. If desired, garnish with lemon peel strips.

2g carbs   **1**g fiber   **1**g net carbs

Nutrition Facts per serving: 176 cal., 5 g total fat (1 g sat. fat), 68 mg chol., 329 mg sodium, 2 g carbo., 1 g fiber, 28 g pro.

Spiced Game Hens

Prep: 25 minutes Roast: 35 minutes Oven: 400°F Makes: 4 servings

1. In a small bowl combine lemon juice, oil, paprika, salt, coriander, turmeric, pepper, and garlic. Set mixture aside.

2. Using a long, heavy knife or kitchen shears, halve Cornish hens lengthwise. Cut through the breast bone of each hen, just off center; cut through the center of the backbone. If desired, remove backbone of each hen.

3. Use your fingers to loosen the skin over the breast meat of each game hen. Rub half of the lemon juice mixture under the skin directly on the meat. Rub remaining lemon juice mixture over the hens. Twist wing tips under back. Place hen halves, cut sides down, in a 3-quart rectangular baking dish. Pour broth around hens in dish. Roast, uncovered, in a 400° oven about 35 minutes or until hens are no longer pink (180°F), basting occasionally with pan juices.

4. Remove hens from baking dish; cover with foil to keep warm. Skim fat from pan juices. Pour ½ cup of the pan juices into a small saucepan; discard the remainder. Bring to boiling; boil gently for 5 minutes. Remove saucepan from heat. Whisk in butter, a piece at a time, until completely combined. Stir in marjoram. Drizzle butter mixture over hens.

¼ cup lemon juice

2 tablespoons olive oil

1 tablespoon hot paprika

1 teaspoon salt

1 teaspoon ground coriander

½ teaspoon ground turmeric

¼ teaspoon black pepper

4 cloves garlic, minced

2 1½-pound Cornish game hens

½ cup reduced-sodium chicken broth

2 tablespoons unsalted butter,
    cut into pieces

1 tablespoon snipped fresh marjoram

4 g carbs   **1** g fiber   **3** g net carbs

Nutrition Facts per serving: 477 cal., 36 g total fat (10 g sat. fat), 136 mg chol., 751 mg sodium, 4 g carbo., 1 g fiber, 37 g pro.

Quick and Easy Cooking Methods for Poultry

Direct Grilling Poultry

If desired, remove skin from poultry. For a charcoal grill, place poultry on grill rack, bone side up, directly over medium coals. Grill, uncovered, for the time given below or until the proper temperature is reached and meat is no longer pink, turning once halfway through grilling. For a gas grill, preheat grill. Reduce heat to medium. Place poultry on grill rack, bone side down, over heat. Cover and grill.

Test for doneness using a meat thermometer. (Use an instant-read thermometer to test smaller portions.) Thermometer should register 180°F, except in breast meat when thermometer should register 170°F. Poultry should be tender and no longer pink.

Type of Bird	Weight	Grilling Temperature	Approximate Indirect-Grilling Time	Doneness
Chicken Chicken, broiler-fryer	1½- to 1¾-pound half or 12-to 14-ounce quarters	Medium	40 to 50 minutes	180°F
Chicken, breast half, skinned and boned	4 to 5 ounces	Medium	12 to 15 minutes	170°F
Meaty chicken pieces (breast halves, thighs, and drumsticks)	2½ to 3 pounds total	Medium	35 to 45 minutes	180°F
Turkey Turkey breast tenderloin steak	4 to 6 ounces	Medium	12 to 15 minutes	170°F

All cooking times are based on poultry removed directly from refrigerator.

Broiling Poultry

If desired, remove the skin from the poultry; sprinkle with salt and black pepper. Remove broiler pan from the oven and preheat the broiler for 5 to 10 minutes. Arrange the poultry on the unheated rack of the broiler pan with the bone side up. If desired, brush poultry with cooking oil. Place the pan under the broiler so the surface of the poultry is 4 to 5 inches from the heat; chicken and Cornish game hen halves should be 5 to 6 inches from the heat. Turn the pieces over when browned on one side, usually after half of the broiling time. Chicken halves and quarters and meaty pieces should be turned after 20 minutes. Brush again with oil. The poultry is done when the meat is no longer pink and the juices run clear.

Type of Bird	Thickness/ Weight	Broiling Time
Chicken Broiler-fryer, half Broiler-fryer, quarter	1¼ to 1½ pounds each 10 to 12 ounces	28 to 32 minutes 28 to 32 minutes
Kabobs (boneless breast, cut into 2x½-inch strips and threaded loosely onto skewers)		8 to 10 minutes
Meaty pieces (breast halves, drumsticks, and thighs with bone)	2½ to 3 pounds total	25 to 35 minutes
Skinless, boneless breast halves	4 to 5 ounces	12 to 15 minutes
Game Cornish game hen, half	10 to 12 ounces	25 to 35 minutes
Turkey Breast steak or slice	2 ounces	6 to 8 minutes
Breast tenderloin steak	4 to 6 ounces	8 to 10 minutes
Patties (ground raw turkey)	¾ inch thick ½ inch thick	14 to 18 minutes 11 to 13 minutes

All cooking times are based on poultry removed directly from refrigerator.

Indirect-Grilling Poultry

If desired, remove skin from poultry. Rinse whole birds; pat dry. For a charcoal grill, arrange medium-hot coals around a drip pan. Test for medium heat above the pan. Place unstuffed poultry, breast side up, on grill rack over drip pan. Cover and grill for the time given below or until the proper temperature is reached and meat is no longer pink, adding more charcoal to maintain heat as necessary. For large poultry cuts and whole birds, we suggest placing the poultry on a rack in a roasting pan and omitting the drip pan. For a gas grill, preheat grill. Reduce heat to medium. Adjust heat for indirect cooking.

Test for doneness using a meat thermometer. (Use an instant-read thermometer to test smaller portions.) For whole birds, insert thermometer into the center of the inside thigh muscle, not touching the bone. Thermometer should register 180°F, except in breast meat when thermometer should register 170°F. Poultry should be tender and no longer pink. (Note: Birds vary in size and shape. Use these times as general guides.)

Type of Bird	Weight	Grilling Temperature	Approximate Indirect-Grilling Time	Doneness
Chicken				
Chicken, whole	2½ to 3 pounds 3½ to 4 pounds 4½ to 5 pounds	Medium Medium Medium	1 to 1¼ hours 1¼ to 1¾ hours 1¾ to 2 hours	180°F 180°F 180°F
Chicken breast half (skinned and boned)	4 to 5 ounces	Medium	15 to 18 minutes	170°F
Chicken broiler-fryer, half	1½ to 1¾ pounds	Medium	1 to 1¼ hours	180°F
Chicken broiler-fryer, quarters	12 to 14 ounces each	Medium	50 to 60 minutes	180°F
Meaty chicken pieces (breast halves, thighs, and drumsticks)	2½ to 3 pounds total	Medium	50 to 60 minutes	180°F
Game				
Cornish game hen, whole	1¼ to 1½ pounds	Medium	50 to 60 minutes	180°F
Pheasant, whole	2 to 3 pounds	Medium	1 to 1½ hours	180°F
Quail, semiboneless	3 to 4 ounces	Medium	15 to 20 minutes	180°F
Squab	12 to 16 ounces	Medium	¾ to 1 hour	180°F
Turkey				
Turkey, whole	6 to 8 pounds 8 to 12 pounds 12 to 16 pounds	Medium Medium Medium	1¾ to 2¼ hours 2½ to 3½ hours 3 to 4 hours	180°F 180°F 180°F

Fish & Seafood

Delicious, nutritious, and quick, fish and seafood supply everything we want in a weeknight entrée. Choose from delicate fillets, meaty steaks, or tender seafood. No matter how you prepare it, fish and seafood provide an abundance of protein, along with heart-healthy omega-3 fatty acids.

Tangy Thyme Fish

Start to Finish: 25 minutes Makes: 4 servings

1 pound fresh or frozen salmon, sole, cod, or orange roughy fillets, ½ to ¾ inch thick

1 cup reduced-sodium chicken broth

¼ cup chopped onion

¼ teaspoon dried thyme or marjoram, crushed

⅛ teaspoon black pepper

¼ cup bottled low-carb ranch salad dressing

2 tablespoons snipped fresh parsley

Lemon slices (optional)

1. Thaw fish, if frozen. Rinse fish; pat dry with paper towels. Set fish aside.

2. In a large skillet combine broth, onion, thyme, and pepper. Bring to boiling. Place fish in skillet, tucking under any thin edges. Simmer, covered, until fish flakes easily when tested with a fork. Allow 4 to 6 minutes per ½-inch thickness of fish. Using a slotted spatula, transfer fish to a serving platter.

3. For sauce, stir salad dressing and parsley into cooking liquid. Serve fish with sauce and if desired, lemon slices.

1 g carbs

0 g fiber

1 g net carbs

Nutrition Facts per serving: 245 cal., 16 g total fat (3 g sat. fat), 66 mg chol., 428 mg sodium, 1 g carbo., 0 g fiber, 24 g pro.

Dijon Mustard Fillets

Start to Finish: 15 minutes Makes: 4 servings

1. Thaw fish, if frozen. Rinse fish; pat dry with paper towels. Cut into four serving-size pieces. Preheat broiler. Place fish on the greased unheated rack of a broiler pan. Tuck under any thin portions to make uniform thickness. Sprinkle with lemon-pepper seasoning.

2. Broil 4 inches from the heat until fish flakes easily when tested with a fork. Allow 4 to 6 minutes per $\frac{1}{2}$-inch thickness of fish. If fillets are 1 inch thick, turn once halfway through broiling.

3. Meanwhile, in a small saucepan stir together sour cream, cream, mustard, and chives. Cook and stir over low heat until heated through (do not boil). Spoon over fish. If desired, sprinkle with capers.

1 pound fresh or frozen fish fillets, $\frac{1}{2}$ to 1 inch thick

$\frac{1}{2}$ teaspoon lemon-pepper seasoning

$\frac{1}{4}$ cup dairy sour cream

1 tablespoon light cream

1 tablespoon Dijon-style mustard

2 teaspoons snipped fresh chives or chopped green onion tops

2 to 3 teaspoons capers, drained (optional)

2g carbs **0**g fiber **2**g net carbs

Nutrition Facts per serving: 113 cal., 4 g total fat (2 g sat. fat), 29 mg chol., 305 mg sodium, 2 g carbo., 0 g fiber, 18 g pro.

Lemon-Parsley Fish

Prep: 15 minutes Marinate: 30 minutes Broil: 8 minutes Makes: 4 servings

1 pound fresh or frozen halibut,
　　swordfish, or salmon steaks,
　　1 inch thick

1 teaspoon finely shredded
　　lemon peel

3 tablespoons lemon juice

2 tablespoons snipped fresh
　　flat-leaf parsley

2 tablespoons olive oil

2 cloves garlic, minced

　　Salt and black pepper

1. Thaw fish, if frozen. Rinse fish; pat dry with paper towels. Cut into 4 serving-size pieces. Place fish in a self-sealing plastic bag set in a shallow bowl. For marinade, combine lemon peel, lemon juice, parsley, oil, and garlic. Pour over fish; seal bag. Marinate in the refrigerator for 30 minutes to 2 hours, turning bag occasionally.

2. Drain fish, reserving marinade. Place fish on the greased unheated rack of a broiler pan. Sprinkle with salt and pepper. Broil 4 inches from the heat for 5 minutes. Using a wide spatula, carefully turn over fish. Brush with marinade. Broil for 3 to 7 minutes more or until fish flakes easily when tested with a fork. Discard any remaining marinade.

2 g carbs　　**0** g fiber　　**2** g net carbs

Nutrition Facts per serving: 190 cal., 9 g total fat (1 g sat. fat),
36 mg chol., 208 mg sodium, 2 g carbo., 0 g fiber, 24 g pro.

Grilled Rosemary Trout with Lemon Butter

Prep: 15 minutes Grill: 6 minutes Makes: 4 servings

1. In a small bowl stir together butter, half of the shallot, and lemon peel; sprinkle with salt and pepper. Set aside.

2. Rinse fish; pat dry with paper towels. Spread each fish open and place skin sides down. Rub remaining shallot and the rosemary onto trout. Sprinkle with additional salt and pepper; drizzle with lemon juice and oil.

3. For a charcoal grill, grill fish, skin side down, on the greased rack of an uncovered grill directly over medium coals for 6 to 8 minutes or until fish flakes easily when tested with a fork. Meanwhile, place tomatoes, cut side up, on grill rack; dot each with 1/4 teaspoon of the butter mixture. Grill tomatoes about 5 minutes or until heated through. (For a gas grill, preheat grill. Reduce heat to medium. Place fish and tomatoes on grill rack over heat. Cover and grill as above.) Remove fish and tomatoes from grill. Cut each fish in half lengthwise.

4. In a small saucepan melt remaining butter mixture. Sprinkle fish with parsley. Serve with butter mixture and tomatoes.

4 teaspoons butter, softened

1 tablespoon finely chopped shallot
   or onion

1 teaspoon finely shredded lemon
   peel

   Salt and black pepper

2 fresh rainbow trout, pan-dressed
   and boned

1 tablespoon snipped fresh rosemary

   Salt and black pepper

1 tablespoon lemon juice

2 teaspoons olive oil

2 medium tomatoes, halved crosswise

1 tablespoon snipped fresh parsley

3g carbs   **1**g fiber   **2**g net carbs

Nutrition Facts per serving: 227 cal., 13 g total fat (4 g sat. fat), 77 mg chol., 145 mg sodium, 3 g carbo., 1 g fiber, 24 g pro.

Rocky Mountain Trout

Prep: 15 minutes Grill: 6 minutes Makes: 4 servings

4 8- to 10-ounce fresh or frozen
   pan-dressed rainbow trout

¼ cup finely chopped red onion

¼ cup finely chopped green
   sweet pepper

2 tablespoons snipped fresh
   cilantro or basil

½ teaspoon ground cumin

¼ teaspoon salt

¼ teaspoon black pepper

   Cooking oil

1. Thaw fish, if frozen. In a bowl stir together onion, sweet pepper, cilantro, cumin, salt, and black pepper.

2. Rinse fish; pat dry with paper towels. Brush the outsides and cavities of fish with oil. Spoon onion mixture into fish cavities.

3. Place fish in a well-greased wire grill basket. For a charcoal grill, grill fish on the rack of an uncovered grill directly over medium-hot coals for 6 to 10 minutes or until fish flakes easily when tested with a fork, turning once. (For a gas grill, preheat grill. Reduce heat to medium-high. Place fish on grill rack over heat. Cover and grill as above.)

2g carbs   **1**g fiber   **1**g net carbs

Nutrition Facts per serving: 340 cal., 14 g total fat (4 g sat. fat), 133 mg chol., 227 mg sodium, 2 g carbo., 1 g fiber, 48 g pro.

Grilled Trout with Cilantro & Lime

Prep: 15 minutes Grill: 8 minutes Makes: 4 servings

1. Thaw fish, if frozen. Rinse fish; pat dry with paper towels. In a small bowl combine lime juice and oil; brush cavity and outside of each fish with the lime juice mixture. Sprinkle cavity of each fish with cilantro, salt, and pepper.

2. For a charcoal grill, place fish in a well-greased grill basket. Grill on the rack of an uncovered grill directly over medium coals for 8 to 12 minutes or until fish flakes easily when tested with a fork, turning basket once halfway through grilling. (Or preheat a well-greased grill pan on the rack of an uncovered grill over medium coals for 5 minutes. Place fish in preheated pan. Grill for 8 to 12 minutes or until fish flakes easily when tested with a fork, turning fish over once halfway through grilling.) Serve fish with lime wedges.

4 8- to 10-ounce fresh or frozen
   dressed trout, heads removed

3 tablespoons lime juice

2 tablespoons olive oil

2 tablespoons snipped fresh
   cilantro or parsley

½ teaspoon salt

¼ teaspoon black pepper

   Lime wedges

1g carbs   **0**g fiber   **1**g net carbs

Nutrition Facts per serving: 376 cal., 19 g total fat (4 g sat. fat), 133 mg chol., 372 mg sodium, 1 g carbo., 0 g fiber, 47 g pro.

Broiled Scrod with Lemon Butter

Start to Finish: 20 minutes Makes: 6 servings

1½ pounds fresh or frozen scrod

     fillets, about 1 inch thick

2 tablespoons butter, melted

1 to 2 tablespoons lemon juice

    Salt and black pepper

    Snipped fresh parsley

    Lemon wedges

1. Thaw fish fillets, if frozen. Rinse fish; pat dry with paper towels. Preheat broiler. Place fish on the greased unheated rack of a broiler pan. Tuck under any thin edges to make even thickness.

2. Combine butter and lemon juice; brush over fillets. Sprinkle with salt and pepper.

3. Broil 4 inches from the heat for 8 to 12 minutes or until fish flakes easily when tested with a fork, brushing occasionally with butter mixture. Garnish with parsley and lemon wedges.

0_g carbs 0_g fiber 0_g net carbs

Nutrition Facts per serving: 129 cal., 5 g total fat (2 g sat. fat), 59 mg chol., 187 mg sodium, 0 g carbo., 0 g fiber, 20 g pro.

Grouper with Summer Vegetables

Prep: 20 minutes Bake: 4 minutes per ½-inch thickness
Cook: 5 minutes Oven: 450°F Makes: 4 servings

1. Thaw fish, if frozen. Cut into 4 serving-size pieces. Rinse fish; pat dry with paper towels. Place fish in a 2-quart rectangular baking dish; sprinkle with salt and black pepper. Set aside.

2. In a small bowl stir together lemon juice and 1 tablespoon of the oil. Drizzle over fish. Bake, uncovered, in a 450° oven until fish flakes easily when tested with a fork. Allow 4 to 6 minutes per ½-inch thickness of fish.

3. Meanwhile, in a large skillet cook zucchini, sweet pepper, and garlic in remaining 1 tablespoon oil until crisp-tender. Stir in 2 teaspoons of the marjoram. Season to taste with salt and black pepper. Sprinkle fish with remaining 2 teaspoons marjoram. Serve fish with vegetables.

See photo, page 306.

1 pound fresh or frozen grouper fillets, ½ to ¾ inch thick

Salt and black pepper

2 tablespoons lemon juice

2 tablespoons olive oil

1 small zucchini, halved lengthwise and thinly sliced

½ of a medium yellow sweet pepper, cut into bite-size strips

1 clove garlic, minced

4 teaspoons snipped fresh marjoram or basil

Salt and black pepper

3g carbs **1**g fiber **2**g net carbs

Nutrition Facts per serving: 178 cal., 8 g total fat (1 g sat. fat), 42 mg chol., 209 mg sodium, 3 g carbo., 1 g fiber, 23 g pro.

Cajun-Flavored Catfish

Prep: 10 minutes Bake: 15 minutes Oven: 350°F Makes: 4 servings

4 skinned catfish fillets, about
     ½ inch thick

1 tablespoon black pepper

1 tablespoon dried oregano,
     crushed

2 to 3 teaspoons seasoned salt

2 teaspoons onion powder

1 teaspoon crushed red pepper

¾ teaspoon chili powder

½ teaspoon ground cumin

1. Rinse fish; pat dry with paper towels. In a small bowl stir together black pepper, oregano, seasoned salt, onion powder, crushed red pepper, chili powder, and cumin. Use about 1 tablespoon seasoning mixture to coat both sides of fish.* Arrange fish in a lightly greased shallow baking pan.

2. Bake in a 350° oven for 10 minutes. Turn over fish and bake for 5 to 8 minutes more or until fish flakes easily when tested with a fork.

*Note: Store remaining seasoning mix in an airtight container at room temperature up to 1 month. Use for fish or pork.

1g carbs   **0**g fiber   **1**g net carbs

Nutrition Facts per serving: 157 cal., 6 g total fat (2 g sat. fat),
53 mg chol., 252 mg sodium, 1 g carbo., 0 g fiber, 18 g pro.

Fragrant Swordfish Brochettes

Prep: 25 minutes Marinate: 1 hour Grill: 8 minutes Makes: 4 servings

1. Thaw fish, if frozen. Rinse fish; pat dry. Cut into 1 1/2-inch cubes. Place fish in a shallow dish. For marinade, in a blender container or food processor bowl combine parsley, mint, cilantro, lemon juice, oil, garlic, paprika, coriander, and cumin. Cover and blend or process until combined, scraping down sides as necessary. Pour over fish; turn fish to coat. Cover and marinate in the refrigerator for 1 to 2 hours, turning fish once.

2. Drain fish, discarding marinade. Onto 4 long metal skewers, alternately thread fish and bay leaves.

3. For a charcoal grill, grill kabobs on the greased rack of an uncovered grill directly over medium coals for 8 to 12 minutes or until fish flakes easily when tested with a fork, gently turning once halfway through grilling. (For a gas grill, preheat grill. Reduce heat to medium. Place kabobs on greased grill rack over heat. Cover and grill as above.) Slide fish and bay leaves off skewers; discard bay leaves.

1 1/2 pounds fresh or frozen swordfish or salmon steaks, cut 1 1/2 inches thick

1/3 cup lightly packed fresh parsley leaves

1/3 cup lightly packed fresh mint leaves

1/3 cup lightly packed fresh cilantro leaves

3 tablespoons lemon juice

3 tablespoons olive oil

6 cloves garlic

2 teaspoons paprika

1/2 teaspoon ground coriander

1/2 teaspoon ground cumin

8 bay leaves

4 g carbs   1 g fiber   3 g net carbs

Nutrition Facts per serving: 312 cal., 17 g total fat (3 g sat. fat), 64 mg chol., 163 mg sodium, 4 g carbo., 1 g fiber, 35 g pro.

Lemon-Herb Swordfish Steaks

Prep: 15 minutes Marinate: 30 minutes Grill: 8 minutes Makes: 4 to 6 servings

1½ **pounds fresh or frozen**

swordfish, tuna, or shark

steaks, cut 1 inch thick

¼ **cup snipped fresh parsley**

¼ **cup chicken broth**

1 **teaspoon finely shredded**

lemon peel

2 **tablespoons lemon juice**

1 **tablespoon snipped**

fresh rosemary

1 **tablespoon olive oil**

1 **shallot, finely chopped**

3 **cloves garlic, minced**

1½ **teaspoons snipped**

fresh tarragon

¼ **teaspoon salt**

1. Thaw fish, if frozen. Rinse fish; pat dry with paper towels. Place fish in a self-sealing plastic bag set in a shallow dish. For marinade, in a bowl combine parsley, broth, lemon peel, lemon juice, rosemary, oil, shallot, garlic, tarragon, and salt. Pour over fish; seal bag. Marinate in the refrigerator for 30 minutes, turning bag occasionally.

2. Drain fish, reserving marinade. For a charcoal grill, grill fish on the greased rack of an uncovered grill directly over medium coals for 8 to 12 minutes, or until fish flakes easily when tested with a fork, turning and brushing with reserved marinade halfway through grilling. (For a gas grill, preheat grill. Reduce heat to medium. Place fish on grill rack over heat. Cover and grill as above.) Discard any remaining marinade.

2g carbs   **0**g fiber   **2**g net carbs

Nutrition Facts per serving: 248 cal., 10 g total fat (2 g sat. fat),
22 mg chol., 337 mg sodium, 2 g carbo., 0 g fiber, 34 g pro.

Blackened Swordfish

Prep: 15 minutes   Grill: 8 minutes   Makes: 4 serving

1. Thaw fish, if frozen. Rinse fish; pat dry with paper towels. In a small bowl combine garlic, black pepper, paprika, cayenne pepper, white pepper, thyme, and salt. Stir in melted butter. Brush both sides of fish with butter mixture.

2. For a charcoal grill, grill fish on the greased rack of an uncovered grill directly over medium coals for 8 to 12 minutes or until fish flakes easily when tested with a fork, turning once halfway through grilling. (For a gas grill, preheat grill. Reduce heat to medium. Place fish on greased grill rack over heat. Cover and grill as above.)

1 pound fresh or frozen
  swordfish or tuna steaks, cut
  1 inch thick
2 teaspoons minced garlic
1 teaspoon black pepper
1 teaspoon paprika
½ teaspoon cayenne pepper
½ teaspoon ground white pepper
½ teaspoon dried thyme, crushed
½ teaspoon salt
3 tablespoons butter, melted

2g carbs   **1**g fiber   **2**g net carbs

Nutrition Facts per serving: 227 cal., 14 g total fat (6 g sat. fat), 67 mg chol., 459 mg sodium, 2 g carbo., 1 g fiber, 23 g pro.

Broiled Halibut with Dijon Cream

Start to Finish: 20 minutes Makes: 4 servings

4 fresh or frozen halibut steaks,

cut 1 inch thick

1½ teaspoons Greek-style

seasoning blend

¼ teaspoon coarsely ground

black pepper

¼ cup dairy sour cream

2 tablespoons mayonnaise

1 tablespoon Dijon-style

mustard

1 tablespoon light cream

½ teaspoon dried oregano,

crushed

1. Thaw fish, if frozen. Rinse fish; pat dry with paper towels. Preheat broiler. Place fish on the greased unheated rack of a broiler pan. Sprinkle both sides of fish with Greek-style seasoning and pepper.

2. Broil 4 inches from the heat for 8 to 12 minutes or until fish flakes easily when tested with a fork, turning once halfway through broiling.

3. Meanwhile, for sauce, in a small bowl combine sour cream, mayonnaise, mustard, cream, and oregano. Serve fish with sauce.

4 g carbs   0 g fiber   4 g net carbs

Nutrition Facts per serving: 168 cal., 5 g total fat (2 g sat. fat),
42 mg chol., 300 mg sodium, 4 g carbo., 0 g fiber, 24 g pro.

Smoked Halibut in Hazelnut Butter

Prep: 20 minutes Soak: 1 hour Grill: 30 minutes Makes: 4 servings

1. About one hour before smoking, soak wood chips in enough water to cover.

2. Thaw fish, if frozen. Rinse fish; pat dry with paper towels. For a charcoal grill, arrange medium-hot coals around a drip pan. Test for medium heat above pan. Sprinkle wood chips over coals. Place fish on greased grill rack over drip pan. Cover and grill for 30 to 36 minutes or until fish flakes easily with a fork. (For a gas grill, preheat grill. Reduce heat to medium. Adjust for indirect cooking. Add soaked wood chips according to manufacturer's directions. Place fish on greased grill rack. Grill as above.)

3. For sauce, in a small skillet cook hazelnuts in hot butter over medium heat, stirring occasionally, until nuts are toasted and butter is brown but not burned. Remove from heat. Stir in wine. Serve immediately over fish. If desired, garnish with parsley.

2 cups apple or oak wood chips

4 fresh or frozen halibut steaks, cut 1 inch thick

⅓ cup blanched hazelnuts (filberts)

⅓ cup butter

1 tablespoon dry white wine

1 tablespoon snipped fresh parsley (optional)

2 g carbs   **1** g fiber   **1** g net carbs

Nutrition Facts per serving: 402 cal., 27 g total fat (11 g sat. fat), 98 mg chol., 257 mg sodium, 2 g carbo., 1 g fiber, 37 g pro.

Swordfish with Cucumber Sauce

Prep: 10 minutes Broil: 6 minutes Makes: 4 servings

4 fresh or frozen swordfish
   steaks, cut ¾ inch thick

⅓ cup dairy sour cream

¼ cup finely chopped cucumber

1 teaspoon snipped fresh mint
   or ¼ teaspoon dried mint,
   crushed

   Dash black pepper

   Light cream (optional)

1. Thaw fish, if frozen. Rinse fish; pat dry with paper towels.

2. For sauce, in a small bowl stir together sour cream, cucumber, mint, and pepper. If necessary, stir in 1 to 2 tablespoons light cream to make desired consistency. Cover and chill until serving time.

3. Preheat broiler. Place fish on the greased unheated rack of a broiler pan. Broil 4 inches from the heat for 6 to 9 minutes or until fish flakes easily when tested with a fork.

4. Serve fish with cucumber sauce.

See photo, page 305.

2g carbs   **0**g fiber   **2**g net carbs

Nutrition Facts per serving: 149 cal., 5 g total fat (1 g sat. fat),
44 mg chol., 116 mg sodium, 2 g carbo., 0 g fiber, 24 g pro.

Swordfish with Cucumber Sauce p. 304

Grouper
with Summer
Vegetables
p. 297

Grilled
Salmon with
Basil Butter
p. 323

Grilled Tuna with Roasted Pepper Sauce p. 330

Lemony
Shrimp
Kabobs
p. 335

Shrimp
& Greens
Soup
p. 338

Shrimp
& Greens
Soup
p. 338

Lobster Tails
with Chive
Butter
p. 341

Minty
Halibut with
Squash
p. 313

Minty Halibut with Squash

Prep: 15 minutes Grill: 8 minutes Makes: 4 servings

1. Rinse fish; pat dry with paper towels. In a small bowl whisk together lemon juice, oil, and garlic. Reserve 3 tablespoons of the mixture. Brush remaining lemon juice mixture on fish and on cut sides of the squash. Lightly sprinkle fish and squash with salt and pepper.

2. For a charcoal grill, grill fish on the lightly greased rack of an uncovered grill directly over medium coals for 8 to 12 minutes or until fish flakes easily when tested with a fork, turning once. Add squash during the last 5 to 6 minutes of grilling; grill just until tender, turning once. (For a gas grill, preheat grill. Reduce heat to medium. Place fish and squash on grill rack over heat. Cover and grill as above.)

3. Meanwhile, stir basil and mint into reserved lemon juice mixture.

4. Transfer squash to a cutting board; cool slightly. Slice 1/8 inch to 1/4 inch thick. Place squash on a serving platter; drizzle with some of the basil mixture. Top with fish; drizzle with the remaining basil mixture. If desired, garnish with mint leaves.

See photo, page 312.

1 1/4 to 1 1/2 pounds fresh halibut or salmon steaks, cut 1 inch thick

1/4 cup lemon juice

2 tablespoons olive oil

3 cloves garlic, minced

2 medium yellow summer squash and/or zucchini, halved lengthwise

Salt and black pepper

2 tablespoons finely snipped fresh basil

1 tablespoon snipped fresh mint

Fresh mint leaves (optional)

4g carbs

1g fiber

3g net carbs

Nutrition Facts per serving: 232 cal., 10 g total fat (1 g sat. fat), 45 mg chol., 224 mg sodium, 4 g carbo., 1 g fiber, 30 g pro.

Mustard-Glazed Halibut Steaks

Prep: 10 minutes Grill: 8 minutes Makes: 4 servings

4 6-ounce fresh or frozen
   halibut steaks, cut 1 inch
   thick

2 tablespoons butter

2 tablespoons lemon juice

1 tablespoon Dijon-style
   mustard

2 teaspoons snipped fresh basil
   or ½ teaspoon dried basil,
   crushed

1. Thaw fish, if frozen. Rinse fish; pat dry with paper towels. In a small saucepan heat butter, lemon juice, mustard, and basil over low heat until melted. Brush both sides of fish with mustard mixture.

2. For a charcoal grill, grill fish on the greased rack of an uncovered grill directly over medium coals for 8 to 12 minutes or until fish flakes easily when tested with a fork, turning once and brushing occasionally with mustard mixture. Discard remaining mustard mixture. (For a gas grill, preheat grill. Reduce heat to medium. Place fish on grill rack over heat. Cover and grill as above.)

1 g carbs   0 g fiber   1 g net carbs

Nutrition Facts per serving: 243 cal., 10 g total fat (2 g sat. fat),
55 mg chol., 254 mg sodium, 1 g carbo., 0 g fiber, 36 g pro.

Orange Roughy
with Tarragon Sauce

Prep: 15 minutes Broil: 6 minutes Makes: 4 servings

1. Thaw fish, if frozen. Rinse fish; pat dry with paper towels. Set fish aside.

2. For sauce, in a small bowl stir together mayonnaise, parsley, green onion, tarragon, and vinegar; set aside.

3. Preheat broiler. Brush fish with oil. Sprinkle with salt and pepper. Place fish on the greased unheated rack of a broiler pan. Broil 4 inches from the heat for 6 to 9 minutes or until fish flakes easily when tested with a fork. Serve with sauce.

4 fresh or frozen orange roughy
   or other fish fillets, ¾ inch thick

½ cup mayonnaise

2 tablespoons snipped fresh
   parsley

1 tablespoon thinly sliced
   green onion

2 teaspoons snipped fresh
   tarragon or ½ teaspoon dried
   tarragon, crushed

2 teaspoons white wine vinegar

1 tablespoon olive oil

   Salt and black pepper

0g carbs

0g fiber

0g net carbs

Nutrition Facts per serving: 310 cal., 26 g total fat (3 g sat. fat),
42 mg chol., 388 mg sodium, 0 g carbo., 0 g fiber, 17 g pro.

Orange Roughy
with Cilantro Pesto

Prep: 20 minutes Broil: 4 to 6 minutes per ½-inch thickness Makes: 4 servings

1 to 1¼ pounds fresh or frozen
   orange roughy or cod fillets

1½ cups loosely packed fresh
   cilantro leaves

1 fresh jalapeño pepper, seeded
   and chopped (see note,
   page 51)

1 clove garlic, halved

2 tablespoons olive oil

1 tablespoon lime juice

¼ teaspoon salt

¼ teaspoon black pepper

1. Thaw fish, if frozen. Rinse fish; pat dry with paper towels. Cut fish into 4 serving-size pieces, if necessary. Set fish aside.

2. For cilantro pesto, in a small food processor bowl or blender container combine cilantro, jalapeño, garlic, 1 tablespoon of the olive oil, and lime juice. Cover and process or blend with on/off turns until almost smooth, stopping the machine and scraping sides several times. Set aside.

3. Preheat broiler. Place fish on the greased unheated rack of a broiler pan, tucking under any thin edges. Brush with remaining 1 tablespoon olive oil. Sprinkle with salt and pepper. Broil 4 inches from the heat until fish flakes easily when tested with a fork. Allow 4 to 6 minutes per ½-inch thickness of fish. If fish is 1 inch or more thick, turn once halfway through broiling. Serve with cilantro pesto.

2g carbs   **1**g fiber   **1**g net carbs

Nutrition Facts per serving: 148 cal., 8 g total fat (1 g sat. fat),
22 mg chol., 233 mg sodium, 2 g carbo., 1 g fiber, 17 g pro.

Broiled Red Snapper with Cream Sauce

Prep: 15 minutes Marinate: 30 minutes
Broil: 4 minutes per ½-inch thickness Makes: 4 servings

1. Rinse fish; pat dry with paper towels. Place fish fillets in a self-sealing plastic bag set in a shallow dish. In a small bowl combine wine, oil, green onion, ¼ teaspoon salt, and ⅛ teaspoon pepper. Pour wine mixture over fish; seal bag. Marinate in the refrigerator for 30 minutes, turning bag once. Drain fish, discarding marinade.

2. Preheat broiler. Place fillets on the greased unheated rack of a broiler pan. Broil 4 inches from the heat until fish flakes easily when tested with a fork. Allow 4 to 6 minutes per ½-inch thickness of fish.

3. Meanwhile, for sauce, in a small bowl stir together sour cream, parsley, thyme, lemon peel, dry mustard, ⅛ teaspoon salt, and ⅛ teaspoon pepper; set aside.

4. In a medium mixing bowl beat whipping cream with an electric mixer on medium speed or with a wire whisk until soft peaks form. Fold whipped cream into sour cream mixture. Serve fish with sauce.

4 6 to 8-ounce red snapper
   fillets, skinned

¼ cup dry white wine

2 tablespoons olive oil

1 green onion, thinly sliced

¼ teaspoon salt

⅛ teaspoon black pepper

¼ cup dairy sour cream

1 tablespoon snipped fresh
   flat-leaf parsley

1 teaspoon snipped fresh thyme

1 teaspoon finely shredded
   lemon peel

½ teaspoon dry mustard

⅓ cup whipping cream

2 g carbs **0** g fiber **2** g net carbs

Nutrition Facts per serving: 309 cal., 17 g total fat (7 g sat. fat), 94 mg chol., 305 mg sodium, 2 g carbo., 0 g fiber, 36 g pro.

Salmon with Ginger Cream

Prep: 20 minutes Broil: 4 to 6 minutes per ½-inch thickness Makes: 4 servings

1 to 1¼ pounds fresh or frozen
   skinless salmon fillets

2 teaspoons lime juice

2 teaspoons olive oil

¼ teaspoon salt

¼ teaspoon ground cumin

⅛ teaspoon freshly ground
   black pepper

½ cup dairy sour cream

1 teaspoon grated fresh ginger

1 small clove garlic, minced

1 green onion, thinly sliced

2 teaspoons snipped fresh mint

⅛ teaspoon salt

1. Thaw fish, if frozen. Rinse fish; pat dry with paper towels. Cut into 4 serving-size pieces. Set fish aside. In a small bowl stir together lime juice, oil, ¼ teaspoon salt, cumin, and pepper. Brush lime juice mixture onto both sides of fish.

2. Preheat broiler. Place fish on the greased unheated rack of a broiler pan, tucking under any thin edges. Broil 4 inches from the heat until fish flakes easily when tested with a fork. Allow 4 to 6 minutes per ½-inch thickness of fish. If fish is 1 inch or more thick, turn once halfway through broiling.

3. Meanwhile, for sauce, in a small bowl stir together sour cream, ginger, garlic, green onion, mint, and ⅛ teaspoon salt. Serve fish with sauce.

2g carbs **0**g fiber **2**g net carbs

Nutrition Facts per serving: 236 cal., 15 g total fat (5 g sat. fat),
71 mg chol., 309 mg sodium, 2 g carbo., 0 g fiber, 24 g pro.

Smoked Salmon with Lemon-Dill Aïoli

Prep: 20 minutes Soak: 1 hour Smoke: 2½ hours Makes: 4 to 6 servings

1. Thaw fish, if frozen. Rinse fish; pat dry with paper towels. At least 1 hour before smoke cooking, soak wood chunks in enough water to cover.

2. Meanwhile, for sauce, in a small bowl combine mayonnaise, snipped dill, lemon peel, lemon juice, and lemon-pepper seasoning. Cover and chill until serving time.

3. Fill fish cavity with fresh dill sprigs. Place salmon on an 18×12-inch piece of greased heavy foil.

4. In a smoker arrange preheated coals, drained wood chunks, and water pan according to manufacturer's directions. Pour water into pan. Place fish and foil on grill rack over water pan. Cover and smoke for 2½ to 3 hours or until fish flakes easily when tested with a fork. Add more coals, wood chunks, and water as needed.

5. To serve, remove skin from one side of salmon; cut salmon into serving-size pieces. Serve fish with sauce.

1 3½- to 4-pound fresh or frozen dressed salmon

10 to 12 alder or apple wood chunks

¾ cup mayonnaise

2 tablespoons snipped fresh dill

1½ teaspoons finely shredded lemon peel

1 tablespoon lemon juice

¼ teaspoon lemon-pepper seasoning

8 fresh dill sprigs

2g carbs   **0**g fiber   **2**g net carbs

Nutrition Facts per serving: 661 cal., 46 g total fat (8 g sat. fat), 95 mg chol., 541 mg sodium, 2 g carbo., 0 g fiber, 57 g pro.

Pepper-Poached Salmon

Start to Finish: 25 minutes Makes: 4 servings

1 to 1½ pounds fresh or
  frozen salmon fillets

1 cup water

½ teaspoon salt

1 cup loosely packed
  watercress leaves

2 tablespoons snipped
  fresh tarragon

½ of a lemon, cut into thick slices

2 teaspoons whole peppercorns

3 bay leaves

½ cup dairy sour cream

1 teaspoon snipped fresh tarragon

½ teaspoon ground black pepper

¼ teaspoon salt

1 tablespoon snipped fresh chives

1. Thaw fish, if frozen. Cut into 4 serving-size pieces. Rinse fish; pat dry with paper towels. In a large skillet combine 1 cup water and ½ teaspoon salt.

2. For the bouquet garni, place ½ cup of the watercress, 2 tablespoons tarragon, lemon slices, peppercorns, and bay leaves in the center of a double-thick, 9-inch-square piece of 100-percent-cotton cheesecloth. Bring the corners of the cheesecloth together and tie with clean 100-percent-cotton string. Place the bouquet garni in the skillet. Bring water to boiling; reduce heat. With a slotted spatula, gently lower the fish fillets into the water. Simmer, covered, until fish flakes easily when tested with a fork. Allow 4 to 6 minutes per ½-inch thickness of fish. Using a slotted spoon, carefully remove the fish fillets to a platter. Cover fish; keep warm.

3. For sauce, in a blender container or food processor bowl combine sour cream, remaining ½ cup watercress, 1 teaspoon tarragon, ½ teaspoon black pepper, and ¼ teaspoon salt. Cover and blend or process until smooth. Stir in chives. Spoon sauce onto plates; top with fish.

2g carbs **0**g fiber **2**g net carbs

Nutrition Facts per serving: 215 cal., 13 g total fat (5 g sat. fat),
71 mg chol., 385 mg sodium, 2 g carbo., 0 g fiber, 24 g pro.

Salmon with Crème Fraîche Sauce

Prep: 10 minutes   Broil: 8 minutes   Makes: 4 servings

1. Thaw fish, if frozen. Rinse fish; pat dry with paper towels. Preheat broiler. Place fish on the greased unheated rack of a broiler pan. Brush with butter. Sprinkle with salt and pepper. Broil 4 inches from the heat for 8 to 12 minutes or until fish flakes easily when tested with a fork, turning once.

2. For sauce, in a small saucepan combine crème fraîche, whipping cream, thyme, lemon peel, lemon juice, and salt. Cook and stir over low heat until hot (do not boil). Serve salmon with sauce.

4   6-ounce fresh or frozen salmon
    steaks, cut 1 inch thick

1   tablespoon butter, melted
    Salt and black pepper

¼   cup crème fraîche

2   tablespoons whipping cream

1   teaspoon snipped fresh thyme
    or ¼ teaspoon dried thyme,
    crushed

¼   teaspoon finely shredded
    lemon peel

1   teaspoon lemon juice
    Dash salt

1 g carbs   0 g fiber   1 g net carbs

Nutrition Facts per serving: 335 cal., 21 g total fat (9 g sat. fat), 122 mg chol., 327 mg sodium, 1 g carbo., 0 g fiber, 35 g pro.

Speedy Salmon Fillets

Prep: 15 minutes Grill: 8 minutes Makes: 6 servings

1½ pounds boneless, skinless
fresh salmon fillets or tuna,
halibut, or swordfish steaks,
cut 1 inch thick

3 tablespoons lemon juice

2 cloves garlic, minced

2 tablespoons snipped fresh
basil or 1 teaspoon dried
basil, crushed

1 tablespoon cooking oil

1 tablespoon soy sauce

1 teaspoon Worcestershire
sauce

¼ teaspoon black pepper

Lemon wedges (optional)

1. Rinse fish; pat dry with paper towels. In a small bowl combine lemon juice, garlic, basil, oil, soy sauce, Worcestershire sauce, and pepper; brush mixture over fish. If desired, place fish fillets in a greased grill basket, turning under thin ends to make an even thickness.

2. For a charcoal grill, grill on the rack of an uncovered grill directly over medium coals for 8 to 12 minutes or until fish flakes easily when tested with a fork, turning and brushing with remaining sauce halfway through grilling. (For a gas grill, preheat grill. Reduce heat to medium. Place fish on grill rack over heat. Cover and grill as above.)

3. If desired, serve with lemon wedges.

1g carbs   **0**g fiber   **1**g net carbs

Nutrition Facts per serving: 187 cal., 10 g total fat (2 g sat. fat),
60 mg chol., 241 mg sodium, 1 g carbo., 0 g fiber, 24 g pro.

Grilled Salmon with Basil Butter

Prep: 15 minutes Grill: 8 minutes Makes: 6 servings

1. For basil butter, in a small food processor bowl or blender container combine basil, lime juice, garlic, butter, dash salt, and dash pepper. Cover and process or blend until basil is finely chopped, stopping to scrape down sides as necessary.

2. Rinse fish; pat dry with paper towels. Brush both sides of the fish with oil; sprinkle with salt and pepper. For a charcoal grill, grill fish on the greased rack of an uncovered grill directly over medium coals for 8 to 12 minutes or until fish flakes easily when tested with a fork, turning once. (For a gas grill, preheat grill. Reduce heat to medium. Place fish on greased grill rack over heat. Cover and grill as above.) Serve with the basil butter.

See photo, page 307.

1½ cups lightly packed fresh basil leaves

1 tablespoon lime juice

2 cloves garlic, minced

6 tablespoons butter, melted

Dash salt

Dash black pepper

6 6-ounce fresh skinless salmon fillets, 1 inch thick

1 tablespoon olive oil or cooking oil

Salt and black pepper

1g carbs   0g fiber   1g net carbs

Nutrition Facts per serving: 373 cal., 26 g total fat (10 g sat. fat), 122 mg chol., 274 mg sodium, 1 g carbo., 0 g fiber, 35 g pro.

Spicy Grilled Salmon

Prep: 15 minutes Grill: 4 minutes per ½-inch thickness Makes: 4 servings

1 pound fresh or frozen salmon fillets, ¾ to 1 inch thick, skin on

2 teaspoons ground coriander

2 teaspoons ground cumin

½ teaspoon salt

¼ teaspoon cayenne pepper

1 medium lime, cut into wedges

1. Thaw fish, if frozen. Rinse fish; pat dry with paper towels. Set aside.

2. For rub, in a small bowl combine coriander, cumin, salt, and cayenne pepper. Rub mixture onto salmon.

3. For a charcoal grill, grill fish, skin side down, on the greased rack of a uncovered grill directly over medium coals until fish flakes easily when tested with a fork. Allow 4 to 6 minutes per ½-inch thickness of fish. (For a gas grill, preheat grill. Reduce heat to medium. Place fish on greased grill rack over heat. Cover and grill as above.) Serve with lime wedges.

2 g carbs **1** g fiber **1** g net carbs

Nutrition Facts per serving: 173 cal., 8 g total fat (2 g sat. fat),
60 mg chol., 370 mg sodium, 2 g carbo., 1 g fiber, 47 g pro.

Salmon Fillets Bathed in Garlic

Prep: 15 minutes Bake: 8 minutes Oven: 425°F Makes: 6 servings

1. Thaw fish, if frozen. Rinse fish; pat dry with paper towels. Sprinkle both sides of fillets with salt and pepper; set aside.

2. In a small bowl combine parsley, broth, wine, oil, garlic, and crushed red pepper.

3. In a 2-quart rectangular baking dish place fillets, flat sides down in a single layer. Pour parsley mixture evenly over fillets.

4. Bake, uncovered, in a 425° oven for 8 to 12 minutes or until fish flakes easily when tested with a fork.

6 4-ounce fresh or frozen
skinless salmon fillets, about
1 inch thick

Salt and black pepper

¼ cup snipped fresh
flat-leaf parsley

¼ cup reduced-sodium
chicken broth

¼ cup dry white wine

1 tablespoon olive oil

4 large cloves garlic, minced

½ teaspoon crushed red pepper

1 g carbs 0 g fiber 1 g net carbs

Nutrition Facts per serving: 163 cal., 6 g total fat (1 g sat. fat), 50 mg chol., 201 mg sodium, 1 g carbo., 0 g fiber, 23 g pro.

Basil-Buttered Salmon Steaks

Start to Finish: 15 minutes Makes: 4 servings

4 fresh or frozen salmon or

halibut steaks, cut 1

inch thick

3 tablespoons butter, softened

1 tablespoon snipped fresh

basil, or savory; or 1

teaspoon dried basil or

savory, crushed

1 tablespoon snipped

fresh parsley

2 teaspoons lemon juice

1. Thaw fish, if frozen. Rinse fish; pat dry with paper towels. Set fish aside. In a small bowl stir together butter, basil, parsley, and lemon juice.

2. Preheat broiler. Place fish on the greased unheated rack of a broiler pan. Lightly brush fish with some of the butter mixture. Broil 4 inches from the heat for 5 minutes. Using a wide spatula, carefully turn over fish. Lightly brush with more of the butter mixture. Broil for 3 to 7 minutes more or until fish flakes easily when tested with a fork.

0_g carbs 0_g fiber 0_g net carbs

Nutrition Facts per serving: 231 cal., 14 g total fat (7 g sat. fat), 54 mg chol., 190 mg sodium, 0 g carbo., 0 g fiber, 24 g pro.

Double-Smoked Salmon with Horseradish Cream

Prep: 15 minutes Soak: 1 hour Smoke: 30 minutes Makes: 4 servings

1. At least 1 hour before smoke cooking, soak wood chunks in enough water to cover.

2. Thaw fish, if frozen. Rinse fish; pat dry. Make a pocket in each fish fillet by cutting horizontally from one side almost through to the other side. Fill with slices of smoked salmon and 2 teaspoons of the dill, folding salmon slices as necessary to fit. Brush each fillet with lemon juice and top with 2 teaspoons of the dill. Sprinkle with salt and pepper.

3. Drain wood chunks. In a smoker arrange preheated coals, drained wood chunks, and water pan according to the manufacturer's directions. Pour water into pan. Place fish fillets, skin side down, on grill rack over water pan. Cover and smoke about 30 minutes or until fish flakes easily when tested with a fork.

4. Meanwhile, for sauce, in a small bowl combine the remaining 2 teaspoons dill, sour cream, horseradish, and green onion. Serve fish with sauce.

4 hickory or apple wood chunks

4 6-ounce fresh or frozen salmon
   fillets (with skin), about 1
   inch thick

4 slices smoked salmon (about
   3 ounces)

2 tablespoons snipped fresh dill

1 tablespoon lemon juice
   Salt and black pepper

½ cup dairy sour cream

4 teaspoons prepared
   horseradish

1 green onion, thinly sliced

2 g carbs   **0** g fiber   **2** g net carbs

Nutrition Facts per serving: 245 cal., 13 g total fat (5 g sat. fat),
48 mg chol., 337 mg sodium, 2 g carbo., 0 g fiber, 29 g pro.

Dilly Salmon Fillets

Prep: 20 minutes Marinate: 30 minutes Broil: 4 minutes per ½-inch thickness Makes: 4 servings

4 6-ounce fresh or frozen
   skinless salmon fillets,
   ½ to ¾ inch thick

3 tablespoons lemon juice

2 tablespoons snipped
   fresh dill

2 tablespoons olive oil

¼ cup mayonnaise

1 tablespoon Dijon-style
   mustard

   Salt and black pepper

   Lemon wedges (optional)

1. Thaw fish, if frozen. Rinse fish; pat dry with paper towels. Place fish in a self-sealing plastic bag set in a shallow dish. In a small bowl stir together lemon juice, 1 tablespoon of the dill, and oil. Pour over fish; seal bag. Marinate in the refrigerator for 30 minutes to 2 hours. Drain fish, discarding marinade.

2. Meanwhile, for sauce, in a small bowl stir together the remaining 1 tablespoon dill, mayonnaise, and mustard. Cover and chill until serving time.

3. Preheat broiler. Sprinkle fish with salt and pepper. Place fish on the greased unheated rack of a broiler pan. Broil 4 inches from heat until fish flakes easily when tested with a fork. Allow 4 to 6 minutes per ½-inch thickness of fish.

4. Serve fish with sauce and if desired, lemon wedges.

1 g carbs   0 g fiber   1 g net carbs

Nutrition Facts per serving: 385 cal., 27 g total fat (5 g sat. fat),
100 mg chol., 432 mg sodium, 1 g carbo., 0 g fiber, 35 g pro.

Grilled Tuna with Rosemary

Prep: 10 minutes Grill: 8 minutes Makes: 4 servings

1. Thaw fish, if frozen. Rinse fish; pat dry with paper towels. Cut fish into 4 serving-size pieces. Brush both sides with oil and lemon juice; sprinkle with salt and pepper. Rub garlic and rosemary onto fish.

2. For a charcoal grill, grill fish on the greased rack of an uncovered grill directly over medium-hot coals for 8 to 12 minutes or until fish flakes easily when tested with a fork, turning once halfway through grilling. (For a gas grill, preheat grill. Reduce heat to medium. Place fish on grill rack. Cover and grill as above.)

3. Top fish with capers. If desired, garnish with fresh rosemary springs.

1 pound fresh or frozen tuna,
    halibut, or salmon steaks, cut
    1 inch thick

2 teaspoons olive oil

2 teaspoons lemon juice

1/8 teaspoon salt

1/8 teaspoon black pepper

2 cloves garlic, minced

2 teaspoons snipped fresh
    rosemary or tarragon or
    1 teaspoon dried rosemary
    or tarragon, crushed

1 tablespoon drained capers,
    slightly crushed

  Fresh rosemary sprigs
  (optional)

1g carbs **0**g fiber **1**g net carbs

Nutrition Facts per serving: 145 cal., 3 g total fat (1 g sat. fat), 51 mg chol., 179 mg sodium, 1 g carbo., 0 g fiber, 27 g pro.

Grilled Tuna with Roasted Pepper Sauce

Prep: 25 minutes Grill: 8 minutes Makes: 4 servings

4 5- to 6-ounce fresh or frozen

 tuna or halibut steaks,

 cut 1 inch thick

1 tablespoon olive oil

1 7-ounce jar roasted red

 sweet peppers, drained

3 tablespoons lime juice

2 tablespoons water

2 teaspoons snipped fresh

 thyme or ½ teaspoon dried

 thyme, crushed

¼ teaspoon salt

⅛ teaspoon black pepper

2 tablespoons butter

 Fresh dill sprigs (optional)

4 thin lime wedges (optional)

1. Thaw fish, if frozen. Rinse fish; pat dry with paper towels. Brush both sides of fish with some of the oil. For a charcoal grill, grill on the rack of an uncovered grill directly over medium coals for 8 to 12 minutes or until fish flakes easily when tested with a fork, turning once and brushing with remaining oil halfway through. (For a gas grill, preheat grill. Reduce heat to medium. Place fish on grill rack over heat. Cover and grill as above.)

2. Meanwhile, for sauce, in a blender container or food processor bowl combine roasted peppers, lime juice, water, thyme, salt, and black pepper. Cover and blend or process until smooth. Pour into a small saucepan. Cook and stir over low heat until heated through. Stir in butter.

3. To serve, pour warm sauce onto 4 plates. Top with fish steaks and, if desired, dill sprigs. If desired, serve with lime wedges.

See photo, page 308.

5 g carbs   **0** g fiber   **5** g net carbs

Nutrition Facts per serving: 306 cal., 17 g total fat (5 g sat. fat), 70 mg chol., 245 mg sodium, 5 g carbo., 0 g fiber, 34 g pro.

Shrimp with Serranos

Start to Finish: 25 minutes Makes: 4 servings

1. Thaw shrimp, if frozen. Rinse shrimp; pat dry with paper towels. In a large skillet heat oil over medium-high heat. Add sweet pepper, serrano peppers, garlic, and shallots; cook and stir for 2 minutes. Add shrimp; cook and stir for 2 to 3 minutes or until shrimp turn opaque. Sprinkle with cilantro.

1 pound fresh or frozen shrimp, peeled and deveined

2 tablespoons cooking oil

¼ cup chopped red sweet pepper

2 or 3 fresh serrano peppers, seeded and chopped (see note, page 51)

3 cloves garlic, minced

¼ cup chopped shallots

1 tablespoon snipped fresh cilantro

4 g carbs   0 g fiber   4 g net carbs

Nutrition Facts per serving: 165 cal., 8 g total fat (1 g sat. fat), 129 mg chol., 129 mg sodium, 4 g carbo., 0 g fiber, 18 g pro.

Cajun Barbecue Shrimp

Prep: 10 minutes Cook: 21 minutes Makes: 8 servings

2 pounds medium unshelled
  shrimp*

⅓ cup butter

⅓ cup olive oil

8 cloves garlic, minced

1 cup chicken broth

2 tablespoons lemon juice

2 tablespoons snipped
  fresh basil

4 teaspoons Worcestershire
  sauce

1 tablespoon finely snipped
  fresh rosemary

1½ teaspoons crushed red
  pepper

1 teaspoon paprika

1. Rinse shrimp; pat dry with paper towels. In a 12-inch cast iron or heavy skillet melt butter. Add oil and garlic. Cook and stir over medium heat for 1 minute. Add chicken broth, lemon juice, basil, Worcestershire sauce, rosemary, crushed red pepper, and paprika; bring to boiling. Reduce heat. Simmer, uncovered, over low heat for 15 minutes. Add shrimp; cook and stir over medium heat about 5 minutes or until shrimp are opaque. Transfer shrimp and juices to a deep serving platter.

*Note: If possible, purchase deveined shrimp in shells.

3g carbs   **0**g fiber   **3**g net carbs

Nutrition Facts per serving: 255 cal., 18 g total fat (6 g sat. fat),
151 mg chol., 432 mg sodium, 3 g carbo., 0 g fiber, 18 g pro.

Shrimp with Tomato & Garlic

Start to Finish: 20 minutes Makes: 4 servings

1. Thaw shrimp, if frozen. Peel and devein shrimp; if desired, leave tails intact. Rinse shrimp; pat dry with paper towels. Set shrimp aside.

2. In a large skillet cook shallots and garlic in hot oil over medium-high heat about 2 minutes or until tender. Add shrimp; cook for 2 to 4 minutes until shrimp turn opaque. Stir in tomato, parsley, salt, lemon peel, and pepper. If desired, garnish with lemon wedges.

1½ pounds fresh or frozen large shrimp in shells

2 tablespoons finely chopped shallots

2 cloves garlic, minced

1 tablespoon olive oil

1 Roma tomato, seeded and chopped (about ½ cup)

2 tablespoons snipped fresh flat-leaf parsley

½ teaspoon salt

½ teaspoon finely shredded lemon peel

¼ teaspoon freshly ground black pepper

Lemon wedges (optional)

4g carbs

0g fiber

4g net carbs

Nutrition Facts per serving: 176 cal., 6 g total fat (1 g sat. fat), 194 mg chol., 483 mg sodium, 4 g carbo., 0 g fiber, 26 g pro.

Shrimp & Feta

Prep: 30 minutes   Marinate: 30 minutes   Makes: 8 to 10 servings

½ cup bottled olive oil and
    vinegar salad dressing or
    Italian salad dressing

1 teaspoon finely shredded
    lime peel

3 pounds fresh or frozen large
    shrimp in shells, peeled,
    deveined, and cooked*

¼ cup snipped fresh herbs,
    such as dill, cilantro,
    and/or parsley

¼ cup crumbled feta cheese
    (1 ounce)
    Salt and black pepper
    Lime wedges

1. In a self-sealing plastic bag set in a shallow dish combine salad dressing and lime peel. Add shrimp; seal bag. Marinate in the refrigerator for 30 minutes to 4 hours, turning bag occasionally.

2. To serve, combine undrained shrimp, herbs, and feta cheese. Stir gently to combine; season to taste with salt and pepper. Spoon into a bowl. Serve with lime wedges.

*Note: To cook shrimp, in a Dutch oven bring lightly salted water to boiling. Add shrimp. Simmer, uncovered, for 1 to 3 minutes or until shrimp turn opaque, stirring occasionally. Rinse under cold running water; drain.

2g carbs   **0**g fiber   **2**g net carbs

Nutrition Facts per serving: 221 cal., 11 g total fat (2 g sat. fat),
197 mg chol., 339 mg sodium, 2 g carbo., 0 g fiber, 26 g pro.

Lemony Shrimp Kabobs

Prep: 25 minutes Grill: 8 minutes Makes: 4 servings

1. Thaw shrimp, if frozen. Peel shrimp leaving tails intact. Devein shrimp; rinse and pat dry with paper towels. Set aside.

2. In a saucepan cook zucchini in a small amount of boiling lightly salted water for 2 minutes; drain. On eight 12-inch skewers, alternately thread shrimp, zucchini, and sweet pepper.

3. In a small saucepan cook garlic in butter. Stir in lemon peel, lemon juice, cayenne pepper, and salt; set aside.

4. For a charcoal grill, grill kabobs on the rack of an uncovered grill directly over hot coals for 5 minutes. Brush kabobs with lemon mixture. Turn kabobs and brush again. Grill for 3 to 7 minutes more or until shrimp turn opaque. (For a gas grill, preheat grill. Reduce heat to high. Place kabobs on grill rack over heat. Cover and grill as above.) If desired, serve with lemon wedges.

See photo, page 309.

1 pound fresh or frozen large
   shrimp in shells
2 small zucchini, cut into ¾-inch
   slices (2 cups)
1 large red sweet pepper, cut
   into 1-inch pieces
   (about 1½ cups)
1 clove garlic, minced
2 tablespoons butter
1 teaspoon finely shredded
   lemon peel
2 tablespoons lemon juice
¼ teaspoon cayenne pepper
⅛ teaspoon salt
   Lemon wedges (optional)

6 g carbs   **1** g fiber   **5** g net carbs

Nutrition Facts per serving: 166 cal., 8 g total fat (3 g sat. fat), 145 mg chol., 248 mg sodium, 6 g carbo., 1 g fiber, 18 g pro.

Seafood Kabobs

Prep: 20 minutes Marinate: 2 hours Grill: 12 minutes Makes: 6 servings

8 ounces fresh or frozen
   medium shrimp in shells

1 pound skinless fresh fish
   fillets, such as salmon,
   halibut, and/or red snapper,
   1 inch thick

2 medium fennel bulbs

¼ cup olive oil

2 tablespoons lemon juice

4 cloves garlic, minced

3 tablespoons snipped fresh
   oregano or 2 teaspoons
   dried oregano, crushed

¼ teaspoon salt

1. Thaw shrimp, if frozen. Peel and devein shrimp, leaving tails intact. Rinse shrimp; pat dry with paper towels. Set aside. Rinse fish; pat dry. Cut fish into 1-inch cubes; set aside.

2. Cut off and discard upper stalks of fennel, reserving some of the leafy fronds. Snip 2 tablespoons of the fronds for use in the marinade. Remove any wilted outer layers from fennel bulbs; cut off a thin slice from the base of each bulb. Wash and cut each bulb lengthwise into 6 wedges. Cook wedges, covered, in a small amount of boiling water about 5 minutes or until nearly tender; drain.

3. Place shrimp, fish, and fennel wedges in a self-sealing plastic bag set in a shallow dish. For marinade, in a bowl stir together oil, lemon juice, garlic, oregano, salt, and the reserved 2 tablespoons snipped fennel fronds. Pour marinade over seafood and fennel; seal bag. Marinate in the refrigerator for 2 hours, turning the bag occasionally.

4. Drain seafood and fennel, discarding marinade. Thread seafood and fennel wedges onto skewers, leaving a ¼-inch space between pieces. For a charcoal grill, grill kabobs on the greased rack of an uncovered grill directly over medium-hot coals for 12 to 14 minutes or until fish flakes easily when tested with a fork and shrimp turn opaque; turn often. (For a gas grill, preheat grill. Reduce heat to medium-high. Place kabobs on grill rack over heat. Cover and grill as above.)

3g carbs **1**g fiber **2**g net carbs

Nutrition Facts per serving: 189 cal., 10 g total fat (2 g sat. fat), 83 mg chol., 157 mg sodium, 3 g carbo., 1 g fiber, 22 g pro.

Garlic-Buttered Shrimp

Prep: 20 minutes Grill: 6 minutes Makes: 4 servings

1. Thaw shrimp, if frozen. Peel and devein shrimp, keeping tails intact. Rinse shrimp; pat dry with paper towels. Thread shrimp onto 4 long metal skewers. Set aside.

2. For sauce, in a small saucepan melt butter. Stir in garlic, parsley, and cayenne pepper; cook for 1 minute. Stir in wine; heat through. Set sauce aside.

3. For a charcoal grill, grill kabobs on the greased rack of an uncovered grill directly over medium coals for 6 to 10 minutes or until shrimp turn opaque, turning once and brushing frequently with sauce. (For a gas grill, preheat grill. Reduce heat to medium. Place kabobs on greased grill rack over heat. Cover and grill as above.)

1 pound fresh or frozen large
 shrimp in shells

2 tablespoons butter

2 cloves garlic, minced

1 tablespoon snipped
 fresh parsley

Dash cayenne pepper

2 tablespoons dry white wine

Nutrition Facts per serving: 159 cal., 8 g total fat (4 g sat. fat), 156 mg chol., 199 mg sodium, 1 g carbo., 0 g fiber, 19 g pro.

Shrimp & Greens Soup

Start to Finish: 30 minutes Makes: 4 servings

12 ounces peeled and deveined
      fresh or frozen shrimp

 1 large leek, sliced

 2 cloves garlic, minced

 1 tablespoon olive oil

 3 14-ounce cans reduced-
      sodium chicken broth or
      vegetable broth

 1 tablespoon snipped fresh
      flat-leaf parsley or parsley

 1 tablespoon snipped fresh
      marjoram or thyme

¼ teaspoon lemon-pepper
      seasoning

 2 cups shredded bok choy or
      spinach leaves

1. Thaw shrimp, if frozen.

2. In a large saucepan cook leek and garlic in hot oil over medium heat until leek is tender. Carefully add broth, parsley, marjoram, and lemon-pepper seasoning. Bring to boiling; add shrimp. Return to boiling; reduce heat.

3. Simmer, uncovered, for 2 minutes. Stir in bok choy. Cook about 1 minute more or until shrimp turn opaque.

See photo, page 310.

6 g carbs   **1** g fiber   **5** g net carbs

Nutrition Facts per serving: 159 cal., 6 g total fat (1 g sat. fat),
132 mg chol., 1,642 mg sodium, 6 g carbo., 1 g fiber, 21 g pro.

Callaloo Soup

Prep: 20 minutes Cook: 25 minutes Makes: 4 servings

1. Rinse shrimp; pat dry with paper towels. In a large saucepan cook bacon over medium heat for 5 to 6 minutes or until crisp. Remove bacon from pan with a slotted spoon; set aside. Reserve 1 tablespoon bacon drippings in pan. Add onion, celery, habanero pepper, and garlic to pan. Cook and stir for 4 to 5 minutes or until vegetables are tender.

2. Carefully add broth to pan. Increase heat to medium-high and bring broth to boiling. Add okra. Reduce heat and simmer, covered, for 10 minutes. Add shrimp and simmer, covered, for 5 minutes more or until shrimp turn opaque. Stir in spinach and heat through. Stir in cooked bacon. Season to taste with salt.

12 fresh or frozen medium shrimp, peeled and deveined

3 slices thick-sliced bacon, chopped

½ cup finely chopped onion (1 medium)

¼ cup finely chopped celery

1 habañero or other fresh hot pepper, stemmed, seeded, and minced (see note, page 51)

1 clove garlic, minced

4 14-ounce cans chicken or vegetable broth

1 cup sliced fresh or frozen okra

2 cups shredded fresh spinach

Salt

5g carbs   **3**g fiber   **2**g net carbs

Nutrition Facts per serving: 121 cal., 7 g total fat (3 g sat. fat), 40 mg chol., 541 mg sodium, 5 g carbo., 3 g fiber, 9 g pro.

Lobster Tails with Basil Butter

Prep: 15 minutes Grill: 12 minutes Makes: 4 servings

4 8-ounce frozen lobster tails

2 teaspoons olive oil

⅓ cup butter

2 tablespoons snipped
    fresh basil

1 clove garlic, minced

1. Thaw lobster. Rinse lobster; pat dry with paper towels. Place lobster, shell side down, on a cutting board. To butterfly, with kitchen scissors, cut each lobster in half lengthwise, cutting to but not through the back shell. Bend backward to crack back shell and expose the meat. Brush lobster meat with oil.

2. For a charcoal grill, grill lobster, shell side down, on the greased rack of an uncovered grill directly over medium coals for 12 to 15 minutes or until lobster meat is opaque and shells are bright red, turning once halfway through grilling. (For a gas grill, preheat grill. Reduce heat to medium. Place lobster, shell side down, on greased grill rack over heat. Cover and grill as above.)

3. Meanwhile, in a small saucepan melt butter over low heat without stirring; cool slightly. Pour off clear top layer; discard milky bottom layer. In a small bowl combine butter, basil, and garlic. Spoon butter mixture over lobster meat.

1 g carbs   0 g fiber   1 g net carbs

Nutrition Facts per serving: 291 cal., 20 g total fat (9 g sat. fat), 177 mg chol., 534 mg sodium, 1 g carbo., 0 g fiber, 27 g pro.

Lobster Tails with Chive Butter

Prep: 20 minutes Grill: 10 minutes Makes: 4 servings

1. Thaw lobster, if frozen. Rinse lobster; pat dry with paper towels. Place lobster, shell side down, on a cutting board. To butterfly, with kitchen scissors, cut each lobster in half lengthwise, cutting to but not through the back shell. Bend backward to crack back shell and expose the meat.

2. For sauce, in a small saucepan melt butter. Remove from heat. Stir in chives and lemon peel. Remove 2 tablespoons of the sauce; set remaining sauce aside.

3. For a charcoal grill, grill lobster tails on the greased rack of an uncovered grill directly over medium coals for 10 to 12 minutes or until lobster meat is opaque, turning and brushing with the 2 tablespoons sauce once halfway through grilling. (For a gas grill, preheat grill. Reduce heat to medium. Place lobster tails on greased grill rack over heat. Cover and grill as above.)

4. Heat reserved sauce, stirring occasionally. Transfer sauce to small bowls for dipping. Serve lobster with butter mixture.

See photo, page 311.

4 5-ounce fresh or frozen rock lobster tails

⅓ cup butter

2 tablespoons snipped fresh chives

1 teaspoon finely shredded lemon peel

1g carbs **0**g fiber **1**g net carbs

Nutrition Facts per servings: 214 cal., 17 g total fat (10 g sat. fat), 118 mg chol., 395 mg sodium, 1 g carbo., 0 g fiber, 15 g pro.

Pan-Seared Scallops with Lemon

Prep: 20 minutes   Cook: 6 minutes   Makes: 4 servings

12 ounces fresh or frozen
   sea scallops

1 lemon

1 pound asparagus spears, cut
   into 2-inch pieces

1 medium red onion, cut into
   thin wedges

3 tablespoons olive oil
   Salt and black pepper

2 or 3 fresh basil sprigs
   Salt and black pepper

1. Thaw scallops, if frozen. Rinse scallops; pat dry with paper towels. Set scallops aside.

2. Score lemon into four lengthwise sections with a sharp knife; remove peel from lemon. Scrape off white portion from peel; discard. Cut peel into very thin strips; set aside. Squeeze 2 tablespoons juice from lemon; set juice aside.

3. In a large skillet cook asparagus and red onion in 1 tablespoon of the oil for 2 to 3 minutes or until crisp-tender. Season to taste with salt and pepper. Transfer asparagus mixture to a serving platter; keep warm.

4. In the same skillet combine reserved lemon peel, the 2 remaining tablespoons olive oil, and basil sprigs. Cook for 30 seconds to 1 minute or until heated through. Remove lemon peel and basil sprigs with a slotted spoon, reserving oil in skillet. Discard lemon peel and basil sprigs.

5. Cook scallops in the hot flavored oil for 3 to 5 minutes or until scallops turn opaque, turning once. Stir in reserved lemon juice. Season to taste with salt and pepper. Serve scallops with asparagus mixture.

6g carbs   **1**g fiber   **5**g net carbs

Nutrition Facts per serving: 190 cal., 11 g total fat (1 g sat. fat),
28 mg chol., 147 mg sodium, 6 g carbo., 1 g fiber, 16 g pro.

Broiled Crab Legs

Start to Finish: 15 minutes Makes: 4 servings

1. Thaw crab legs, if frozen. Rinse and pat dry with paper towels. Preheat boiler. Place crab legs on the greased unheated rack of a broiler pan. Stir together butter, basil, lemon peel, and lemon juice. Brush crab legs with butter mixture. Broil 4 to 6 inches from the heat for 3 to 4 minutes or until heated through.

1½ pounds fresh or frozen split
    crab legs

3 tablespoons butter, melted

1 tablespoon snipped fresh basil
    or 1 teaspoon dried basil,
    crushed

½ teaspoon finely shredded
    lemon peel

1 tablespoon lemon juice

4 g carbs   0 g fiber   4 g net carbs

Nutrition Facts per serving: 176 cal., 10 g total fat (7 g sat. fat),
24 mg chol., 358 mg sodium, 4 g carbo., 0 g fiber, 16 g pro.

Scallops with Fresh Herb Tartar Sauce

Prep: 20 minutes Broil: 8 minutes Makes: 4 servings

12 ounces fresh or frozen sea scallops

2 tablespoons butter, melted

1/4 teaspoon black pepper

1/8 teaspoon paprika

2/3 cup mayonnaise

1 tablespoon finely chopped onion

1/2 teaspoon finely shredded
   lemon peel

2 teaspoons lemon juice

1 1/2 teaspoons snipped fresh parsley

1 1/2 teaspoons snipped fresh dill or
   1/2 teaspoon dried dill

1 1/2 teaspoons snipped fresh thyme, or
   1/2 teaspoon dried thyme, crushed

Lemon wedges (optional)

1. Thaw scallops, if frozen. Rinse scallops; pat dry with paper towels. Halve any large scallops. Thread scallops onto four 8- to 10-inch skewers, leaving a 1/4-inch space between pieces. Preheat broiler. Place skewers on the greased unheated rack of a broiler pan.

2. In a small bowl stir together butter, pepper, and paprika. Brush half of the mixture over scallops. Broil about 4 inches from the heat for 8 to 10 minutes or until scallops are opaque, turning and brushing often with the remaining melted butter mixture.

3. For tartar sauce, in a medium bowl stir together mayonnaise, onion, lemon peel, lemon juice, parsley, dill, and thyme. Serve scallops with tartar sauce and if desired, lemon wedges.

3g carbs   **0**g fiber   **3**g net carbs

Nutrition Facts per serving: 400 cal., 36 g total fat (7 g sat. fat), 71 mg chol., 388 mg sodium, 3 g carbo., 0 g fiber, 14 g pro.

Grilled Clams

Prep: 15 minutes Soak: 45 minutes Grill: 6 minutes Makes: 4 servings

1. Scrub clams under cold running water. In a 6- to 8-quart Dutch oven stir together 4 quarts water and $\frac{1}{3}$ cup salt. Add clams; let soak for 15 minutes. Drain, discarding water. Rinse clams. Repeat soaking twice.

2. For a charcoal grill, grill clams in a single layer on the rack of an uncovered grill directly over medium-hot coals for 6 to 8 minutes or until opened at least $\frac{1}{2}$ inch, turning once. (For a gas grill, preheat grill. Reduce heat to medium-hot. Place clams on grill rack over heat. Cover and grill as above.) Remove clams as they open and keep warm while others cook. Discard any unopened clams.

36 small hard-shell clams, such as

littlenecks (about 5 pounds)

Water

Salt

Nutrition Facts per serving: 126 cal., 2 g total fat (0 g sat. fat), 57 mg chol., 96 mg sodium, 4 g carbo., 0 g fiber, 22 g pro.

Scallops in Garlic Butter

Start to Finish: 20 minutes Makes: 4 servings

1 pound fresh or frozen
    sea scallops

3 cloves garlic, minced

2 tablespoons butter

2 tablespoons dry white wine

1 tablespoon snipped fresh
    chives or parsley

⅛ teaspoon salt

1. Thaw scallops, if frozen. Rinse scallops; pat dry with paper towels.

2. In a 12-inch skillet cook garlic in 1 tablespoon of the butter over medium-high heat for 1 minute. Add scallops. Cook, stirring frequently, for 2 to 3 minutes or until scallops turn opaque. Remove from skillet and transfer to a serving platter. Add remaining 1 tablespoon butter and wine to the skillet. Cook and stir to loosen any browned bits. Pour over scallops; sprinkle with chives and salt.

Shrimp in Garlic Butter: Prepare as above, except substitute 1½ pounds fresh or frozen medium shrimp in shells for the scallops. Thaw shrimp, if frozen. Peel and devein shrimp, leaving tails intact. Rinse shrimp; pat dry with paper towels. Cook shrimp in the butter and garlic for 1 to 3 minutes or until shrimp turn opaque. Continue as above.

2g carbs **0**g fiber **2**g net carbs

Nutrition Facts per serving: 183 cal., 8 g total fat (4 g sat. fat), 189 mg chol., 303 mg sodium, 2 g carbo., 0 g fiber, 23 g pro.

Soft-Shell Crabs with Lemon Butter

Prep: 25 minutes Grill: 5 minutes Makes: 4 servings

1. To clean each soft-shell crab, hold the crab between the back legs. Using kitchen scissors, remove the head by cutting horizontally across the body about 1/2 inch behind the eyes, removing the face. Lift the pointed, soft top shell to expose the "devil's fingers" (the spongy projectiles) on one side. Using your fingers, push up on the devil's fingers and pull off. Replace the soft top shell over the body. Repeat on the other side. Turn over crab. Pull off the apron-shaped piece and discard. Handle each crab carefully while thoroughly rinsing under cold running water to remove the mustard-colored substance; pat dry. Brush crabs with cooking oil. Cover and chill until ready to grill.

2. For a charcoal grill, grill crabs, back side down, on the greased rack of an uncovered grill directly over medium coals for 5 to 7 minutes or until golden brown, turning once halfway through grilling. (For a gas grill, preheat grill. Reduce heat to medium. Place crabs, back side down, on greased grill rack over heat. Cover and grill as above.)

3. Meanwhile, for lemon butter, in a small saucepan melt butter. Stir in lemon peel and juice. Serve crabs with lemon butter.

4 large or 8 small soft-shell crabs

Cooking oil

2 tablespoons butter

1 teaspoon finely shredded lemon peel

1 tablespoon lemon juice

1 g carbs   0 g fiber   1 g net carbs

Nutrition Facts per serving: 135 cal., 11 g total fat (4 g sat. fat), 96 mg chol., 373 mg sodium, 1 g carbo., 0 g fiber, 9 g pro.

Quick and Easy Cooking Methods for Fish and Seafood

Direct Grilling Fish and Seafood

Thaw fish or seafood, if frozen. Place fish fillets in a well-greased grill basket. For fish steaks and whole fish, grease grill rack. Thread scallops or shrimp onto skewers, leaving a ¼-inch space between pieces. For a charcoal grill, place fish on grill rack directly over medium coals. Grill, uncovered, for the time given below or until fish flakes easily when tested with a fork (seafood should look opaque), turning once halfway through grilling. For a gas grill, preheat grill. Reduce heat to medium. Place fish on grill rack over heat. Cover the grill. If desired, brush fish with melted butter after turning.

Form of Fish	Thickness, Weight, or Size	Grilling Temperature	Approximate Direct Grilling Time	Doneness
Dressed whole fish	½ to 1 ½ pounds	Medium	6 to 9 minutes per 8 ounces	Flakes
Fillets, steaks, cubes (for kabobs)	½ to 1 inch thick	Medium	4 to 6 minutes per ½-inch thickness	Flakes
Lobster tails	6 ounces 8 ounces	Medium Medium	6 to 10 minutes 12 to 15 minutes	Opaque Opaque
Sea scallops (for kabobs)	12 to 15 per pound	Medium	5 to 8 minutes	Opaque
Shrimp (for kabobs)	Medium (20 per pound) Jumbo (12 to 15 per pound)	Medium Medium	5 to 8 minutes 7 to 9 minutes	Opaque Opaque

All cooking times are based on fish or seafood removed directly from refrigerator.

Indirect Grilling Fish and Seafood

Thaw fish or seafood, if frozen. Place fish fillets in a well-greased grill basket. For fish steaks and whole fish, grease grill rack. Thread scallops or shrimp on skewers, leaving a ¼-inch space between pieces. For a charcoal grill, arrange medium-hot coals around a drip pan. Test for medium heat above the pan. Place fish on grill rack over drip pan. Cover and grill for the time given below or until fish flakes easily when tested with a fork (seafood should look opaque), turning once halfway through grilling, if desired. For a gas grill, preheat grill. Reduce heat to medium. Adjust heat for indirect cooking. If desired, brush with melted butter halfway through grilling.

Form of Fish	Thickness, Weight, or Size	Grilling Temperature	Approximate Indirect Grilling Time	Doneness
Dressed whole fish	½ to 1½ pounds	Medium	15 to 20 minutes per 8 ounces	Flakes
Fillets, steaks, cubes (for kabobs)	½ to 1 inch thick	Medium	7 to 9 minutes per ½ inch thick	Flakes
Sea scallops (for kabobs)	12 to 15 per pound	Medium	11 to 14 minutes	Opaque
Shrimp (for kabobs)	Medium (20 per pound)	Medium	8 to 10 minutes	Opaque
	Jumbo (12 to 15 per pound)	Medium	9 to 11 minutes	Opaque

Indoor Electric Grilling Fish and Seafood

Lightly grease the rack of an indoor electric grill or lightly coat with cooking spray. Preheat grill. Place fish, or seafood on grill rack. (For fish fillets, tuck under any thin edges.) If using a grill with a cover, close the lid. Grill for the time given below or until done. If using a grill without a cover, turn food once halfway through grilling. The following timings should be used as general guidelines. Refer to your owner's manual for preheating directions and recommended grilling times.

Fish and Seafood	Thickness, Weight, or Size	Covered Grilling Time	Uncovered Grilling Time	Doneness
Dillets or steaks	½ to 1 inch	2 to 3 minutes per ½-inch thickness	4 to 6 minutes per ½-inch thickness	Flakes
Sea scallops	15 to 20 per pound	2½ to 4 minutes	6 to 8 minutes	Opaque
Shrimp	Medium (20 per pound)	2½ to 4 minutes	6 to 8 minutes	Opaque

Cooking Shellfish

Refer to these directions for cooking fresh shellfish. Many types of shellfish are available partially prepared or even cooked. Ask at the fish and shellfish counter for additional information when making purchases.

Shellfish Type	Amount	Preparing	Cooking
Clams	6 clams in the shell	Scrub live clams under cold running water. For 24 clams in shells, in an 8-quart kettle combine 4 quarts of cold water and ⅓ cup salt. Add clams and soak for 1 hour; drain and rinse. Discard water.	For 24 clams in shells, add ½ inch water to an 8-quart kettle; bring to boiling. Place clams in a steamer basket. Steam, covered, 5 to 7 minutes or until clams open. Discard any that do not open.
Crabs (hard shell)	1 pound live crabs	Grasp live crabs from behind, firmly holding the back two legs on each side. Rinse under cold running water.	To boil 3 pounds live hard-shell blue crabs, in a 12- to 16-quart kettle, bring 8 quarts water and 2 teaspoons salt to boiling. Add crabs. Simmer, covered, for 10 minutes or until crabs turn pink; drain.
Lobster tails	One 8-ounce frozen lobster tail	Thaw frozen lobster tails in the refrigerator.	For four 8-ounce lobster tails, in a 3-quart saucepan bring 6 cups water and 1½ teaspoons salt to boiling. Add tails; simmer, uncovered, for 8 to 12 minutes or until shells turn bright red and meat is tender; drain.
Mussels	12 mussels in shells	Scrub live mussels under cold running water. Using your fingers, pull out the beards that are visible between the shells. Soak as for clams, above.	For 24 mussels, add ½ inch water to an 8-qt. kettle; bring to boiling. Boil 7 minutes or until shells open. Discard any that do not open.

Side Dishes

Turn the freshest low-carb produce into spectacular phase 1 taste sensations. Along with colorful dishes like Summer Squash Combo and Lemony Mixed Vegetables, this chapter contains new twists on much-loved favorites, such as Bacon & Spinach Salad and Napa Cabbage Slaw.

Swiss Chard with Peppered Bacon

Start to Finish: 20 minutes Makes: 4 servings

2 slices thick-sliced

   peppered bacon

½ cup chopped onion

8 cups coarsely chopped

   Swiss chard leaves

½ teaspoon finely shredded

   lemon peel

   Salt and black pepper

1. In a 12-inch skillet cook bacon over medium heat until crisp. Remove bacon from skillet, reserving 1 tablespoon drippings in skillet. Drain bacon on paper towels. Crumble bacon; set aside.

2. Cook onion in reserved drippings over medium heat until tender. Add Swiss chard. Cook and stir about 5 minutes or until just tender. Stir in bacon and lemon peel. Season to taste with salt and pepper.

5g
carbs

2g
fiber

3g
net carbs

Nutrition Facts per serving: 45 cal., 2 g total fat (1 g sat. fat),
3 mg chol., 253 mg sodium, 5 g carbo., 2 g fiber, 3 g pro.

Roasted Asparagus in Mustard-Dill Sauce

Start to Finish: 25 minutes Oven: 425°F Makes: 4 servings

1. Snap off and discard woody bases from asparagus. Arrange asparagus in a shallow baking dish. Combine broth and mustard. Pour over asparagus, turning asparagus to coat with mustard mixture.

2. Bake in a 425° oven, uncovered, for 15 to 20 minutes or until asparagus is crisp-tender. Transfer to a serving dish. Sprinkle with pepper. If desired, garnish with cheese, lemon slice, and dill sprig.

*Note: If dill mustard is not available, substitute 2 tablespoons Dijon-style mustard plus 1 teaspoon snipped fresh dill.

2 pounds asparagus spears

¼ cup reduced-sodium
    chicken broth

2 tablespoons dill mustard*
    Freshly ground black pepper

2 tablespoons grated Parmesan
    or Asiago cheese (optional)

Lemon slice (optional)

Fresh dill sprig (optional)

6g carbs   **3**g fiber   **3**g net carbs

Nutrition Facts per serving: 38 cal., 1 g total fat (0 g sat. fat),
0 mg chol., 84 mg sodium, 6 g carbo., 3 g fiber, 3 g pro.

Baby Broccoli with Lemon

Start to Finish: 15 minutes Makes: 6 servings

½ cup chicken broth

2 tablespoons butter

1 pound baby broccoli or

broccoli rabe

⅛ teaspoon freshly ground

black pepper

½ of a medium lemon, cut into

6 wedges

1. In a large skillet bring chicken broth to boiling. Add butter and baby broccoli to skillet. Cook, covered, over medium heat for 6 to 8 minutes or until broccoli is tender. Transfer to a serving bowl. Drizzle with cooking liquid, if desired. Sprinkle with pepper. Serve with lemon wedges.

See photo, page 378.

6g
carbs

2g
fiber

4g
net carbs

Nutrition Facts per serving: 64 cal., 4 g total fat (2 g sat. fat),
11 mg chol., 136 mg sodium, 6 g carbo., 2 g fiber, 2 g pro.

Lemony Mixed Vegetables

Prep: 20 minutes Cook: 15 minutes Makes: 8 servings

1. In a large saucepan, cook green beans, covered, in a small amount of salted boiling water for 8 minutes. Add cauliflower and sweet pepper. Cook, covered, 5 minutes more or until vegetables are crisp-tender. Drain vegetables.

2. In same saucepan melt butter. Stir in coriander, lemon peel, and lemon juice. Add drained vegetables to saucepan; stir to coat.

See photo, page 379.

½ pound green beans, cut into
   2-inch lengths (about 2 cups)

2 cups cauliflower florets

1 medium red sweet pepper, cut
   into 1-inch pieces

2 tablespoons butter

½ teaspoon ground coriander

½ teaspoon finely shredded
   lemon peel

4 teaspoons lemon juice

4 g carbs **2** g fiber **2** g net carbs

Nutrition Facts per serving: 46 cal., 3 g total fat (2 g sat. fat),
8 mg chol., 30 mg sodium, 4 g carbo., 2 g fiber, 1 g pro.

Grilled Asparagus with Parmesan Curls

Prep: 15 minutes Marinate: 30 minutes Grill: 3 minutes Makes: 6 servings

1½ pounds asparagus spears, trimmed

2 tablespoons olive oil

2 tablespoons lemon juice

½ teaspoon salt

¼ teaspoon black pepper

1 2-ounce block Parmesan cheese

1. In a large skillet cook asparagus in a small amount of boiling water for 3 minutes. Drain well. Meanwhile, for marinade, in a 2-quart rectangular baking dish stir together olive oil, lemon juice, salt, and pepper. Add drained asparagus, turning to coat. Cover and marinate at room temperature for 30 minutes. Drain asparagus, discarding marinade. Place asparagus on a grill tray or in a grill basket.

2. For a charcoal grill, grill asparagus on the rack of an uncovered grill directly over medium coals for 3 to 5 minutes or until asparagus is tender and beginning to brown, turning once halfway through grilling. (For a gas grill, preheat grill. Reduce heat to medium. Place asparagus on grill rack over heat. Cover and grill as above.)

3. Arrange asparagus on a serving platter. Working over asparagus, use a cheese plane or vegetable peeler to cut thin, wide strips from the side of Parmesan cheese block.

4g carbs   **1**g fiber   **3**g net carbs

Nutrition Facts per serving: 95 cal., 7 g total fat (1 g sat. fat),
7 mg chol., 287 mg sodium, 4 g carbo., 1 g fiber, 6 g pro.

Garlicky Mushrooms

Start to Finish: 20 minutes Makes: 4 servings

1. Cut off the mushroom stems even with the caps; discard stems. Rinse mushroom caps. Gently pat dry with paper towels.

2. In a small bowl stir together butter, garlic, salt, and pepper. Brush over mushrooms.

3. For a charcoal grill, grill mushrooms on the rack of an uncovered grill directly over medium coals for 6 to 8 minutes or until mushrooms are just tender, turning once halfway through grilling. (For a gas grill, preheat grill. Reduce heat to medium. Place mushrooms on grill rack over heat. Cover and grill as above.)

4. Sprinkle mushrooms with chives.

1 pound portobello mushrooms

¼ cup butter, melted

1½ bottled minced garlic (3 cloves)

¼ teaspoon salt

⅛ teaspoon black pepper

1 tablespoon snipped fresh
   chives

6g carbs   **2**g fiber   **4**g net carbs

Nutrition Facts per serving: 133 cal., 12 g total fat (7 g sat. fat), 31 mg chol., 252 mg sodium, 6 g carbo., 2 g fiber, 3 g pro.

Peppers Stuffed with Goat Cheese

Start to Finish: 25 minutes Makes: 4 servings

1 ounce soft goat cheese

   (chèvre)

¼ cup shredded Monterey Jack

   cheese (1 ounce)

1 tablespoon snipped

   fresh chives

1 tablespoon snipped fresh

   basil or 1 teaspoon dried

   basil, crushed

2 medium red, yellow, and/or

   green sweet peppers,

   quartered lengthwise

1. For filling, in a small bowl combine goat cheese, Monterey Jack cheese, chives, and basil. Set aside.

2. For a charcoal grill, grill peppers on the rack of an uncovered grill directly over medium-hot coals about 8 minutes or until peppers are crisp-tender and beginning to brown, turning once halfway through grilling. (For a gas grill, preheat grill. Reduce heat to medium-hot. Place peppers on grill rack over heat. Cover and grill as above.) Remove peppers from grill.

3. Spoon cheese mixture into sweet pepper pieces; return to grill. Grill for 2 to 3 minutes more or until cheese is melted. Serve immediately.

3g carbs   **0**g fiber   **3**g net carbs

Nutrition Facts per serving: 60 cal., 4 g total fat (2 g sat. fat),
13 mg chol., 80 mg sodium, 3 g carbo., 0 g fiber, 3 g pro.

Green Beans Amandine

Start to Finish: 30 minutes Makes: 3 servings

1. Cut fresh beans into 1-inch pieces (or slice lengthwise for French-cut beans). Cook fresh green beans, covered, in a small amount of salted boiling water for 10 to 15 minutes (5 to 10 minutes for French-cut beans) or until crisp-tender. (Or cook frozen beans according to package directions.) Drain; keep warm.

2. Meanwhile, in a small saucepan cook and stir almonds in hot butter over medium heat until golden. Remove from heat; stir in lemon juice. Stir almond mixture into beans.

8 ounces fresh green beans or

one 9-ounce package frozen

cut or French-cut green beans

2 tablespoons slivered almonds

1 tablespoon butter or margarine

1 teaspoon lemon juice

6g carbs **3**g fiber **3**g net carbs

Nutrition Facts per serving: 89 cal., 7 g total fat (3 g sat. fat), 11 mg chol., 45 mg sodium, 6 g carbo., 3 g fiber, 2 g pro.

Collard Greens with Bacon

Prep: 30 minutes   Cook: 1¼ hours   Makes: 6 servings

1½   pounds collard greens

3   slices bacon, chopped

2   cups water

1   7- to 8-ounce smoked
     pork hock

½   cup chopped onion
     (1 medium)

½   cup chopped green
     sweet pepper

¼   teaspoon salt

⅛   teaspoon cayenne pepper

4   cloves garlic, minced

Red wine vinegar (optional)

1. Wash collard greens thoroughly in cold water; drain well. Remove and discard stems; trim bruised leaves. Coarsely chop leaves to measure 6 cups; set aside.

2. In a large saucepan cook bacon until crisp. Remove bacon, reserving drippings in saucepan. Drain bacon and set aside. Add water, pork hock, onion, sweet pepper, salt, cayenne pepper, and garlic to saucepan. Bring to boiling; add chopped collard greens. Reduce heat. Simmer, covered, about 1¼ hours or until greens are tender. Remove from heat. Remove pork hock. Cover greens; keep warm.

3. When cool enough to handle, cut meat off pork hock. Chop or shred meat; discard bone. Return meat to greens mixture along with cooked bacon; heat through. Serve with a slotted spoon. If desired, sprinkle with vinegar.

5 g carbs   **2** g fiber   **3** g net carbs

Nutrition Facts per serving: 158 cal., 13 g total fat (5 g sat. fat),
22 mg chol., 267 mg sodium, 5 g carbo., 2 g fiber, 5 g pro.

Brussels Sprouts with Prosciutto

Start to Finish: 20 minutes   Makes: 8 servings

1. Trim stems and remove any wilted outer leaves from Brussels sprouts. In a saucepan cook Brussels sprouts, covered, in enough salted boiling water to cover for 7 to 9 minutes or until just tender. Drain. Rinse with cold water; drain again.

2. Thinly slice Brussels sprouts. In a large skillet cook sliced Brussels sprouts in hot oil for 2 to 3 minutes until heated through. Stir in prosciutto, lemon peel, salt, and pepper.

1 **pound Brussels sprouts**

1 **tablespoon olive oil**

3 **ounces prosciutto, chopped**

1 **teaspoon finely shredded lemon peel**

½ **teaspoon salt**

¼ **teaspoon freshly ground black pepper**

5g carbs   **2**g fiber   **3**g net carbs

Nutrition Facts per serving: 58 cal., 3 g total fat (1 g sat. fat), 7 mg chol., 444 mg sodium, 5 g carbo., 2 g fiber, 5 g pro.

Lemon Broccoli

Start to Finish: 20 minutes Makes: 6 servings

6 cups broccoli florets

2 tablespoons olive oil

½ teaspoon finely shredded

lemon peel

4 teaspoons lemon juice

¼ teaspoon salt

⅛ teaspoon black pepper

1 clove garlic, minced

1. Place a steamer basket in a saucepan. Add water to just below the bottom of the basket. Bring water to boiling. Add broccoli to steamer basket. Cover and reduce heat. Steam for 8 to 10 minutes or until crisp-tender.

2. Meanwhile, combine oil, lemon peel, lemon juice, salt, pepper, and garlic. Drizzle over hot broccoli; toss to coat.

5 g
carbs

3 g
fiber

2 g
net carbs

Nutrition Facts per serving: 66 cal., 5 g total fat (1 g sat. fat),
0 mg chol., 121 mg sodium, 5 g carbo., 3 g fiber, 3 g pro.

Asparagus Dijon

Start to Finish: 15 minutes   Makes: 6 servings

1. Snap off and discard woody bases from fresh asparagus. If desired, scrape off scales. Cook fresh asparagus, covered, in a small amount of boiling water for 4 to 6 minutes or until crisp-tender. (Or cook frozen asparagus according to package directions.) Drain; keep warm.

2. Meanwhile, for sauce, beat whipping cream just until stiff peaks form. Fold in mayonnaise, mustard, and if desired, egg. Spoon sauce over asparagus; top with green onion. Serve immediately.

See photo, page 380.

1½ pounds asparagus spears or two

    10-ounce packages frozen

    asparagus spears

¼ cup whipping cream

2 tablespoons mayonnaise

3 to 4 teaspoons Dijon-style mustard

1 hard-cooked egg, chopped

   (optional)

2 tablespoons sliced green onion

2g carbs   **1**g fiber   **1**g net carbs

Nutrition Facts per serving: 88 cal., 8 g total fat (3 g sat. fat),
17 mg chol., 100 mg sodium, 2 g carbo., 1 g fiber, 2 g pro.

Rosemary Roasted Vegetables

Prep: 30 minutes Roast: 20 minutes Oven: 425°F Makes: 12 servings

12 ounces green beans

1 pound Brussels sprouts

6 green onions, trimmed and cut

12 fresh rosemary sprigs

8 slices pancetta or bacon,

   partially cooked, drained,

   and cut up

2 tablespoons olive oil

   Salt

   Freshly ground black pepper

1 lemon, halved

1. Wash green beans and Brussels sprouts; drain. Halve large sprouts. In a large saucepan cook sprouts in a small amount of lightly salted boiling water for 3 minutes; add beans and cook 5 minutes more. Drain.

2. Place Brussels sprouts and beans in a shallow roasting pan. Add green onions and rosemary sprigs; toss to combine. Top with pancetta.

3. Drizzle vegetable mixture with oil. Sprinkle with salt and pepper. Roast, uncovered, in a 425° oven for 20 minutes or until vegetables are crisp-tender and pancetta is crisp. Remove to serving platter. Squeeze juice from lemon over vegetables.

6g carbs **3**g fiber **3**g net carbs

Nutrition Facts per serving: 143 cal., 10 g total fat (4 g sat. fat), 10 mg chol., 275 mg sodium, 6 g carbo., 3 g fiber, 4 g pro.

Broiled Zucchini Slices

Start to Finish: 20 minutes   Makes: 4 servings

1. In a saucepan cook garlic in hot oil over medium heat for 30 seconds. Stir in rosemary, pepper, and salt. Drizzle mixture over zucchini; toss to coat. Arrange zucchini in a single layer in a 15×10×1-inch baking pan. Broil about 5 inches from heat for 5 to 6 minutes or until tender, turning once halfway through broiling.

See photo, page 381.

2 cloves garlic, minced

2 tablespoons olive oil or butter

1 tablespoon snipped fresh
   rosemary or ½ teaspoon
   dried rosemary, crushed

½ teaspoon cracked black pepper

⅛ teaspoon salt

2 medium zucchini and/or yellow
   summer squash, cut
   lengthwise into ¼-inch slices

3g carbs   **1**g fiber   **2**g net carbs

Nutrition Facts per serving: 74 cal., 7 g total fat (1 g sat. fat),
0 mg chol., 7 mg sodium, 3 g carbo., 1 g fiber, 1 g pro.

Summer Squash Combo

Start to Finish: 20 minutes Makes: 6 servings

2 tablespoons white wine or red
   wine vinegar

2 tablespoons olive oil

2 teaspoons snipped fresh
   oregano or thyme or
   ½ teaspoon dried oregano
   or thyme, crushed

¼ teaspoon salt

⅛ to ¼ teaspoon crushed
   red pepper

3 green onions, trimmed

1 medium zucchini, quartered
   lengthwise

1 medium yellow summer
   squash, quartered
   lengthwise

1. In a small bowl stir together vinegar, oil, oregano, salt, and crushed red pepper. Brush the onions, zucchini, and yellow squash with some of the vinegar mixture.

2. For a charcoal grill, grill vegetables on the rack of an uncovered grill directly over medium coals until crisp-tender, turning occasionally. Allow 3 to 4 minutes for green onions and 5 to 6 minutes for zucchini and yellow summer squash. (For a gas grill, preheat grill. Reduce heat to medium. Place vegetables on grill rack over heat. Cover and grill as above.)

3. Cut grilled vegetables into bite-size pieces; transfer to a serving bowl. Toss with the remaining vinegar mixture. Serve warm.

2 g carbs **1** g fiber **1** g net carbs

Nutrition Facts per serving: 51 cal., 5 g total fat (1 g sat. fat),
0 mg chol., 101 mg sodium, 2 g carbo., 1 g fiber, 1 g pro.

Lemony Brussels Sprouts

Start to Finish: 25 minutes Makes: 4 servings

1. Trim stems and remove any wilted outer leaves from Brussels sprouts. Cut sprouts in half lengthwise.

2. In a medium saucepan cook Brussels sprouts, covered, in a small amount of salted boiling water for 10 to 12 minutes or until crisp-tender. Drain well. Add butter, lemon juice, lemon-pepper seasoning, and salt; toss gently to coat.

1 **pound Brussels sprouts**

   (4 cups)

1 **tablespoon butter**

2 **teaspoons lemon juice**

¼ **teaspoon lemon-pepper**

   seasoning

⅛ **teaspoon salt**

9g carbs **4**g fiber **5**g net carbs

Nutrition Facts per serving: 72 cal., 3 g total fat (2 g sat. fat), 8 mg chol., 188 mg sodium, 9 g carbo., 4 g fiber, 3 g pro.

Grilled Summer Squash with Cheese

Start to Finish: 20 minutes Makes: 6 servings

3 small yellow summer squash

   or zucchini

   (about 12 ounces)

2 teaspoons cooking oil

¼ teaspoon salt

⅛ teaspoon black pepper

3 tablespoons picante sauce

   (with no added sugar)

¼ cup shredded Monterey

   Jack cheese

1 tablespoon snipped

   fresh cilantro

1. Trim ends from squash; halve squash lengthwise. Brush squash with oil; sprinkle cut surface with salt and pepper.

2. For a charcoal grill, grill squash on the rack of an uncovered grill directly over medium coals for 8 minutes or until crisp-tender, turning once and brushing occasionally with picante sauce. (For a gas grill, preheat grill. Reduce heat to medium. Place squash on grill rack over heat. Cover and grill as above.) Transfer squash to a serving platter; sprinkle with cheese and cilantro.

2 g carbs **1** g fiber **1** g net carbs

Nutrition Facts per serving: 42 cal., 3 g total fat (1 g sat. fat), 4 mg chol., 186 mg sodium, 2 g carbo., 1 g fiber, 2 g pro.

Bacon-&-Cheese-Stuffed Mushrooms

Prep: 15 minutes Bake: 18 minutes Oven: 425°F Makes: 4 servings

1. For filling, in a small bowl stir together cream cheese, Parmesan cheese, basil, and pepper. Stir in bacon; set aside. Rinse and drain mushrooms. Pat dry with paper towels. Remove and discard stems. Place mushroom caps, stem sides down, in a shallow baking pan. Bake in a 425° oven for 10 minutes. Remove from pan and drain mushrooms, stem sides down, on paper towels. Return mushrooms, stem sides up, to baking pan. Divide filling among caps. Bake for 8 to 10 minutes more or until heated through.

1 3-ounce package cream cheese, softened

2 tablespoons finely shredded Parmesan cheese

1 tablespoon snipped fresh basil or 1 teaspoon dried basil, crushed

⅛ teaspoon freshly ground black pepper

2 slices bacon, crisp-cooked and crumbled

12 large fresh mushrooms (1½ to 2 inches in diameter)

3g carbs   **0**g fiber   **3**g net carbs

Nutrition Facts per serving: 182 cal., 15 g total fat (8 g sat. fat), 39 mg chol., 412 mg sodium, 3 g carbo., 0 g fiber, 11 g pro.

Herb-Salt Sprinkle

Prep: 5 minutes Stand: 24 hours Makes: ½ cup

¼ cup coarse-grain sea salt or
  kosher salt

¼ cup snipped fresh herbs, such
  as basil, tarragon, thyme,
  dill, savory, or rosemary

Radishes or other raw or fresh
  vegetables (optional)

1. Place 1 tablespoon salt in a 1-pint screw-top jar. Sprinkle about half of the herbs over the salt. Sprinkle 1 tablespoon salt over herbs. Sprinkle remaining herbs over salt and top with remaining salt. Cover and let stand for 24 hours or up to 6 months.

2. Serve the herb salt, if desired, with radishes or other raw or fresh vegetables.

0g carbs   0g fiber   0g net carbs

Nutrition Facts per ¼ teaspoon: 0 cal., 0 g total fat (0 g sat. fat),
0 mg chol., 241 mg sodium, 0 g carbo., 0 g fiber, 0 g pro.

Kale with Garlic

Start to Finish: 30 minutes Makes: 8 servings

1. Preheat a Dutch oven over medium-high heat. Add kale, water, garlic, and salt. Cook and stir about 2 minutes or until greens wilt. Reduce heat to medium. Cook, uncovered, for 10 to 15 minutes or until greens are tender, stirring occasionally. Remove from heat; toss with oil. Sprinkle with freshly ground black pepper.

1 pound kale, trimmed and
    chopped (about 12 cups)

¼ cup water

4 cloves garlic, minced

¼ teaspoon salt

1 teaspoon olive oil

    Freshly ground black pepper

Nutrition Facts per serving: 25 cal., 1 g total fat (0 g sat. fat), 0 mg chol., 87 mg sodium, 4 g carbo., 1 g fiber, 1 g pro.

Broiled Roma Tomatoes with Goat Cheese

Start to Finish: 15 minutes Makes: 4 servings

4 medium Roma tomatoes, halved lengthwise

2 tablespoons olive oil

2 tablespoons red wine or white wine vinegar

2 teaspoons snipped fresh oregano or ½ teaspoon dried oregano, crushed

¼ teaspoon salt

⅛ teaspoon freshly ground black pepper

1 ounce semisoft goat cheese (chèvre), crumbled

1. Preheat broiler. Place tomato halves, cut side up, on the unheated rack of a broiler pan. Whisk together oil, vinegar, oregano, salt, and pepper. Brush tomatoes with some of the oil mixture. Broil 3 to 4 inches from the heat for 5 to 8 minutes or until tomatoes are heated through and begin to soften.

2. Transfer tomatoes to a serving platter. Drizzle with any remaining oil mixture and sprinkle with goat cheese.

3g carbs **1**g fiber **2**g net carbs

Nutrition Facts per serving: 94 cal., 8 g total fat (2 g sat. fat), 3 mg chol., 176 mg sodium, 3 g carbo., 1 g fiber, 2 g pro.

Grilled Endive with Prosciutto

Prep: 15 minutes   Grill: 25 minutes   Makes: 4 servings

1. In a small bowl combine olive oil, mustard, and black pepper; brush over endive halves. Wrap each endive half in a thin slice of prosciutto; secure with wooden toothpicks.

2. For a charcoal grill, arrange medium-hot coals around a drip pan. Test for medium heat above the pan. Place endive on grill rack over drip pan. Cover and grill about 25 minutes or until endive is tender and prosciutto is golden brown, turning once halfway through grilling. (For a gas grill, preheat grill. Reduce heat to medium. Adjust grill for indirect grilling. Place endive on grill rack. Grill as above.)

3. Meanwhile, in a small bowl combine sweet peppers and green onion; divide among 4 salad plates. Top with grilled endive. Drizzle each serving with Herbed Oil. Discard any remaining oil. Serve immediately.

Herbed Oil: In a blender container combine $1/4$ cup olive oil, $1/3$ cup coarsely chopped fresh flat-leaf parsley, 3 tablespoons snipped fresh chives, 4 teaspoons snipped fresh thyme, and $1/4$ teaspoon salt. Cover and blend until smooth. Strain herb mixture through a fine-mesh sieve, pressing on solids to extract all oil; discard herb mixture. Place oil in a squeeze bottle. Refrigerate for up to 2 days. (For food safety reasons, do not hold oil any longer than 2 days.) To serve, bring to room temperature; shake well.

1   tablespoon olive oil

1   tablespoon Dijon-style mustard

$1/4$ teaspoon black pepper

2   heads Belgian endive, trimmed
    and halved lengthwise

4   thin slices prosciutto ($1\frac{1}{2}$ to
    2 ounces)

$1/2$ of a medium red sweet pepper,
    cut into thin strips

$1/2$ of a medium yellow sweet
    pepper, cut into thin strips

1   green onion, bias-sliced

1   recipe Herbed Oil

4g carbs   **1**g fiber   **3**g net carbs

Nutrition Facts per serving: 206 cal., 20 g total fat (2 g sat. fat),
0 mg chol., 361 mg sodium, 4 g carbo., 1 g fiber, 4 g pro.

Minted French Green Beans

Prep: 15 minutes Cook: 2 minutes Chill: 2 hours Makes: 4 servings

8 ounces haricots vert or other

  small, thin green beans

  (2 cups)

1 tablespoon finely chopped

  shallot

2 teaspoons olive oil

2 teaspoons snipped fresh mint

Salt

Freshly ground black pepper

1. Rinse beans. If desired, trim tips off beans; drain.

2. Place a steamer basket in a large skillet. Add water to just below the bottom of basket. Bring water to boiling. Place beans in steamer basket. Cover and steam for 2 minutes. Drain. Rinse with cold water. (Or plunge into ice water.) Drain well.

3. In a medium bowl lightly toss together beans, shallot, oil, and mint. Season to taste with salt and pepper. Cover and chill for 2 hours.

See photo, page 382.

4 g
carbs

2 g
fiber

2 g
net carbs

Nutrition Facts per serving: 38 cal., 2 g total fat (0 g sat. fat),
0 mg chol., 140 mg sodium, 4 g carbo., 2 g fiber, 1 g pro.

Herb-Lover's Salad

Prep: 10 minutes Chill: 1 hour Makes: 4 to 6 servings

1. Place mesclun in a large bowl of cold water. After a few minutes, lift out mesclun and discard water. Dunk mesclun again, if necessary, to remove any dirt or sand particles. Drain mesclun in a colander.

2. Gently pat mesclun dry with a clean kitchen towel or paper towels or use a salad spinner. Wrap dried mesclun in a dry kitchen towel or paper towels; chill at least 1 hour or up to several hours to crisp.

3. For vinaigrette, in a screw-top jar combine oil, vinegar, tarragon, marjoram, chives, and garlic. Cover and shake well to mix. Season to taste with salt and pepper.

4. Arrange mesclun on a large serving platter or in a salad bowl. Arrange edible flower petals on top of mesclun. Shake vinaigrette well; drizzle desired amount over the salad. Toss gently to coat. Serve immediately. If desired, pass additional vinaigrette. Cover and store any remaining vinaigrette in the refrigerator for up to 1 week. Let stand at room temperature for 20 minutes before serving; shake well.

8 cups mesclun or torn mixed salad greens

½ cup olive oil

⅓ cup white wine vinegar

2 teaspoons snipped fresh tarragon

2 teaspoons snipped fresh marjoram

2 teaspoons snipped fresh chives

1 to 2 cloves garlic, minced

Salt and freshly ground black pepper

2 cups edible flower petals such as chives
   (with flowers), corianders, pansies,
   marigolds, and/or geraniums

3g carbs **2**g fiber **1**g net carbs

Nutrition Facts per serving: 138 cal., 14 g total fat (0 g sat. fat),
0 mg chol., 11 mg sodium, 3 g carbo., 2 g fiber, 1 g pro.

Bacon & Spinach Salad

Start to Finish: 20 minutes Makes: 6 servings

6 cups baby spinach

½ cup sliced mushrooms

4 slices thick-sliced peppered

   bacon, cut into 1-inch pieces

1 tablespoon chopped shallots

½ cup bottled oil-and-vinegar

   salad dressing (with no

   added sugar)

6 hard-cooked eggs, quartered

1. In a large heatproof bowl combine spinach and mushrooms; set aside.

2. For dressing, in a large skillet cook bacon over medium heat until crisp. Using a slotted spoon, remove bacon, reserving 1 tablespoon drippings in skillet. Drain bacon on paper towels; set aside.

3. Add shallots to drippings in skillet. Cook and stir over medium heat until tender. Stir in salad dressing; bring to boiling. Drizzle dressing over spinach mixture; toss to coat. Divide mixture among 6 dishes or salad plates. Top with cooked bacon and hard-cooked eggs.

See photo, page 377.

3g carbs   **1**g fiber   **2**g net carbs

Nutrition Facts per serving: 219 cal., 19 g total fat (4 g sat. fat), 217 mg chol., 271 mg sodium, 3 g carbo., 1 g fiber, 9 g pro.

Bacon &
Spinach
Salad
p. 376

Baby
Broccoli with
Lemon
p. 354

Lemony
Mixed
Vegetables
p. 355

Asparagus
Dijon
p. 363

Broiled
Zucchini
Slices
p. 365

Minted
French Green
Beans
p. 374

Asparagus-
Squash
Salad
p. 388

Napa
Cabbage
Slaw
p. 385

Napa Cabbage Slaw

Start to Finish: 15 minutes Makes: 6 servings

1. In a large bowl combine cabbage, bok choy, and sweet pepper.

2. For dressing, in a small bowl stir together vinegar, salad oil, and sesame oil. Pour over cabbage mixture; toss gently to coat. If desired, cover and chill for up to 2 hours.

See photo, page 384.

3 cups finely shredded Chinese (Napa) cabbage

1 cup finely shredded bok choy

¼ of a small red sweet pepper, cut into very thin strips (about ¼ cup)

¼ cup rice vinegar or white wine vinegar

1 tablespoon salad oil

½ teaspoon toasted sesame oil

2g carbs   **2**g fiber   **0**g net carbs

Nutrition Facts per serving: 40 cal., 3 g total fat (0 g sat. fat), 0 mg chol., 81 mg sodium, 2 g carbo., 2 g fiber, 1 g pro.

Fresh Greens with Shallot-Mustard Vinaigrette

Start to Finish: 20 minutes Makes: 4 servings

2 cups torn watercress,

    tough stems removed

2 cups baby spinach

½ cup thinly sliced cucumber

8 cherry tomatoes, quartered

¼ cup tarragon vinegar

    or white wine vinegar

¼ cup olive oil or salad oil

1 tablespoon finely chopped

    shallot

1 teaspoon Dijon-style mustard

¼ teaspoon salt

¼ teaspoon coarsely ground

    black pepper

1. Divide watercress and spinach among 4 chilled salad plates. Top with cucumber and tomatoes. In a screw-top jar combine vinegar, oil, shallot, mustard, salt, and pepper. Cover; shake well. Drizzle dressing over salads.

4g carbs   **1**g fiber   **3**g net carbs

Nutrition Facts per serving: 142 cal., 14 g total fat (2 g sat. fat),
0 mg chol., 199 mg sodium, 4 g carbo., 1 g fiber, 2 g pro.

Tossed Crisp
Vegetable Salad

Start to Finish: 25 minutes Makes: 6 servings

1. Snap off and discard woody bases from asparagus. Wash asparagus and drain. Using a sharp knife, cut spears lengthwise into very thin strips. Wash beet; trim ends. Using a mechanical slicer or sharp peeler, peel thin strips of beet. Rinse under cold water; set aside. Trim carrot, parsnip, celery root, and fennel bulb. Using a mechanical slicer or sharp peeler, cut vegetables into wide, thin strips.

2. In a large salad bowl combine vegetables. Season to taste with salt and pepper. Toss with low-carb Italian dressing.

4 thin asparagus spears

1 small beet

1 small carrot

1 small parsnip or parsley root

1 small celery root

1 small fennel bulb

Salt

Freshly ground black pepper

⅓ cup bottled low-carb Italian
   salad dressing

6g carbs   **2**g fiber   **4**g net carbs

Nutrition Facts per serving with 1 tablespoon dressing: 79 cal., 6 g total fat (1 g sat. fat), 4 mg chol., 159 mg sodium, 6 g carbo., 2 g fiber, 1 g pro.

Asparagus-Squash Salad

Start to Finish: 25 minutes Makes: 8 servings

8 ounces asparagus, cut into

    1-inch pieces

8 ounces yellow summer

    squash, cut in half

    lengthwise and sliced

1 recipe Mustard-Herb Dressing

8 cups packaged baby salad

    greens (about 10 ounces) or

    torn mixed salad greens

1. In a saucepan cook asparagus, covered, in a small amount of boiling salted water about 4 minutes or until crisp-tender. (Or steam asparagus about 4 minutes.) Immediately drain and plunge into ice water. Drain.

2. In a saucepan cook squash, covered, in a small amount of salted boiling water about 3 minutes or until crisp-tender. (Or steam squash about 3 minutes.) Immediately drain and plunge into ice water. Drain.

3. In a salad bowl combine asparagus and squash. Toss with Mustard-Herb Dressing to coat. Serve vegetables over salad greens.

Mustard-Herb Dressing: In a blender container combine 3 tablespoons white wine vinegar; 1 tablespoon fresh tarragon or thyme or 1 teaspoon dried tarragon or thyme, crushed; 1 tablespoon Dijon-style mustard; and a dash freshly ground black pepper. With blender running, add ⅓ cup salad oil in a thin, steady stream. Continue blending until mixture is thick. Cover and store in the refrigerator.

See photo, page 383.

2 g carbs **1** g fiber **1** g net carbs

Nutrition Facts per serving: 98 cal., 9 g total fat (1 g sat. fat), 0 mg chol., 51 mg sodium, 2 g carbo., 1 g fiber, 1 g pro.

Italian Coleslaw

Prep: 25 minutes   Chill: 1 hour   Makes: 5 (½-cup) servings

1. Trim any brown spots from fennel and cut a thin slice off base of bulb. Discard green stems. Cut fennel in half lengthwise; cut crosswise into very thin slices.

2. In a medium bowl combine fennel and olives. For dressing, in a screw-top jar combine oil, vinegar, oregano, garlic, salt, and pepper. Cover; shake well. Pour dressing over fennel mixture; toss to coat. Cover and chill for 1 to 24 hours.

1 medium fennel bulb (about 1 pound)

⅓ cup sliced pitted green olives

2 tablespoons olive oil

1 white wine vinegar

1 tablespoon snipped fresh oregano or 1 teaspoon dried oregano, crushed

1 clove garlic, minced

⅛ teaspoon salt

⅛ teaspoon crushed red pepper

5g carbs   **2**g fiber   **3**g net carbs

Nutrition Facts per serving: 81 cal., 7 g total fat (1 g sat. fat), 0 mg chol., 306 mg sodium, 5 g carbo., 2 g fiber, 1 g pro.

Creamy Lemon-Pepper Coleslaw

Prep: 10 minutes Chill: 2 hours Makes: 6 servings

½ cup mayonnaise

1 teaspoon lemon-pepper
  seasoning

½ teaspoon dried thyme,
  crushed

5 cups shredded cabbage

¼ cup shelled sunflower seeds

1. In a large salad bowl combine mayonnaise, lemon-pepper seasoning, and thyme. Stir in shredded cabbage and sunflower seeds. Toss lightly to coat. Cover and chill for 2 to 24 hours.

5 g carbs   **2** g fiber   **3** g net carbs

Nutrition Facts per serving: 188 cal., 18 g total fat (2 g sat. fat),
7 mg chol., 328 mg sodium, 5 g carbo., 2 g fiber, 2 g pro.

Carb Count Journal

It's easier to stick with your low-carb diet when you keep track of how you're doing. This handy journal lets you record your carb grams for each meal so you don't go overboard. You also can write down how you're feeling while on the diet. After a few days, look back at your journal and note how your energy level or hunger have changed while on phase 1 of your low-carb diet.

Week 1, Day 1

	Food or Beverages	Net Carb Count
Breakfast		
Lunch		
Dinner		
Snacks		

Energy Level

(low) (medium) (high)

Hunger Level

(low) (medium) (high)

Carb Cravings

(low) (medium) (high)

Week 1, Day 2

	Food or Beverages	Net Carb Count
Breakfast		
Lunch		
Dinner		
Snacks		

Energy Level

low   medium   high

Hunger Level

low   medium   high

Carb Cravings

low   medium   high

Week 1, Day 3

	Food or Beverages	Net Carb Count
Breakfast		
Lunch		
Dinner		
Snacks		

Energy Level

low · medium · high

Hunger Level

low · medium · high

Carb Cravings

low · medium · high

Week 1, Day 4

	Food or Beverages	Net Carb Count
Breakfast		
Lunch		
Dinner		
Snacks		

Energy Level

low   medium   high

Hunger Level

low   medium   high

Carb Cravings

low   medium   high

Week 1, Day 5

	Food or Beverages	Net Carb Count
Breakfast		
Lunch		
Dinner		
Snacks		

Energy Level

(low) (medium) (high)

Hunger Level

(low) (medium) (high)

Carb Cravings

(low) (medium) (high)

Week 1, Day 6

	Food or Beverages	Net Carb Count
Breakfast		
Lunch		
Dinner		
Snacks		

Energy Level

low | medium | high

Hunger Level

low | medium | high

Carb Cravings

low | medium | high

Week 1, Day 7

	Food or Beverages	Net Carb Count
Breakfast		
Lunch		
Dinner		
Snacks		

Energy Level

(low) (medium) (high)

Hunger Level

(low) (medium) (high)

Carb Cravings

(low) (medium) (high)

Week 2, Day 1

	Food or Beverages	Net Carb Count
Breakfast		
Lunch		
Dinner		
Snacks		

Energy Level

(low) (medium) (high)

Hunger Level

(low) (medium) (high)

Carb Cravings

(low) (medium) (high)

Week 2, Day 2

	Food or Beverages	Net Carb Count
Breakfast		
Lunch		
Dinner		
Snacks		

Energy Level

low medium high

Hunger Level

low medium high

Carb Cravings

low medium high

Week 2, Day 3

	Food or Beverages	Net Carb Count
Breakfast		
Lunch		
Dinner		
Snacks		

Energy Level

(low) (medium) (high)

Hunger Level

(low) (medium) (high)

Carb Cravings

(low) (medium) (high)

Week 2, Day 4

	Food or Beverages	Net Carb Count
Breakfast		
Lunch		
Dinner		
Snacks		

Energy Level

(low) (medium) (high)

Hunger Level

(low) (medium) (high)

Carb Cravings

(low) (medium) (high)

Week 2, Day 5

	Food or Beverages	Net Carb Count
Breakfast		
Lunch		
Dinner		
Snacks		

Energy Level

(low) (medium) (high)

Hunger Level

(low) (medium) (high)

Carb Cravings

(low) (medium) (high)

Week 2, Day 6

	Food or Beverages	Net Carb Count
Breakfast		
Lunch		
Dinner		
Snacks		

Energy Level

low   medium   high

Hunger Level

low   medium   high

Carb Cravings

low   medium   high

Week 2, Day 7

	Food or Beverages	Net Carb Count
Breakfast		
Lunch		
Dinner		
Snacks		

Energy Level

(low) (medium) (high)

Hunger Level

(low) (medium) (high)

Carb Cravings

(low) (medium) (high)

Index

S

Metric Information

The charts on this page provide a guide for converting measurements from the U.S. customary system, which is used throughout this book, to the metric system.

Product Differences

Most of the ingredients called for in the recipes in this book are available in most countries. However, some are known by different names. Here are some common American ingredients and their possible counterparts:

- **Sugar** (white) is granulated, fine granulated, or castor sugar.
- **Powdered sugar** is icing sugar.
- **All-purpose flour** is enriched, bleached or unbleached white household flour. When self-rising flour is used in place of all-purpose flour in a recipe that calls for leavening, omit the leavening agent (baking soda or baking powder) and salt.
- **Light-colored corn syrup** is golden syrup.
- **Cornstarch** is cornflour.
- **Baking soda** is bicarbonate of soda.
- **Vanilla or vanilla extract** is vanilla essence.
- **Green, red, or yellow sweet peppers** are capsicums or bell peppers.
- **Golden raisins** are sultanas.

Volume and Weight

The United States traditionally uses cup measures for liquid and solid ingredients. The chart at right shows the approximate imperial and metric equivalents. If you are accustomed to weighing solid ingredients, the following approximate equivalents will be helpful.

- 1 cup butter, castor sugar, or rice = 8 ounces = ½ pound = 250 grams
- 1 cup flour = 4 ounces = ¼ pound = 125 grams
- 1 cup icing sugar = 5 ounces = 150 grams
- Canadian and U.S. volume for a cup measure is 8 fluid ounces (237 ml), but the standard metric equivalent is 250 ml.
- 1 British imperial cup is 10 fluid ounces.
- In Australia, 1 tablespoon equals 20 ml, and there are 4 teaspoons in the Australian tablespoon.

Spoon measures are used for smaller ingredient amounts. Although the size of the tablespoon varies slightly in different countries, for practical purposes and for recipes in this book, a straight substitution is all that's necessary. Measurements made using cups or spoons always should be level unless stated otherwise.

Common Weight Range Replacements

Imperial / U.S.	Metric
½ ounce	15 g
1 ounce	25 g or 30 g
4 ounces (¼ pound)	115 g or 125 g
8 ounces (½ pound)	225 g or 250 g
16 ounces (1 pound)	450 g or 500 g
1¼ pounds	625 g
1½ pounds	750 g
2 pounds or 2¼ pounds	1,000 g or 1 Kg

Oven Temperature Equivalents

Fahrenheit Setting	Celsius Setting*	Gas Setting
300°F	150°C	Gas Mark 2 (very low)
325°F	160°C	Gas Mark 3 (low)
350°F	180°C	Gas Mark 4 (moderate)
375°F	190°C	Gas Mark 5 (moderate)
400°F	200°C	Gas Mark 6 (hot)
425°F	220°C	Gas Mark 7 (hot)
450°F	230°C	Gas Mark 8 (very hot)
475°F	240°C	Gas Mark 9 (very hot)
500°F	260°C	Gas Mark 10 (extremely hot)
Broil	Broil	Grill

*Electric and gas ovens may be calibrated using celsius. However, for an electric oven, increase celsius setting 10 to 20 degrees when cooking above 160°C. For convection or forced air ovens (gas or electric), lower the temperature setting 25°F/10°C when cooking at all heat levels.

Baking Pan Sizes

Imperial / U.S.	Metric
9×1½-inch round cake pan	22- or 23×4-cm (1.5 L)
9×1½-inch pie plate	22- or 23×4-cm (1 L)
8×8×2-inch square cake pan	20×5-cm (2 L)
9×9×2-inch square cake pan	22- or 23×4.5-cm (2.5 L)
11×7×1½-inch baking pan	28×17×4-cm (2 L)
2-quart rectangular baking pan	30×19×4.5-cm (3 L)
13×9×2-inch baking pan	34×22×4.5-cm (3.5 L)
15×10×1-inch jelly roll pan	40×25×2-cm
9×5×3-inch loaf pan	23×13×8-cm (2 L)
2-quart casserole	2 L

US/Standard Metric Equivalents

⅛ teaspoon = 0.5 ml	
¼ teaspoon = 1 ml	
½ teaspoon = 2 ml	
1 teaspoon = 5 ml	
1 tablespoon = 15 ml	
2 tablespoons = 25 ml	
¼ cup = 2 fluid ounces = 50 ml	
⅓ cup = 3 fluid ounces = 75 ml	
½ cup = 4 fluid ounces = 125 ml	
⅔ cup = 5 fluid ounces = 150 ml	
¾ cup = 6 fluid ounces = 175 ml	
1 cup = 8 fluid ounces = 250 ml	
2 cups = 1 pint = 500 ml	
1 quart = 1 litre	